FIRESIDE

Eugene A. Sloane's
BICYCLE MAINTENANCE MANUAL

A Fireside Book
Published by Simon and Schuster
New York

A Fireside Book
Published by Simon and Schuster
A Division of Gulf & Western Corporation
Simon & Schuster Building
Rockefeller Center
1230 Avenue of the Americas
New York, New York 10020

FIRESIDE and colophon are registered trademarks of Simon & Schuster
Designed by Irving Perkins Associates
Manufactured in the United States of America

3 4 5 6 7 8 9 10

Library of Congress Cataloging in Publication Data

Sloane, Eugene A.
Eugene A. Sloane's bicycle maintenance manual.
(A Fireside book)
"Based on material from The all new complete book
of bicycling."—verso t.p.
1. Bicycles—Maintenance and repair—Handbooks,
manuals, etc.   2. Cycling.   I. Title.   II. Title:
Bicycle maintenance manual.
GV1043.7.S58   629.2'272   81-1846
AACR2

ISBN 0-671-42806-3

Grateful acknowledgment is made for permission to reprint
from the following articles:

"Frame Repairing and Refinishing," by Otis Childress, from *Bike World*
(October 1977, Volume 6, Number 10).

"Tips to Inexpensive Frame Painting," by Otis Childress, from *Bike World*
(January/February 1979, Volume 8, Number 1).

CONTENTS

INTRODUCTION

If you can handle a screwdriver, a wrench and a few other simple tools, you can learn to keep your bicycle in tip-top working condition. A bicycle is not a simple machine, but it's not that complicated either. If you possess even rudimentary mechanical skills, you should be able to do most of the basic maintenance of your bicycle yourself. We will explain how to adjust the brakes for safe, reliable stopping power. You will see how to keep the over 100 ball bearings in the working parts of your bicycle clean and the bearing surfaces correctly adjusted for smoother, easier pedaling and longer component life. And you will find that the chain, your link between muscles and wheels, can, when properly maintained or replaced, withstand the stress of uphill climbs without breaking.

Best of all will be the knowledge that after you have once overhauled your bicycle, nothing can go wrong short of a broken frame that will hold you up for very long on a camping trip, a spin through the park, or commuting to work.

In this book we will concentrate primarily on all aspects of keeping your bicycle safe and in good repair. For details on the prevention of injury, for evaluation of bicycles and their parts, tips on safe riding, commuting and bike tripping, racing and bike history and lore, please refer to my expanded volume, *The All New Complete Book of Bicycling*.

A properly maintained bicycle lets you sail down long, steep hills secure in the knowledge that the wheels will stay on, the brakes will keep speed under control, and the frame will be aligned for safe, accurate steering. You can tour longer distances with saddle, stem and handlebars adjusted to fit your body for comfortable and efficient pedaling. On long uphill climbs, with muscle power applied to cranks, you will know that the seat post and stem are inserted far enough so that they won't snap off under stress. You will be able to repair the inevitable flat tire quickly and without fuss and muss and long delays. Your wheels will be aligned for more accurate steering and effective braking. Spokes will be under correct tension so that they will not break even when carrying all your camping gear over rough roads.

When, not if, your beautiful, costly steed gets its paint scratched, you will learn how to touch up nicks, cuts and scrapes or even refinish the entire frame. And, when brake and derailleur cables stretch, you will learn how to readjust them to restore braking and shifting functions to original efficiency.

In short, you will find that with just a few of these repairs under your belt this book will pay for itself. With a little effort you should be able to do all your own repairs and routine maintenance.

A WORD ABOUT TOOLS

Depending on how much work you want to do yourself, you will need from $30 to $80 worth of tools. If there is a bicycle club in your area, you might check to see if they have a roving bicycle tool set that you can borrow (after joining the club). If there is a club and they do not have a tool set, you might consider persuading them to buy one; however, you should own the more basic tools yourself. The following is a list of the tools that you will need to own, as opposed to the more costly and less frequently needed tools that could be shared.

Basic Bicycle Tools
- Allen wrenches—5, 6 and 7 millimeters
- Small screwdriver
- Box wrench set—5, 6, 7, 8, 9, 10, 11, 12 millimeters
- Hub wrenches (unless you use sealed-bearing hubs) 13, 14, 15, 16 millimeters
- Third hand (to hold brake shoes closed while taking out cable slack)
- Set of tire irons (not for tubular tires)
- Tire tube patch kit (special thin type if you use tubular tires)
- Spoke nipple wrench (for truing wheels, replacing spokes, lacing wheels)
- Chain rivet remover (for removing chain, repairing broken chain on tour)
- Headset lockring wrench (to fit your brand of headset)
- Bottom-bracket adjustable cone wrench (to fit your brand of headset)
- Crank fixing bolt wrench (I like the Park tool, because it fits three bolt sizes)

- Crank puller (to fit your cranks)
- Pin pliers (for bottom-bracket adjustable cup)
- Freewheel remover (to fit your freewheel)

Tools That Can Be Shared

- Wheel truing jig or fixture
- Dishing tool (for rear wheel)

The two tools above can run up to $150 or more, depending on how elaborate a wheel truer you buy.

Now, let's begin our course in basic bicycle maintenance and repair, starting with brakes. First things first: Correctly adjusted brakes can save your life.

Chapter One

BRAKES

TYPES OF BRAKES

There are six types of bicycle brakes:

Center-pull caliper brakes (Fig. 1-1): My experience with these brakes, over many thousands of miles of use, is that in general they offer somewhat better ultimate stopping power than side-pull brakes of equal quality, but that they give less *controlling* stopping power. If you could run a curve comparing the stopping power of center-pulls versus side-pulls, my own empirical riding experience tells me that braking power builds up more quickly with center-pulls but that unless you are careful you can go into a sliding skid as wheels lock up. With side-pulls you can apply braking power much more evenly and stop just as well. That's why the high-priced bikes, and those used by road racing cyclists, use side-pulls; they are much more graduated in braking control. This is not to say that side-pulls won't work as well as center-pulls in an emergency, other things being equal. Not at all. I am saying that center-pulls seem to concentrate stopping power more quickly than side-pulls.

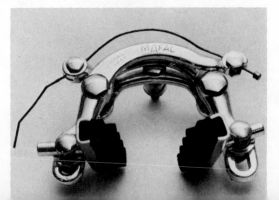

Fig. 1-1: Mafac center-pull brake offers excellent stopping power. Note that brake shoes or pads can be moved up and down the slotted opening in brake stirrups, to adjust brake shoes to fit against rim flats for different size rims and/or frames. Some frames have longer clearances between rim flats and brake-pivot mounting bolt.

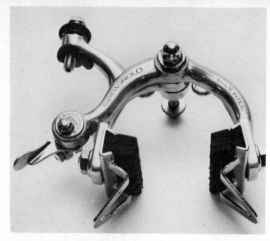

Fig. 1-2: Campagnolo side-pull brake is one of the best brakes made anywhere.

Side-pull caliper brakes (Fig. 1-2): These are less flexible than center-pulls, in general, and as far as I am concerned are more "forgiving" in maintaining stopping power if the rim is out of line. Going back to center-pulls for a moment, you will notice that there is an extra short cable attached to both stirrups (Fig. 1-1) which can also stretch. (Later on in this chapter I will offer suggestions about how to stop safely on the flats and how to control speed on fast downhill runs.)

Fig. 1-3: Shimano disc brake, designed for the juvenile market. Not strong enough for adult use, especially on tandems: (A) brake cable; (B) brake disc; (C) brake body; (D) brake adjustment.

Fig. 1-4: The excellent Phil Wood disc brake mounted on the rear wheel of a Schwinn Paramount tandem, on which these brakes are now standard equipment.

Disc brakes: There are two types of disc brakes, those made for children's bicycles, (Fig. 1-3) where the slight similarity to automotive or motorcycle disc brakes is a marketing feature . . . and the high-quality, much lighter weight disc brakes (Fig. 1-4) designed primarily for tandems, where the extra stopping power is required. I will describe these brakes in more detail later on in this chapter. For now, I can say that they stop better in wet weather than caliper brakes but that they are heavier.

Drum brakes (Fig. 1-5): These are internally expanding brakes and operate just like those on a car. An internal brake shoe, when braking is applied, presses against the brake drum. Because working parts are internal, drum brakes are less affected by water than any other type of bike brakes, and offer excellent stopping power. But because they are far heavier than the high-performance, lighter, more expensive disc brakes, drum brakes are going out of style for general use and for tan-

Fig. 1-5: Phil Wood disc brakes on the front wheel of the Schwinn Paramount tandem. Note straight-in approach of the cable in both this illustration and in Figure 1-4.

dems. Nowadays you seldom see them on new bikes. I might add that you need a special hub for either disc or drum brakes—and that because friction-generated heat is absorbed by the brake lining and dissipated to the air, either disc or drum brakes do not heat up the rim. Caliper brakes, on the other hand, do heat up the rim because brake shoes rub on rims, and friction heat is transferred to the rims. On a fast downhill run, therefore, rims can get hot enough to soften the cement that holds on tubulars. When this occurs, tubulars slide around rims and can tear off the valve and cause a blowout or sudden flat, and loss of control of the bicycle. And on conventional tires, rims can get hot enough to blow out tubes, although this is a far less likely occurrence than the cement-melting problem of tubulars.

Cantilever brakes (Fig. 1-6): These brakes take a lot of effort to work, and they don't let you stop any better than any other brakes I have ever used . . . in fact I suspect they don't stop as well. But they do *look* unusual and expensive and powerful, as they should on a bike that costs today over $1,500. For myself, I would never specify cantilevers on any custom bike. Strangely, though, to be fair, I have found that the shorter-lever cantilevers on the new Raleigh Rampar Tourist 14-speed bicycle do work very well, certainly as well as the excellent Mafac Competition center-pulls, and with less effort at the levers.

Coaster brakes (Fig. 1-7): These are also internal brakes, located in the rear hub, and on some bicycles, notably the single-speed models, this is the only brake on the bike. You stop by backpedaling. Because all working parts are internal, they stop better in wet weather than any of the

Fig. 1-6: Cantilever brakes on the author's Alex Singer touring bicycle. Note that Matthauser shoes are installed. You sharp-eyed experts will notice two items in this photo. The brakes look as though they are touching the fork blades, due to camera angle. I can assure you that they are not; this is **my** bike. The fixing bolt on the right-hand lever is not the original, which fell on the floor and, as in all such incidents, immediately and, apparently permanently, disappeared from view. The replacement is temporary. Also there's some paint off the fork crown, where the Singer front carrier fits. Well, this bike has thousands of miles on it, and has earned the right to have a few nicks and scratches. I'm considering awarding it a Purple Heart.

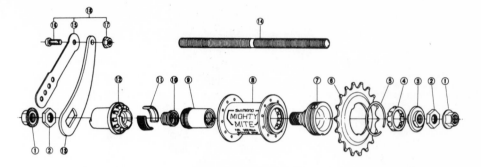

Fig. 1-7: Detailed view of a single-speed coaster brake hub. Part No. 11 is the brake shoe, which under back pedal pressure is forced against the inner perimeter of the brake cone, No. 12, by the clutch cone, No. 9. Coaster brakes are great for children, who have short, weak fingers and so should not have to grasp caliper-brake levers. It is easier for them to use their feet to exert back pressure on the pedal.

three types of caliper brakes. But for two-wheel brakes you still need a caliper brake up front; and some of the bikes, mostly the three-speed models, have a coaster brake rear and a caliper up front.

BRAKE LOCATION

On down-turned handlebars, the brake levers should be where you can reach them quickly and safely, without strain or imbalance. The normal location is about midway on the curve of the bars, as shown in Figure 1-8. To move the levers to another position, remove handlebar tape, loosen the brake lever (Fig. 1-9) with a screwdriver (or a 5- or 6-millimeter Allen wrench if it's one of the newer Campy or Shimano levers) and move the levers to where you want them.

I would also remove the extension levers, the so-called safety levers

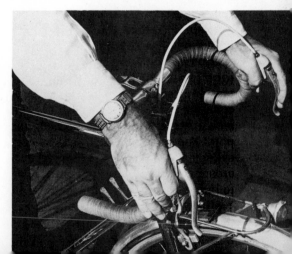

Fig. 1-8: Brake levers should be located at the rise of the bar curve, as shown, where they are convenient for hand-resting points as well as for braking. *(Photo courtesy Dr. Clifford Graves)*

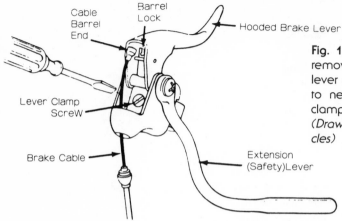

Cable
Barrel
End

Barrel
Lock

Hooded Brake Lever

Lever Clamp
Screw

Brake Cable

Extension
(Safety)Lever

Fig. 1-9: To move brake levers, remove handlebar tape, loosen lever clamp screw, move levers to new location, tighten lever clamp screw, rewind bar tape. *(Drawing courtesy Soma Bicycles)*

(Fig. 1-9), because they do not have nearly the distance of travel of the bar-mounted levers. Squeeze the bar levers as tightly as you can. They should not come all the way to the handlebars. If they do, the brakes need adjustment. Squeeze the extension levers. They will usually come right to the bars, touching them. What this means is that the extension levers will stop you under conditions where mild braking ability is needed but won't work well in the case of a panic stop. Their limitation is amplified by the fact that cables stretch, and if you don't take up the slack the extension levers will be almost worthless. Yet, because they are in such a convenient location, right under the flat of the bars, you come to depend on them and could from habit reach for them in an emergency, and not be able to stop. If you don't have these levers, you won't become addicted to them. Your bike dealer can provide a shorter, replacement axle. All you do is unscrew the side binder bolt, remove and throw away the safety lever, remove the old axle, replace it with the shorter one and screw the side binder bolt back in place. Now you are saved from the "safety" lever addiction curse.

ADJUSTMENT AND MAINTENANCE OF CALIPER BRAKES

First, let's talk about lubrication. Caliper brakes need periodic lubrication—not, of course, on the brake shoes. I know you know better than that. But caliper brakes all have a pair of springs, or one spring with two arms, that hold the caliper arms apart so they won't drag on the rim until you pull on the brake levers. The place to apply a little grease is the point where the spring arms press against the back of the caliper arms or stirrups (let's call them "stirrups" from now on). Lubriplate is fine.

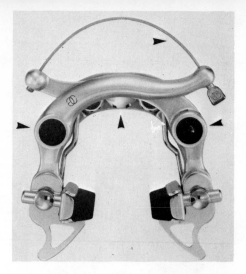

Fig. 1-10: Arrows point to lubrication spots on a Dia-Compe center-pull brake. Top, the stirrup cable should be lightly greased where it passes through yoke. Apply small amount of light oil at stirrup pivot bolts, right and left arrows, and at brake pivot bolt, center arrow. Put a dab of grease on spring ends where they rub on stirrups (not shown, location is on rear of brakes).

You can buy it in most hardware stores, and it can be used on all bike bearings as well. Figure 1-10 shows where lubrication should be applied. Rub off old grease and accumulated dirt with a cloth before applying clean grease. Lightly oil pivot bolts and stirrup cable of center-pull brakes.

At least once a year you should remove brake cables, check them for wear and frayed strands and replace any cable that has a broken strand. If the inside of the cable cover, the spaghetti tubing through which the cable itself runs, is frayed, replace it. Rust inside a cable tube is a sign of neglect, such as having left the bike out in the rain a lot. If you do a lot of commuting, you really need brakes that respond fast to your touch of brake levers. Rusty, frayed or lube-dry cables will delay and make brake action that much harder, so they are a definite safety hazard. Remember, brake shoes should be about one-eighth inch from rims, as noted earlier. As I will point out later, this is so important, because the farther shoes are from the rim the slower the brake reaction time, and the farther brake levers will have to travel to bring the shoes to the rim.

If shoes are too far away, as in an effort to keep a crooked rim from hitting a shoe, the levers may, in a panic stop, travel all the way tightly against the handlebars, and still not stop you. There is a finite relationship between brake-lever travel, cable stretch or slack, shoe wear and distance of shoes from the rim. Unless all these factors are taken into consideration in adjusting brakes, you can have brakes considerably under par in terms of stopping power—yes, even Campagnolo brakes. Any brakes.

TOOLS

Depending on the brand of brake, you will need a 5-, 6-, 7- or 8-millimeter Allen wrench or a 6-, 7-, 8- or 9-millimeter box or open-end wrench. You should also have a "third hand" to hold brake stirrups

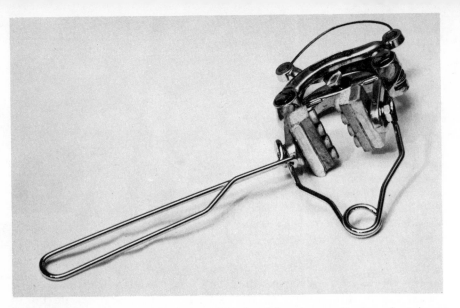

Fig. 1-11: Brake "third hand" tool holds brake shoes close to rim to make takeup of cable slack easier. You apply tool, pull cable end through cable clamp at brake end, tighten clamp, remove tool.

closed while you take up cable slack when installing new brake cables or reinstalling old ones after lubricating them. (Fig. 1-11).

Attaching Points: Here's where some of the other brakes have a slight advantage over Campy. The Campy 8-millimeter T wrench (socket end), which costs around $5 but which is equivalent to a thin wall socket, will fit the Campy Lever mounting nut, the one that locks the clamp section on the handlebars and the cable end attaching nut on the stirrup. If you don't have this wrench, you will have some difficulty using a standard socket, at least on the lever clamp nut. I find so many parts on a bike that this 8-millimeter wrench will fit that I would suggest you buy one, even though it's grossly overpriced. My initials are etched on mine.

Brake housing mounting nuts on the Shimano take an 8-millimeter Allen wrench (the "T" end of a Campy wrench will fit), as does the cable attaching nut on this brake, and the brake lever clamp nut.

The brake lever clamp nut on Dia-Compe levers takes a 5-millimeter Allen wrench, a major convenience in mounting and demounting these levers, as when, for example, you need to change handlebar tape or reposition the levers.

If you commute to work on your bike and leave it out in all sorts of weather, cable lubrication is especially important: first, because the cables are far more likely to run dry of grease and even rust when the bike is out all day; and second, lube-dry or rusty cables or cable tubing makes braking harder and slower, and robs you of braking torque by absorbing some of what should go to the brakes. If you commute you are most likely cycling through city traffic, and your brakes should be in top-

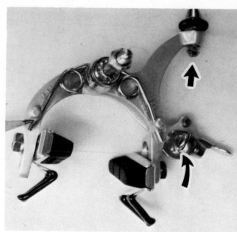

Fig. 1-12: Dia-Compe brakes. Pencil at left points to where grease should be applied to make brakes work smoothly. Arrow at upper right shows cable-adjusting barrel. To remove slack so as to keep shoes about ⅛ inch from rim flats, turn rubber bumper counterclockwise. Bottom right, arrow points to clamp-type cable gripper and quick-release unit.

Fig. 1-13: Center arrow points to cable-end fixing bolt. Note the hole in the bolt, through which cable is to pass. An Allen wrench at other end of bolt is tightened to clamp cable end in place. It is not possible to get a stranded cable end through this small hole, so that if just the end of the cable is stranded, entire cable must be replaced if cable is removed, as for lubrication.

notch condition at all times. To remove and replace cables, follow these steps:

STEP ONE: *Loosen cable holding or fixing bolt nut* (Fig. 1-12) and pull the end of the cable through. If the cable end is frayed and the cable end fixing bolt is the kind with a hole in it, discard the cable, because you will never get the frayed cable end back through the tiny bolt hole (Fig. 1-13).

STEP TWO: *Shove the cable back through the cable tubing* until the bell end comes slightly out of the slotted hole in the brake lever (Fig. 1-14). Or, simply push the cable out at the brake end until enough of the cable shows at the brake lever so you can pull the cable entirely through.

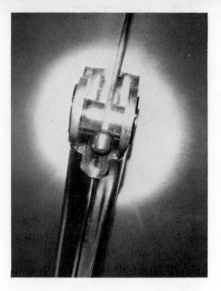

Fig. 1-14: When replacing old cable or installing a new one, thread lead bell end of cable through slot in brake lever. Big hole should be on bottom, because this is what the lead bell end fits into. Otherwise cable will just slip out as soon as brake is applied. Some brake-lever cable studs are not slotted, in which case cable must be threaded up through stud from underneath and then up and into top of brake-housing hole where cable leaves brake lever.

STEP THREE: *If you don't have to replace the cable,* apply a thin layer of Lubriplate or some other light grease to the entire cable and thread it back through the cable tubing.

STEP FOUR: *Fit the bell end of the cable* into the slot in the brake lever.

STEP FIVE: *Apply the "third hand" tool* (Fig. 1-11) to keep brake stirrups closed.

STEP SIX: *Pull brake cable all the way through.* Holding the brake end, pull on the brake lever to make sure the bell end of the cable is firmly inside the slotted hole. The small end of the hole slot must be on top. If the cable is not properly inside the slotted hole, this is when the bell end will pop out. Once the bell end is in place, fasten the other end to the brake-cable-end fixing bolt and tighten the fixing-bolt nut. Solder cable end so ends won't fray.

STEP SEVEN: *Release the "third hand" tool,* check to make sure brake shoes are about one-eighth inch from both sides of the wheel rim flats and that shoes are aligned with the rim. No part of the shoe should touch the tire nor should any part of the shoe be below the inner edge of the rim.

STEP EIGHT: *Spin the wheel, watching the shoes.* If the rim is out of alignment, it will rub on the shoe wherever it is out of line. Align the rim as described in Chapter 10. Again check to make sure the brake shoes have about one-eighth-inch distance from the rim flat on *both* sides (Fig. 1-15). If you have installed a new cable, squeeze the brake levers tightly to take out some of the cable stretch that new cables always have, and readjust the brake shoes again.

Fig. 1-15: An older model of the excellent Dia-Compe 450 center-pull brake. Note that tire is wider than shoe adjustment, so to remove wheel easily, the quick-release is opened to spread shoes back farther from the rim flat, to allow fatter tire to pass through. Parts are:

A. Brake-cable locknut. Loosen to pull cable through.
B. Stirrup cable
C. Cable yoke pulley. Makes brakes work more easily.
D. Brake-shoe locknut. Loosen to move shoe up or down, or tilt until shoe is accurately aligned on rim flat. **Must not touch tire!**

STEP NINE: *There are two places to adjust brake shoes.* If you are tuning up your bike for the season, it's best to remove cable slack at the brake-cable fixing bolt by loosening the fixing-bolt nut and pulling excess cable through, with the "third hand" in place. This way you will have plenty of adjustment room left in the cable-adjusting barrel. On side-pull brakes the adjusting barrel is on one of the stirrups (Fig. 1-16). On center-pull brakes the adjusting barrel can be on the front yoke (Fig. 1-17), the rear yoke (Fig. 1-18) or on the brake lever itself (Fig. 1-19). In either location, to take out cable-stretch slack, just loosen the barrel locknut (Fig. 1-17), and turn the barrel counterclockwise. (Make sure that if you have a quick-release it is closed before adjusting.) This pulls the cable up and removes slack. Brake shoes also wear, and some of the slack can be caused by worn shoes. Replacing shoes is simple enough;

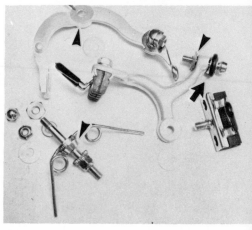

Fig. 1-16: Campy brakes dissected. Top arrow shows precise machining of stirrup pivot-bolt area. Arrow at bottom points to 13-mm. flats on pivot bolt which make it easier to hold brake in position while tightening pivot-bolt fixing nut. Washer, top-right arrow, helps hold cable take-up adjuster in place under vibration of bicycle riding. Pencil at top also points to pivot flat where light oil should be applied from time to time.

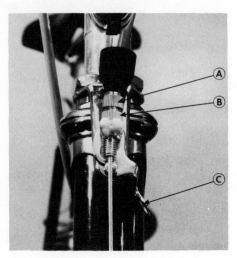

Fig. 1-17: This cable-slack take-up barrel is located on front cable yoke of center-pull brake. Note threaded end of barrel, at bottom.

A. Take-up barrel. Turn counterclockwise to remove cable slack.

B. Barrel locknut. Turn clockwise to tighten after adjusting barrel.

C. Quick-release lever.

just unscrew the brake-shoe-housing fixing nut, remove it and replace with either a new housing and shoe or the shoe alone. Squeeze the worn shoe out of the housing and squeeze a new one in. You can best do this with a vise. *You must reinstall housings with the open end, if it has one, toward the rear of the bike.* Or, install a complete new brake shoe in its housing.

Fig. 1-18: Cable-slack remover (arrow) is on rear center-pull brake yoke. Bottom arrow points to cable-clamp locknut on stirrup. This type of yoke can move up or down. Tighten or loosen brake, if saddle-fixing bolt is adjusted. When adjusting saddle, hold brake yoke so cable comes out of barrel in line with the barrel. In this photo, the yoke is tilted too far down, so cable rubs on top of barrel opening. Note also that a quick-release is part of this yoke.

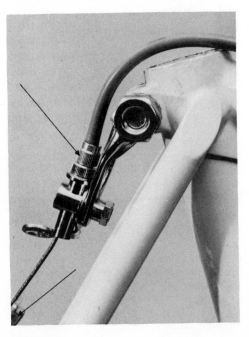

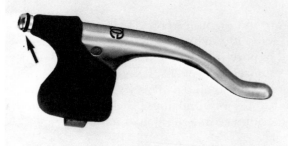

Fig. 1-19: Dia-Compe new Model 450 center-pull brake has cable-slack adjusting barrel located at top of brake lever (arrow), a more convenient location.

Cable Attachment: The Campy, Galli, and SunTour Superbe brakes lock at the end of the brake cable with a fixing clamp. There's no need to thread a cable through a tiny hole, as in the Shimano DuraAce and Dia-Compe brakes. You can attach a frayed cable to the clamp type, but not through the latter type. If you wish, for example, to remove brakes for cleaning, and the cable end is frayed, you won't have to replace a perfectly good cable when you reattach the brake. Of course, you can avoid this situation by soldering cable ends before snipping them off after installing a new cable, so you won't have frayed ends on your cables. Just apply a half inch or so of solder, shake off excess solder, and cut the cable in the middle of the soldered area. Figure 1-13 shows the hole-in-locking-bolt type of cable end attachment. Personally, I applaud the clamp type; it's so much easier to use. And if just one cable thread is loose, this is the one that won't go through the bolt hole.

Cables: All brakes, sold as a set, also come with cables. There's a vast difference, though, in cables. For example, the Campagnolo cables (Fig. 1-20) are considerably thicker than other makes, are soldered up to a couple of inches from the end, and are made with an outer shell or core

Fig. 1-20: Campagnolo brake cable—thicker, stronger, better made than other bike cables —is the cable at bottom. Campy cable is soldered for about two inches from the end so cable ends won't fray. If you trim off excess cable-end length, be sure to apply solder for one inch on either side of your intended cut. Soldered cable ends are much easier to deal with when removing cable later on for servicing and lubrication.

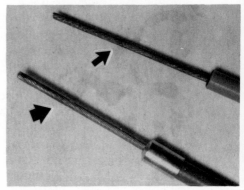

which is reverse wrapped around an inner core. This construction is both stronger and less conducive to fraying at the cut end. The Campy housing is slightly oversized to permit the cable to slide freely. Because the free end of the cable is soldered to prevent fraying, as noted, it may be just a tad thicker at that point and so bind a bit as you shove it through lever tops, cable guides and hole-in-bolt clamps. If this is a problem, pull the cable end through medium coarse sandpaper a few times.

Brake "Reach": In selecting a new set of brakes, you should make sure that those you purchase will have enough "reach" so the brake shoes can be adjusted to rub on the flats of the rims (*not on the tires!*). Some brake stirrups are not long enough for some bike sizes. To make sure that new brakes will fit, measure the distance from the centerline of the brake mounting hole in the brake bridge on the seat stays (rear) and of the same hole in the fork (front) to the centerline of the rim (Fig. 1-21). You may find that the rear brake stirrups should be longer than the front, or vice versa, depending on the frame builder. If, for example, your bike was designed for fender clearance, so that there is considerable space between the brake mounting hole and the rim centerline, you will need a longer brake reach. Some models of the same brake come in various reaches. For example, from Table 1-1 you will notice that Shimano DuraAce brakes come with minimum/maximum reaches of 39/49 and 47/57 millimeters respectively. Some brakes come in only one reach. If you have a bike with very little clearance between the fork and rim, be sure you buy a brake that will fit.

If for some reason you can't find the brakes you want (or can afford) that will have enough reach, or if you have bought them and perhaps are stuck with them, you can increase the reach by using a special brake pivot bolt that is dog-legged shaped or dropped. It drops the brake about 5 millimeters below its normal position if the stock pivot bolt were used. Be sure to buy the pivot bolt that fits your make and model of brake, though. Pivot bolts are not universal, by any means.

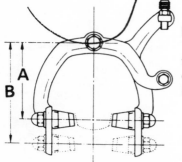

Fig. 1-21: This drawing shows how brake stirrup "reach" is calculated. You need to know the distance from centerline of brake pivot bolt, top, to centerline of rim and select a brake with stirrups long enough, or short enough, to fit.

Table 1-1 High-Quality Brake Selections

Make and Model	Q/R *	Weight †	Min/Max Reach ‡	Type §	Cost"
Campagnolo record	Yes	22	49/52	SP	$89.95
Universal CX	Yes	19.08	NA	SP	74.98
Galli Ti	Yes	15.87	NA	SP	74.98
Dia-Compe 400	Yes	19.50	40/50	SP	66.00
Dia-Compe 450	Yes	19.75	45/57	CP	66.00
SunTour Superbe	Yes	19.50	39/50	SP	NA
Galli 75	Yes	17.64	NA	SP	54.90
Shimano DuraAce EX CS-49	Yes	19.90	39/49	SP	87.75
Shimano DuraAce EX CS-57	Yes	19.90	47/57	SP	87.75
Shimano 600 BB-300	Yes	18.50	43/47	SP	35.00
Shimano 600 BB-400	Yes	20	47/62	SP	35.00
Shimano 600 cc-75	No	20.45	57/75	SP	35.00
Shimano 600 BB 330	Yes	18.5	43/57	SP	35.00

* Quick release.

† In ounces.

‡ Minimum/maximum brake reach, in millimeters (translates to inches by multiplying by .03937).

§ SP = side-pull; CP = center-pull.

" Approximate retail list price.

BRAKE TROUBLESHOOTING

- *If Campagnolo brake shoes drag on one side or the other,* first make sure the pivot-bolt fixing nut is tight. Then, with a 13-millimeter open-end wrench, grasp the pivot bolt just behind the stirrups (Figs. 1-22 and 1-23) and move the brake so the rim is centered between them. Shimano and other side-pull brakes can be adjusted the same way.
- *If brakes squeal,* check shoes for imbedded glass or small stones or other foreign material. Old, hardened brake shoes will also squeal. Brake shoes should slightly "toe-in" at the front. To toe-in, bend the stirrup arms slightly with a crescent wrench. Be careful not to overdo the bending process, so you don't break the stirrup arms.
- *Hand levers on handlebars bind:* Check to find the exact location of the binding. If sides of brake lever rub against the lever body, use a thin screwdriver to gently pry the lever inward (or bend the lever slightly inward). Check to make sure the cables aren't binding and that the cable housings (the spaghetti tubing through which the cables

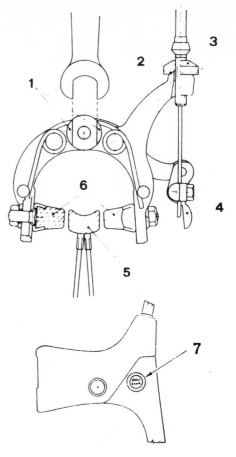

Fig. 1-22: Drawing of Campagnolo brake showing:

1. 13-mm. pivot-bolt flats where pivot bolt can be held from rotating while pivot-bolt fixing nut is tightened. Helps keep brakes aligned while tightening this nut.

2. Rubber bumper on adjusting barrel protects paint finish if fork swings too far.

3. The adjusting nut has a semispheric shape which wedges in the lever to keep it in place under vibrations of cycling.

4. Quick-release lever

5. Rim

6. Brake shoes

7. Knurled cable spindle makes it easier to keep the slotted end in place while you insert cable. You just hold the exterior knurls with fingers.

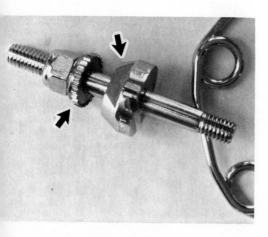

Fig. 1-23: Top arrow points to the flats on the Campy pivot bolt, which you can hold with a 13-mm. open wrench as the bolt is tightened in place in the fork or rear brake bridge. This makes aligning or centering of brake easier. Bottom arrow points to two-sided serrated washer which helps hold brake in place, once tightened.

run) curve gradually from the levers to the frame and from the frame to the brakes without "kinks" at any point.

- *Center-pull brake arms do not pivot freely on trunnions (center bolt):* If the center bolt or trunnion fits too tightly, ream out a small hole in the arm with a drill. Or sand the trunnion to a smaller diameter. If the arms are too thick, file at the pivot area so that the pivot bolt sits against the trunnion without binding the arm. Loosen the pivot bolt; if the arm moves freely, the arm is too thick.

- *Uneven braking:* Check for out-of-round or dented rims. Sometimes the brakes will grab unevenly and, at the same time, "shudder" or "judder." Juddering means that the entire brake assembly is loose on the trunnion bolt holding it to the frame. The brake assembly must be rigid. Loosen the locknut, take up on the adjusting nut and retighten the locknut. The brakes should have no front-to-rear play; they should pivot freely but not loosely. If the brakes still "judder," check the head bearing play on the front fork, and readjust (see Chapter 7).

Chapter Two

FLAT TIRES

Figure 2-1 shows a wired-on tire. You will note that there is a steel wire in the bead of this tire, hence the name "wired-on." The "clincher" tire does not have a wire bead, rather a rubber bead that fits into a groove in the rim. The clincher tire is all but obsolete, has not been used on bicycles sold in this country for years and I for one will be happy to forget that it ever existed. So now we are left with wired-on and tubular tires. The tubular tire (Fig. 2-2) is, as its name implies, tubular in that it is sewn up with the tube inside. It is used for racing, primarily, although a lot of us toured on them until the new lightweight narrow-profile wired-on tires appeared a few years ago.

Because tubulars are quite thin compared to tires, and the tube in particular is even thinner, they are far more likely to get punctured than the thicker casing of the tire and the thicker tube. Once punctured, the

Fig. 2-1: Cross-section of a box-type rim and conventional wired-on tire, showing the wire bead cutaway. Note how the bead seats in the rim. As the tube is expanded under air pressure, the tire bead is held firmly in the slanted rim section, keeping the tire in place. The box-type rim is one of the strongest made.

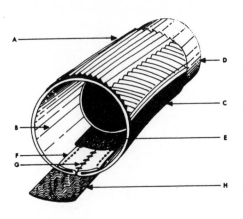

A. Tread.

B. Casing, made of fabric.

C. Outside of casing, between bottom of tread and base tape, is called the "wall."

D. Inner tube.

E. Chafing tape, to prevent inner tube from puncture by rubbing on tire stitching.

F. Hems of casing are made by gluing back the edges of fabric to the inside. In some tires, hems are folded to the outside.

G. Stitching. When repairing, use a simple hand-over-hand stitch.

H. Base tape protects stitching and provides seating for entire tire.

Fig. 2-2: A tubular tire is dissected in this sketch. You will note that the tread, bottom, is a separate part of the tubular, unlike conventional beaded tires, and that the tube is sewn up inside the tubular. Other names for tubulars are "tubs" and "sew-ups."

tubular is a real pain to repair, because you have to cut the stitching, lift out the tube where you hope the puncture is located, patch that spot, resew and remount the tubular on the rim. To fix a flat tire, you do not even need to remove it from the rim, if you are sure you know where the puncture is located. All you do is pry away the tire from the rim, pull out the tube, patch it, push it back in, reseat the tire and pump it up. There's more to repairing both types of rubber things around rims, but I shall treat this subject in depth later.

Tires on Tubular Rims

You can't mount tires on tubular rims, except in the direst of emergencies. If while touring you blow a tire and have no spare, with 700-centimeter rims and some rim cement, you can mount a tubular (if you can find someone who will lend you one) that will get you home or to a bike shop, if you take it easy.

Mounting Lightweight Tires

First of all, the new 27-inch or 700-centimeter × 1-inch tires are not mountable on any but the rims made for them. The wire bead of these narrow-profile tires will not seat securely in the wider rims, and you are likely to have a blowout that will put a large hole in the tube and ruin it. If you are lucky, you won't lose control of the bike if this occurs. It has happened to me.

Different rims have sides of different depths, from 5 to 7 millimeters, so be careful about seating any narrow-profile tire, even the 1⅛-inch-wide tires. I have found that the best way to seat these tires is to pump them up to about five pounds, run my hand all around the bead area, or the sidewall area, and make double sure the tire is well seated, especially around the valve. If the rim strip is doubly thick at the valve hole, you may not be able to seat the tire at all, in which case, use rim tape instead of the rim strip. Pump the tire up to around 20 psi and check seating again. Finally, blow it up to 100 psi, which is the pressure I like, or even to 115 psi to get the lowest possible rolling resistance. Ride the newly mounted tire for a few blocks, stop and recheck the tire seating. The bend should be well into the rim all the way around on both sides. Bicycle Research has a tire-pinching tool that can help seat these tires (Fig. 2-3).

Be particularly careful when seating the new foldable lightweights, such as the Michelin Elan TS. This tire uses a fiberglass instead of a wire rim bead, which is why it is foldable. The fiberglass bead resists seating more than the conventional steel wire bead and is far more likely to pop out.

One note of caution about rims: The Schwinn Super Record tires will not fit on Mavic rims.

TIRE PRESSURE

Probably the most neglected aspect of tire care is air pressure. Use this tire chart as a guide to correct minimum tire pressure, increasing pressure according to the weight of the rider and any extra load carried. For tires used on tandem bicycles, increase above pressures from 10 to 20 pounds per square inch to handle the extra load safely.

NOTE: On cool days one can inflate tires to maximum pressures safely. However, on very hot days, with temperatures in the eighties and higher, it is safer to reduce pressures by 3 to 5 pounds under the maximum to avoid heat buildup. Air expands as it heats, and on a hot day you could experience a blowout if your bike stands exposed to the sun.

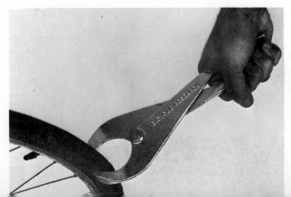

Fig. 2-3: This tool helps seat the new lightweight, high-pressure tires on the rim. The tire bead must be seated in the groove.

Table 2-1 Air Pressure

In general, these are the air pressures you should use with various types of tires. Remember that if you are a bit heavier than average, you should add about five pounds more pressure. If tire bulges markedly, you are too heavy for the pressure used. Tire should not bulge, or at most, bulge very slightly when ridden.

Tire Size	Air Pressure (in lbs. per sq. in.)
12 in. x 1⅜ in.	30–40
16 in. x 1⅜ in.	30–40
18 in. x 1⅜ in.	35–45
20 in. x 1⅜ in.	45–50
24 in. x 2⅛ in.	35–45
26 in. x 1¼ in.	45–50
26 in. x 1⅜ in.	45–50
26 in. x 1¾ in.	30–35
26 in. x 2⅛ in.	35–45
27 in. x 1¼ in.	85–100
700 cm. x 1⅛ in.	85–100
700 cm. x 1 in.	85–100
Tubular tires	Tracks with very smooth surfaces: rear wheels, 100–140; front tires, 90–120
	Tracks with uneven surfaces: rear tires, 90–100; front tires, 90
	Road racing: rear tires, 90–100; front tires, 90, depending on road conditions
	Touring: rear tires, 85–100, depending on load and road conditions; front tires, 85–90

How to Use a Pump

On any valve, be it Presta or Schraeder, there is a correct way to use a pump. Presta valves, being longer and skinnier, are far easier to break off with improper application of the pump. Figure 2-4 shows how easy it is to break off the top half of a Presta valve. The valve core, when the valve tube is broken like that, cannot be threaded down, so the tire or tubular tends to leak, something like a slow leak. The newer Presta valve comes in two pieces, at least on the better tubulars, so if it breaks, you can replace the top half. I haven't seen any tire Presta valve tubes with two-piece valves, and I don't think I'll hold my breath till they come.

Fig. 2-4: If you wiggle a Presta valve pump as you pump air you can easily break off the valve tube, as shown. Hold pump steady so this doesn't occur.

Fig. 2-5: Remove pump with a sharp downward thump with the base of the hand, as shown. Don't wiggle pump off valve or you may damage valve tube.

To pump a Presta valve properly, first open the valve by turning the core counterclockwise (otherwise you can't pump air in). Then, holding the pump with thumb on top of the tubular (or tire), and holding the pump in place so it does not wiggle from side to side as you pump, shove the pump handle in and out until the tubular is filled to your satisfaction. Wiggling the pump from side to side is a sure way to break off the valve tube. When you are finished pumping, knock the pump off the valve with a firm downward blow (Fig. 2-5). Don't try to wiggle the pump off. That breaks valve tubes.

HOW TO REPAIR TIRES

Why Tires Go Flat

Underinflated tires put more tire tread on the road and use up more energy by flexing and creating heat, which makes the bicycle considerably harder to pedal.

An underinflated tire cannot take bumps and stones, and ordinary contact with pavement roughness can be sufficient to force the tire casing inward far enough to pinch the tube against the metal wheel rim. This can cause a blowout and might even bruise the tire casing beyond repair, causing a flat spot on the rim that cannot be pulled out. Here are some common types of tire damage and how to avoid them.

Glass damage causes knifelike cuts on the tread or the sidewall. To avoid running over glass and similar sharp objects, watch the road just in front of you as you ride. If you ride at night, ride only on roads with which you are familiar and know are not likely to have glass, and use a good light to detect glass as far in advance as possible to give you time to swing out of the way. (Watch out for passing cars—swing right instead of left if you can to avoid glass.)

Blowouts can be caused by overinflation (Fig. 2-6), underinflation, and tire-casing damage such as glass cuts. A glass wound (Fig. 2-7) will open and close as the tire casing flexes and will eventually pinch a hole in the tire tube. That is why you should always look for the *cause* of a flat after a patch has been applied to the tube.

Nails and other sharp objects such as fine pieces of wire will cause a flat by piercing both tire and tube. Be sure to remove the nail before reinstalling the tire and tube. If the nail is still in the tire when you go to repair it, at least you will know the location of the leak in the tube.

Ruptures (Fig. 2-8) are *always* a sign of abuse, barring accidents. Riding up and down curbs, into sharp stones and curbs, is a sure invitation to ruptures and a very short tire life.

Rim cuts (Fig. 2-9) are long, thin-looking cuts in the sidewalls and are caused by riding an underinflated tire, rusty rims, or an overloaded bicycle.

Uneven tread wear (Fig. 2-10) can be due to crooked rims, quick stops that grab and lock the wheel (otherwise known as skidding to a stop for kicks), or out-of-adjustment caliper brakes that grab the rim. Out-of-true rims also cause excessive tire wear because the caliper brake will grab at the out-of-true spot. It is a good idea to look far enough ahead to be able to avoid sudden stops, for your own as well as for your tires' longevity.

Other common kinds of tube failures or punctures include:

When the tire is under-inflated, the tube can slide around the rim and pull the valve stem out of the seat, as shown. This could also be a manufacturing defect. Always check new tubes for defects before leaving the store (Fig. 2-11).

Blowout. This is what happens to the new lightweight tires, especially the one-inch-diameter sizes when used on a too large rim or not seated properly in the rim (Fig. 2-12).

Failure at the joining (Fig. 2-13). This is a manufacturer's defect and if found, get your money back.

A genuine puncture. Looks as though it was caused by a nail (Fig. 2-14).

When you pinch the tube with a tire iron, you can cause a slit such as the one in Figure 2-15.

An underinflated tire can move around on the rim and tear the valve out. Check your tires frequently. If valve becomes cocked to one side, deflate and move tire on rim until valve is straightened. Figure 2-16 shows this type of damage.

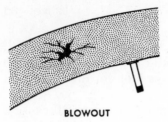

BLOWOUT

Fig. 2-6: Puncture due to overinflation

STAR BREAK

Fig. 2-7: Star break in tire casing caused by riding over stones or other sharp objects. May not be visible from outside, so always check inside of casing when repairing a flat.

RUPTURE

Fig. 2-8: Slit type of damage to tire caused by jumping curbs or hitting sharp objects at high speeds, forcing casing against rim.

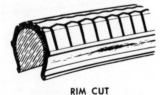

RIM CUT

Fig. 2-9: Rim cuts caused by underinflated tires. Cuts are evidence of excessive flexing.

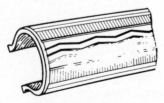

UNEVEN TREAD WEAR

Fig. 2-10: Uneven tire wear caused by skidding brake stops, uneven rims. (*Figs. 2-6 through 2-10 courtesy Schwinn Bicycle Company*)

Fig. 2-11: Arrow points to ruptured valve. This is what happens when the tire is underinflated, permitting the tube to slide around the rim.

Fig. 2-12: Blow-out caused by sudden departure of the tire from the rim. Improperly seated tires will lift out of the rim groove, permitting the section of the tube nearest the point of lift-off to protrude and blow out. Illustrates the importance of being earnest about tire-bead setting when mounting a new tire. Older tires have stretched somewhat and are easier to mount so that beads drop into rim groove.

Fig. 2-13: Failure where the tube is joined illustrates a manufacturer's defect. Get your money back, or a new tube.

Fig. 2-14: This is a puncture, very likely by a nail.

Fig. 2-15: If you are not careful when replacing tire on rim, it's very, very easy to puncture a slit like this in the tube with whatever you are using to pry the tire back on the rim, particularly at those last few mean old stubborn inches. Watch that you don't pinch the tube between the tool and the rim. This is where this type of pinch damage occurs. Use tire irons, not a sharp-edged screwdriver.

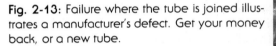

Fig. 2-16: Again, an underinflated tire will permit tube to slip around rim. Because valve is in the rim hole, when the tube slips the valve stays more or less in place until torn loose, as shown. The solution: keep tires inflated to maximum permitted pressure, plus four or five more psi.

Steps in Tire Repair

STEP ONE: If the tire goes flat overnight, you may have either a tiny puncture or a slow leak through the valve. You can check for a valve core leak by removing the valve cap (Figs. 2-17 and 2-18), inflating the tire to normal pressure, and putting a bit of soapy water in the valve. If the valve leaks, you will see bubbles. In this case, all you need to do is tighten the valve core. If the valve still leaks, replace the valve core with a new one. You will need an old-fashioned metal valve cap to tighten or remove the core. This is available from any bicycle shop and most service stations.

STEP TWO: To repair a tube puncture you will need two flat-end tire levers, or two dull-edge, broad-blade screwdrivers, to pry the tire off and put it on. First, remove the valve core from the valve, with a valve cap. If there is a locknut on the valve stem, remove it from the stem. If a Presta valve, unscrew the valve and depress to deflate.

STEP THREE: You usually do not need to remove the wheel if you're on the road and touring. Even with saddlebags or carriers in the way, you can attack the repair by removing the tire in the vicinity of the puncture, pulling out the tube, and patching it as described below. Otherwise, remove the wheel and, with the two tire levers, pry one side of the tire away from the rim until one side is loose enough to pull all the way off. Remove the tire by hand from the other side of the rim.

STEP FOUR: Inflate the tube and rotate it near your ear until you find the location of the puncture by hearing the hiss of escaping air. Draw a

Fig. 2-17: Schraeder valve, used on U.S. auto, motorcycle and bike tubes, has a removable valve core.

Fig. 2-18: Schraeder valve cores can be removed to get all the air out of a slow-leaking tube so that you can pry the tire off the rim, or partially off the rim, to get at the tube.

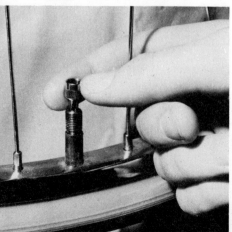
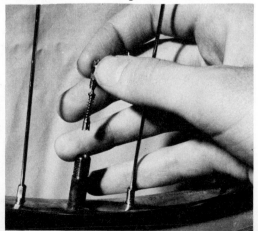

circle around the puncture with a piece of chalk. If you can't find it by listening for escaping air, immerse the tube in a tub of water and watch for bubbles as you rotate the tube in the water. Hold your finger in the puncture area while you dry the tube off thoroughly. Mark the puncture with a piece of chalk.

STEP FIVE: With a piece of sandpaper or the metal abrader that comes with tire repair kits, scrape the tube around the puncture and put a thin layer of rubber cement around it, extending outward about a half inch in all directions. Let the rubber cement get tacky, pull the paper backing off the appropriate-sized tube patch, and press the patch firmly down onto the coated area over the puncture. Be careful, in handling the tube patch, not to finger the patch over the coated area where you have removed the paper covering. Hold the patch carefully by the edges until you have pressed it into place over the puncture.

STEP SIX: While the rubber under the patch is drying, check the outside of the tire carefully and pry out any embedded glass, nails, and the like. Remember, *something* caused that tire to go flat, and that something is most likely still embedded in the tire. Then, spreading the tire apart as you go, check the inside walls for any breaks. Breaks, if not too bad, can be patched with a tire patch. However, if the tire has bad cuts or bruises, discard it and buy a new one. Check for loose spokes, and tighten them. Remove the rubber strip inside the wheel and check to make sure all spokes are flush with the spoke nipples. File down any protruding spokes to prevent a later puncture, and replace the rubber strip. Realign the rim, if necessary, as discussed in Chapter 10.

STEP SEVEN: Install the tire on the wheel. First, make sure most but not all the air is out of the tube. Tuck the tube carefully back into the tire. Put the valve into the valve hole in the rim. Next, starting at the valve, with hands on either side of the wheel, push the beaded edge of the tire all the way around until one side of the tire is on the rim. Then push the other side of the tire on the rim in the same manner. You should not need to use the tire levers to install the tire. But if you do use them, make sure that when you have the lever pushed up under the tire, you do not pinch the tube between the lever and the rim and cause a puncture. Inflate the tire and check for leaks before remounting the wheel. To make sure the bead is set, before inflating, shove down on the valve stem so it will seat. Then inflate to around five pounds. Remove the pump and rotate the wheel to make sure the bead is seated all the way around.

TIRES AND WHEELS

I recommend you switch to the new lightweight narrow-profile tires and abandon tubulars altogether for touring. You can scrap the tubular rims, cut the spokes with cutting pliers and, using the old hub, lace on rims suitable for the lightweight tires.

Another alternative is to simply keep the old tubulars and tubular rims and hubs intact and use them for day trips on country roads. For touring you can then buy a complete tire, rim and hub, ready to install on your bicycle. If you're going to be doing a lot of touring, I would recommend the complete wheel with a sealed-bearing hub such as the Avocet, Phil Wood, Durham or Hi-E. You should be able to get a set of wheels made up with hubs using Robergel high-tension spokes for around $80 to $90, depending on the hub. You can get 48-spoke tandem wheels made up for around $120 each. For stronger wheels, specify Robergel 3 star spokes. These are stainless steel finish, double-butted.

Care of Tubulars

If you do a lot of racing and/or like touring with tubulars, I advise you to stock up a year in advance and age them for longer life. Aging is necessary because new "raw" tubulars, whether the casing is cotton, silk, polyester or nylon, are latex impregnated and the latex is soft when new. As time passes, the latex bonding with casing fibers toughens. If you ride with new tubulars you are much more prone to flats and the tread may separate from the casing, which you definitely do not want to happen to your good $30 silks. The best way to age tubulars is to mount them on old rims and hang them up in a cool, dark, dry place for six months. A year would be better. In the off-season, never leave the bicycle with tubulars on the ground; hang the bike from the ceiling so the tubulars won't take a "set."

With age, tubular casings tend to dry out, become brittle and crack or show "craze" marks. The rubber coating actually evaporates. You can avoid or at least delay this deterioration by applying a latex solution on sidewalls, over sidewall cuts and use it to glue down the base tape onto the tubular casing after repairing (see below). If your bike shop does not have this sealant, order from Palo Alto Bicycles, P.O. Box 1276, Palo Alto, California 94302 for $1.50 for a four-ounce container.

You should, of course, always carry a spare tubular even on day trips. There's where tubulars have a real advantage over tires. You can change a tubular in two minutes or less, even on the back wheel, but replacing a tire takes upwards of ten or fifteen minutes, at least. (It's when you get home that all the time is used in repairing the punctured tubular. But at least on the road, if you're with a group, you won't hold anyone up for long if all you have to do is strip off the punctured tubular and roll on a good one.)

Do not leave spares folded on bicycles longer than two weeks. Remove the spare, inflate lightly, let it stand overnight, deflate, and reroll. This prevents spares from taking a "set" on the folds. In refolding, fold the opposite way so that the part that was on the inside is now on the outside. However, always fold so that the tread is on the outside. When folded, mount the spare so that it cannot rub or chafe anywhere. Ideally, you should carry it in a plastic bag.

Valves should be protected against dirt with a light plastic dust cap. Remember to close the valve on the spare. Open, it can be easily bent.

Extra spares should always be stored lightly inflated, in a warm, dry place. Be very careful not to store tubulars that have become wet, unless you inflate them so they can dry out.

For safety, particularly if you do a lot of riding, check rim cement frequently. If you are on a tour, check rim cement at least weekly, because this cement can dry out and flake off. Rim cement is absolutely essential to keep tires from creeping and crawling.

Never let oil, grease, kerosene, gasoline, rubber cement or any other kind of solvent touch your tubulars. Solvents will eventually eat right through your tubular.

When you're car-carrying tubulars, partially deflate them so the hot sun won't heat the air inside the tube, causing a blowout. Keep tubulars from rubbing anything; preferably use a cover. You can make a cover out of an old 27- $\times$ 1¼-inch tire casing by removing its wire bead.

Don't fill tubulars with CO_2 because it leaks out even faster than air. If you use a pressure cartridge, use nitrogen.

On the road, protect spare tubulars against road dirt with plastic cloth. *And before you leave on a long trip, check rim cement to make sure it hasn't dried out.* Try to pry the tubular off with your fingers. If it lifts easily, the cement is dry. Remove tubular, old cement, and re-cement. Do try to keep rim cement off side walls; that makes for a fast, skidding stop every time, and it's messy, besides.

If you realign your rim, remember that retensioning spokes can cause spoke heads to protrude and puncture the tube. Remove the tubular, and check and file off any protruding spoke heads.

If you carry your bicycle, be careful not to let the tires rub on any metal or wooden parts. Check the placement of wheels against car seats, carrying racks, toe straps, and tie-down straps.

On an airplane trip, if you bring your bicycle, remember to half deflate your tubulars (or tires); because if your bicycle is stored in an unpressurized or partly pressurized baggage compartment, the low pressures at high altitudes may permit the high pressures inside the tube to cause a blowout.

How to Carry Tubular Spares

Because tubulars do not take time to repair, you should always carry at least one spare on any trip. A convenient way to carry the spare is to fold the tire so that the tread is on the outside and not folded back on itself (Fig. 2-19). Wrap the tire under the seat, behind the seat post, with a strap (Fig. 2-20). Better yet, protect folded tubulars from the sunlight, road debris and rain by carrying your spare in a spare-tire carrier that can be fastened under the saddle (Fig. 2-20). From Palo Alto Bicycles for around $7. This is a waterproof nylon pouch with buckle strap.

Tire Savers

Experienced cyclists have learned to rub a gloved hand over the tire every so often during a trip, or whenever they think the tire has rolled over something that might puncture it. Quite often you can remove tiny sharp objects this way, before they've had a chance to work their way

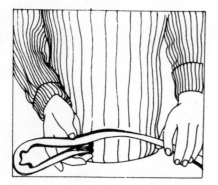 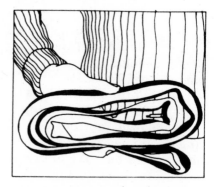

Fig. 2-19: Fold a spare tubular as shown. Valve should be located as indicated at right, where it cannot chafe the tubular.

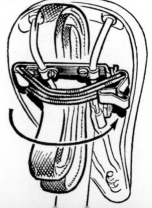

Fig. 2-20: Carry a spare tubular, folded, under the saddle. Tire carrier shown is made by Vittoria. You can also use a pedal strap.

Fig. 2-21: These gloves are made specially for bicyclists. They have a double-thick palm so you can rub over tires as you pedal, to remove any foreign objects that may have become imbedded in the tire, before they can cause a flat. Double palm also protects your palm in case of a fall.

through the casing and the tube. This applies to all tires, but especially to tubulars and the new lightweight tires.

Sometimes it's difficult or impossible to reach tires when panniers or a handlebar bag are in the way; and if you're not careful, it's not too difficult to get your hand caught between the tire and the brake bridge, which can be a painful experience at best and cause a spill at worst. Which is why I strongly urge you to cycle only with double thick palm cool bike gloves (Fig. 2-21), which cost about $8.50 in any good bike store. These gloves can save a lot of skin on the palm of your hand in the event of a fall.

Back to tire savers. You can also mount a pair of tire savers (Fig. 2-22) onto brake bolts, and adjust them to rub lightly over the tires. Use them on tubulars and tires. They cost around $1.50 a pair and are cheap insurance against punctures. At least they help scrape off stuff you do not notice as you ride.

Fig. 2-22: These "tire savers" can be used for both tubulars and conventional tires. They fasten onto brake-mounting bolts and rub lightly over the tire treads to scrape off any small pieces of glass, nails and other objects that would work their way through the tread and casing into the tube. The tire savers do not work well on heavier tires because puncture-causing objects can lodge in the deeper tread indentations where the savers can't reach them. Use savers only on tubulars and on the lightest high-pressure tires.

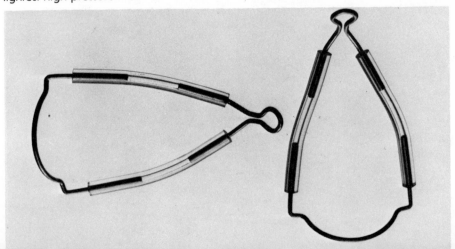

How to Repair Tubular Tires

To repair tubular tires, you will have to cut a few stitches in the area where the puncture is located, repair the puncture, and restitch the tire. To repair tubulars, follow this procedure:

STEP ONE: You will need a patch set (Fig. 2-23) consisting of:

- Special thin tube patches (such as the ones made by Dunlop)
- A triangular-pointed hand-sewing needle
- Tubular tire linen thread
- Rubber cement
- A small tube of talc powder
- A small piece of yellow chalk
- A small screwdriver
- A sharp knife or razor blade
- A small square of fine sandpaper

Many bicycle mail-order houses sell a tubular tire repair kit with most of the above items. The reason for the extra-thin tube patches is that tubulars have a very thin tube. An ordinary tire patch is far too thick for this tube and would cause a lump inside the tubular which would thump

Fig. 2-23: Here is a tubular-tire surgical repair kit, everything you need to repair the tubular—scalpel, needle, suture thread, pincers, patches, scrapers, compounds. Not shown is shellac, used only on nonrubberized base strip of track tubulars. Do not use cement on track tires.

Fig. 2-24: Step Three in tubular repair: Dunk tubular in water to find location of leak before cutting base-strip threads.

as you ride. Thin patches are especially needed for the lighter track-racing tubulars, which are generally handmade from silk cord and rubber latex. An old piece of tubular tube will do in an emergency.

STEP TWO: If you have an old rim, mount the tubular on the rim, inflate it to sixty or seventy pounds of air pressure and set the tire and rim in a half-filled washtub. Or simply remove the tubular from the wheel, inflate as above and put it, a bit at a time, into the washtub. If you can see no puncture, you could have a loose or torn valve or a puncture at the valve area (Fig. 2-24).

STEP THREE: As you insert the tubular into the tub of water, you will notice that a lot of air seems to be bubbling up from around the valve stem first (Fig. 2-25). The tubular is sewn and has a rubber-cemented strip over the sewing, so this is about the only place air *can* escape, except through the puncture itself.

Fig. 2-25: Sometimes you can get a false reading on the location of the leak because air follows the path of least resistance and escapes around valve. Never accept bubbles at the valve as prima facie evidence; keep checking for another air bubble location.

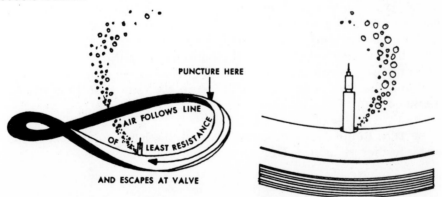

Rotate the tubular slowly until you come to the spot where air is seeping out through a small puncture in the tire casing. With a piece of yellow chalk, mark this area; it is also the location of the tube puncture. Deflate the tubular and remove it from the rim.

STEP FOUR: With the small screwdriver or another flat (but not sharp!) tool, carefully pry about 2½ inches of the tape on both sides of the puncture away from the inner circumference of the tire (Fig. 2-26).

STEP FIVE: With the razor or small sharp knife, carefuly cut the stitching about 2 inches on either side of the puncture. Do not cut down *into* the tire, but insert the knife edge under the stitching and cut upward to avoid cutting into the tube, which lies just under the stitching (Figs. 2-27 and 2-28).

STEP SIX: Pull about 4 inches of the tube out gently and, with a hand pump, inflate the tube enough to find the puncture (Fig. 2-29). With the yellow chalk, outline the puncture, centering it in a chalked circle about the size of a quarter. A simple way to find the puncture is to hold the tube near your lips and rotate it slowly. You should be able to feel the flow of air from the puncture. If you can't find the puncture this way, put a drop of liquid soap in a glass, fill it with warm water, and place this mixture on the tube until you find a bubble marking the location of the puncture.

STEP SEVEN: Dry the tube thoroughly, if you have wet it. With the sandpaper, lightly abrade the area you have marked off around the puncture, putting a small, solid object under the tube to support it as you rub it with the sandpaper (Fig. 2-30).

STEP EIGHT: Apply several light coatings of rubber cement to the abraded area. Let each coating dry to a hard glaze (Fig. 2-31).

STEP NINE: Apply a patch of finest-grade thin rubber to the tube over the puncture. Dust with talcum powder to prevent the tube from sticking to the casing. Note that two patches have been applied to this tube. This is because whatever caused the flat often goes through *both sides* of the tube, so you should check the other side of the tube from where you found the first puncture to make sure *that* side also hasn't been penetrated (Figs. 2-32 and 2-33).

STEP TEN: Reinflate the tube slightly with the hand pump. Check the area for further punctures. Deflate the tube.

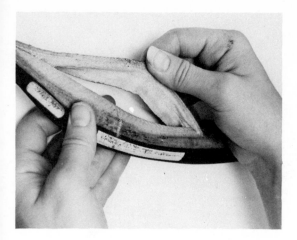

Fig. 2-26: Step Four: Pull away base strip.

Fig. 2-27: Step Five: Cut base stitching.

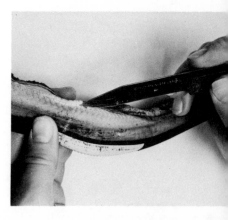

Fig. 2-28: Step Five: Remove old stitching.

Fig. 2-29: Step Six: Pull out tube, locate puncture.

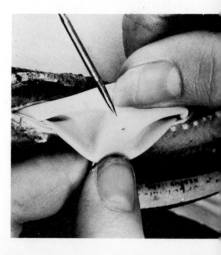

Fig. 2-30: Step Seven: Abrade tube lightly.

Fig. 2-31: Step Eight: Apply rubber cement, let dry till tacky.

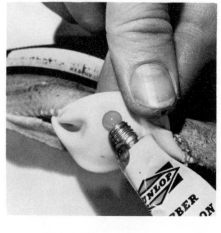

Fig. 2-32: Step Nine: Apply patch.

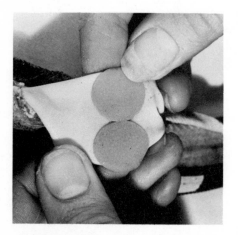

Fig. 2-33: Step Ten: Push tube back in casing.

STEP ELEVEN: Inspect the tire casing for damage, such as bruises, gouges, rips, tears and the rare manufacturing defect (Figs. 2-34 and 2-35). If the tire casing itself is damaged, I recommend relegating the tire to the spare-use-only category, because although the casing damage can be patched with a thin piece of canvas applied with rubber cement if the bruise or hole is small, even this patch will bulge and cause the tire to "thump" annoyingly, especially at high speeds. Tubular-tire repair kits do come with a special piece of canvas for this purpose, but I recommend its use for emergency situations only. Patched tires can, of course, serve ideally as spares.

STEP TWELVE: Sew up the tire, using the triangular-pointed needle and doubled thread. In an emergency, a twelve-pound-test linen thread or double thread *silk* fishing line will do. Nylon line won't serve the purpose; it cuts into the tire. Start by sewing back about a half inch over the cut stitching. Use a simple overhand stitch to finish the stitching, running the thread about a half inch through *existing* holes left from the manufacturer's original stitching. Don't make new holes. Pull stitches firmly, but don't overdo it or you'll cut the tire casing (Fig. 2-36).

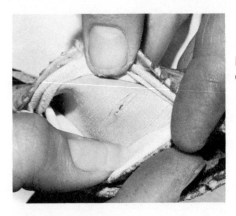

Fig. 2-34: Step Eleven: Reinstall tube cover.

Fig. 2-35: Step Eleven: Make sure tube cover is smooth, like a bed sheet.

Fig. 2-36: Step Twelve: Begin cross-over stitching.

Fig. 2-37: Step Thirteen: With dilute solution of rim cement, replace base strip. Use shellac on track tubulars.

Fig. 2-38: Step Fifteen: Inflate, check for leaks.

STEP THIRTEEN: Apply rubber cement over the area revealed when you peeled back the protective tape over the stitching and on the tape itself (Fig. 2-37). Let dry. Carefully lay tape back in position.

STEP FOURTEEN: Mount the tire, inflate to riding pressure, and check again for leaks. Leave inflated so that rubber cement has a chance to dry thoroughly.

STEP FIFTEEN: Fill in any cuts in the tread with the black rubber cement (*not* patch cement) that comes with your patch kit, or with black plastic rubber cement which you can buy in a hardware store (Fig. 2-38).

Adhering Road Tubulars

Road tubulars should be stuck on the rim with mastic, a form of rubber cement. Look for Tubasti, Vittoria, or Pastali rim glue.

If the track rim is new it should be scored with a rough file so that the smooth bed is roughened for better adhesion. The lighter silks may puncture just from pressure over the nipple holes, so if you wish, these may be filled with tight-fitting corks which should then be filed flush with the rim base so as to present a smooth, unbroken surface.

Don't apply one thick coat of shellac. It's far better to apply two or three coats to the rim, allowing each coat to dry thoroughly before applying the next coat. Drying time depends on temperature and humidity. What we are looking for is a smooth bed of shellac on the rim. Any shellac which has strayed over onto the rim sides should be carefully scraped away.

Now that the rim is prepared, let's work on the tire. Inflate the tire so it is just beginning to feel firm, with around five or six strokes of the pump. Remove any rubber solution which may have adhered to the base tape in the manufacturing process. Thin out the shellac solution and carefully brush it on the base tape and allow it to dry. What we want to do here is fill the cotton- or silk-weave base tape with shellac for proper adhesion. This is an important step, because otherwise the base tape will not adhere firmly to the shellac on the rim.

At this point, go back to the rim and give it one final coat of shellac and let it dry for from ten to forty minutes, depending on the temperature, until it gets tacky, or a bit less than tacky.

If this is not a new rim, remove all old glue (this applies also to track rim shellac) with a paint remover or Bullshot Rimstrip. Apply Rimstrip to the rim, wait for a couple of hours, then wipe the rim clean. Follow with a hot soap-and-water bath to remove the Rimstrip completely. If the rim is new or has not been scored, do so with a rough file for maximum adhesion.

If the road tubular has a nonrubberized cotton base tape, fill the base tape weave with a thinned-out solution of rim cement, using one of the brands noted above. Some of the base tapes of this type of tubular are sort of fluffy, and unless filled with a thin solution of rim cement, adhesion will not be secure. If the road tubular has a rubberized base tape, you need only apply the rim cement to the rim (Fig. 2-39). In either case, do not wait for the cement to dry on the rim or the tubular, but fit the tubular right on the rim as soon as possible. Wipe or scrape any rim cement that may have slopped over onto the rim sides. Now follow these steps in putting the tubular on the rim:

Fig. 2-39: Use thin layer of rim cement for road tubes, shellac for track tubes.

Fig. 2-40: Step One: With valve in rim, start placing tube on rim, pushing from both sides of valve evenly and alternately.

Fig. 2-41: Step Two: Continue pushing tube on rim.

Fig. 2-42: Step Three: Using thumbs and palms of hands, finish placing tube on rim.

Fig. 2-43: Step Four: If tubular is more to one side of rim, move it so that both sides are even, as shown.

STEP ONE: Deflate tubular almost completely, leaving just enough air to give the tire a little body. Hold wheel in an upright position and insert valve through the valve hole in the rim (Fig. 2-40).

STEP TWO: With the valve at the top of the wheel and the wheel on a soft pad on the floor, stand behind the wheel and with both hands push the tubular downward onto the rim, finishing on the side opposite the valve (Fig. 2-41). Hold the rim away from your body while you're doing this—or wear old clothes.

STEP THREE: With the tubular on the rim as far as possible, force the remainder of the tubular onto the rim with both thumbs (Fig. 2-42).

STEP FOUR: True up the tubular with your fingers (Fig. 2-43) so that it sits evenly all the way around the rim and tension is even all the way around. Inflate the tubular partially and inspect it to make sure that it is seated evenly. Leave the tubular inflated for a few hours, if possible, before using it, to give the rim cement time to dry and become fixed.

Road Tubular Replacement

So now you are on the road, in a race or just touring, and your tubular punctures. Obviously, you aren't going to sit around for a couple of hours while the rim cement dries. If you're in a race you should have someone along with a replacement wheel, no fussing with changing tires. On tour, you won't want to leave the group, let them go ahead, while you sit glumly by the side of the road waiting for cement to adhere tubular to rim. What I do is use sticky tape, a special tape made for mounting tubulars on rims. I keep this tape in a sealed plastic bag, the kind used to store food with a self-sealing top. The tape is messy, to be sure, but it works and it will get you home or to your destination. Rim tape loses some of its adhesiveness in the rain, so take it easy on cornering and high-speed downhill runs in the rain. Another solution is to coat the tubular base tape, if rubberized, with a thin solution of rim cement and let it dry. Then I fold the tubular as noted earlier, for a spare, fasten it in this position with rubber bands or a strap, put it in a plastic bag and put the bag in a saddle carrier. There will be enough residual molecular adhesion between the thin layer of rim cement on the base tape and the rim cement still on the rim under the punctured tubular for fair adhesion, good enough for the day's run or to get you home but not good enough for a tough race situation. That's when you need a tire that will adhere to the rim as well as man can make it stick. If in doubt, try to roll the tubular off the rim. If it comes off easily, you have poor adhesion and you will very likely have a tubular roll off the rim in a race, and very possibly cause an accident involving not only you but others.

For Track Tubulars

If you are fastening track tubulars you should always use shellac. Track tires have a cotton or silk nonrubberized base tape which is best cemented with shellac. Road tires have a rubberized base tape, and these are secured best on the rim with a rubber solution such as Clement.

Chapter Three
Seats, Seat Posts,
Handlebars and Stems

There are three saddle types, made out of a variety of leathers and plastics. The three types (Fig. 3-1) are, left to right, mattress, narrow touring and racing saddle, and lightweight racing saddle. I prefer the narrow saddle in the center, for two reasons. First, the wider mattress saddle tends to rub on the inside of the thighs when you ride in the more efficient angle position with dropped bars. Second, the springs in the mattress saddle absorb energy I would rather see go into turning the back wheel.

Scientific Approach to Saddle-Height Adjustment

Experiments conducted at Loughborough University, England, illustrate the importance of saddle height to cycling efficiency.[1]

[1] Vaughn Thomas, "Scientific Setting of Saddle Position," *American Cycling* (now *Bicycling!*), June 1967, p. 12.

Fig. 3-1: The three basic saddle designs are, left to right: mattress, narrow touring and racing, and pure racing.

The experiments, which used well-known racing cyclists and a bicycle ergometer (a stationary bicycle) with a harness to hold the rider in position, showed that cycling energy output varies significantly with minor changes in saddle height. Tests proved that alterations in saddle height of 4 percent of inside leg measurement affected power output by about 5 percent. Experimenters also concluded that the most efficient saddle height is 109 percent of inside leg measurement.

These are average values, however, and it must be expected that some minor variations will be necessary for individual builds and preferences. But it is interesting to note that recent studies of racing cyclists reveal that the better racers tend to have their saddle height conform to this formula.

How does one adjust saddle height to 109 percent of leg length? The method is easy:

First, measure the length of your leg *on the inside,* from the floor to the crotch bone, while standing erect and without shoes.

Then, multiply this length as measured in inches by 109 percent. Let's say, for example, that your leg measures 32 inches from floor to crotch. Multiply 32 × 1.09 = 34.88 inches. With the crank parallel to the plane of the seat tube (Fig. 3-2), measure or adjust the saddle so that the top of the saddle is 34⅞ inches from the pedal spindle.

Some cyclists will not want to follow this formula because they feel more comfortable at some other saddle-to-leg length ratio. But you

Fig. 3-2: A scientific method of adjusting saddle height is measuring leg height from floor to crotch, on inside of leg, and multiplying this measurement by 1.09. Result should equal length from top of saddle to pedal spindle, as shown. If leg measures 32 inches, saddle height should be 34⅞ inches, for example.

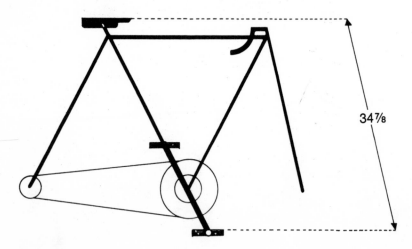

34⅞

should bear in mind that saddle height is something one becomes accustomed to, and any particular saddle adjustment is not necessarily the most efficient because it is, at the moment, the most comfortable. The beginning cyclist who adjusts his saddle according to the formula above will, in my opinion, be more likely to wind up a more efficient cyclist than the experienced cyclist who departs from this formula.

Few people are more opinionated than racing cyclists, or more concerned with the minute details of technique and equipment. Yet, when this formula for saddle-height adjustment was announced in 1967, a fierce controversy arose and many skeptics protested. The furor appears to have died down, and many professional cyclists, as well as their coaches and scientists who are interested in cycling, have adopted the formula.

Don't forget that this formula is the result of tests on 100 racing cyclists, ranging from beginners to the late world champion, Tommy Simpson. Four hundred readings were obtained at four different saddle heights—105, 109, 113, and 117 percent of inside leg measurements. These measurements were made from the top of the saddle to the pedal spindle at the bottom of the stroke, with the *crank* aligned with the seat tube.

If you find that there is a great difference between the formula height and the present height of your saddle, I would suggest that you make the adjustment gradually, in increments of one eighth of an inch, over a period of several months. This will give you time to adjust to the new setting, and give the formula a fair try. If you boost or lower the saddle height an inch or so to adjust to the formula at one time, you might find the new setting uncomfortable. Saddle height, as I said above, is something one must adjust to.

I have tried this formula on long trips. Once I had become used to the minor change I had to make, I found my cycling more efficient.

The Effect of Saddle Height on the Output of Muscular Power

Muscles have ranges of optimum stretch. They will stretch only to a limited degree. Experts say that leg muscles can exert more power as they approach the fully extended position—one reason why people who use a child's bicycle without readjusting the saddle huff and puff so ridiculously. But if leg muscles are stretched beyond their maximum capacity by a saddle that is too high, fluidity of leg movement will be disrupted.

The saddle height of 109 percent of leg measurement seems to give the best combination of maximum muscle stretch and maximum pedaling fluidity.

ADJUSTMENT OF SADDLE HEIGHT

As is shown in Figure 3-3, you must have at least 2½ inches of the seat post *inside* the seat tube, or you risk breaking off the post when you are straining uphill. The post may also break off because of the extra lever effect when too much of it is left outside the seat tube. Or, the post may break from metal fatigue if it is stressed unduly with just a little in the seat tube. Note also from Figure 3-3 that the saddle is raised or lowered by loosening the binder bolt, shown just below the bottom part of the caliper ruler. This spreads the seat-post cluster and top of the seat tube that is slotted, and permits the seat post to move up and down. If the seat post sticks, grasp the saddle and twist it from side to side while exerting upward pressure. You may need to straddle the top tube while doing so, or have someone hold the bike down while you twist and pull upward.

Saddle Tilt

I strongly recommend that you tilt the saddle slightly downward, at an angle of about 10 degrees. This downward angle throws more of your weight on the broader, rear section of the saddle and keeps pressure off more sensitive areas. Further, the slight forward tilt permits you to take more pressure off the saddle and put it onto the arms, which can then act as shock absorbers.

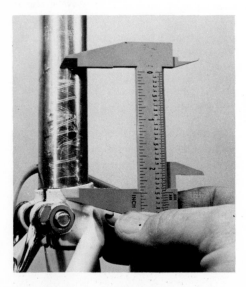

Fig. 3-3: You must have at least 2½ inches of the seat post inside the seat tube for safety, so that the post won't break under stress.

Fig. 3-4: A high-quality alloy seat post with microtilt adjustment of the saddle

Seat Posts: Seat posts on fine bicycles are made of aluminum alloy and have a unique microtilt adjustment (Fig. 3-4) that lets you move the saddle up or down in as small an increment as you wish, to accommodate the curves of your you-know-what. These seat posts are made by Campagnolo, Zeus, Unica-Nitor, t.t.t., and Sakae Ringyo, Ltd.

Some saddles, such as the Avocet, need only be tilted about 5 degrees down, in my experience, or perhaps can even be left flat, parallel to the top tube. Ride each position for a week or so, change it slightly, and try again until you have just the right tilt for you.

Saddle tilt on less expensive bikes is adjusted by loosening the saddle clamp (Fig. 3-5) and forcing the nose up or down and retightening the

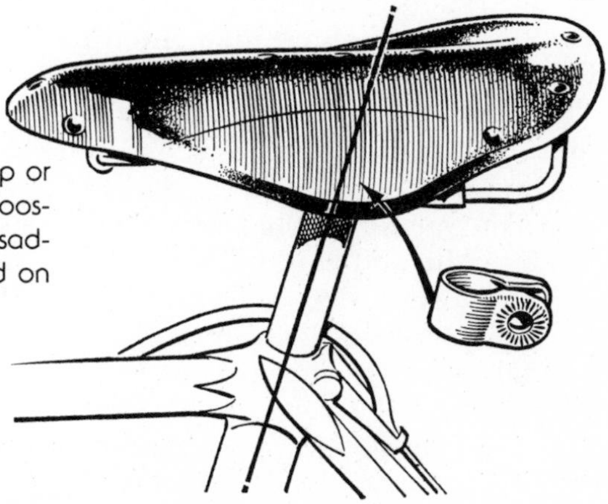

Fig. 3-5: You can tilt the saddle up or down, or move it horizontally, by loosening the saddle clamp bolt, on saddles with this type of fitting. Found on less expensive bicycles.

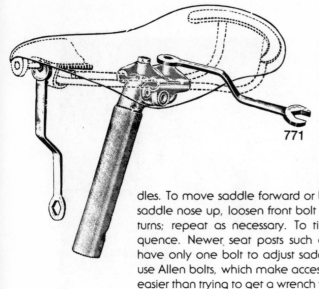

Fig. 3-6: Typical aluminum alloy micro-adjusting seat post, this Campagnolo post is adjusted by loosening the two top bolts with the special Campy No. 771 spanner (or a 10-mm. socket, which, with a ratchet wrench, is a lot easier to use). The other end of the Campy spanner is 13 mm., for taking up stretch from leather saddles. To move saddle forward or backward, loosen both bolts. To tilt saddle nose up, loosen front bolt two turns and tighten rear bolt two turns; repeat as necessary. To tilt saddle nose down, reverse sequence. Newer seat posts such as the Campagnolo Brevett Inter. have only one bolt to adjust saddle tilt; others, such as the Avocet, use Allen bolts, which make access to the seat post adjustment much easier than trying to get a wrench way up under the saddle, as shown here.

clamp binder bolt when you have the saddle where you want it. On better bikes using Campagnolo-style alloy seat posts the saddle tilt can be micro-adjusted by tightening the rear bolt to tilt up and the front bolt to tilt down (Fig. 3-6). You will have to loosen the opposite bolt to permit the facing bolt to be tightened.

Two Horizontal Saddle Adjustments

For most cyclo-tourists, the favored location of the saddle from the handlebars is where the nose of the saddle is from 2 to 2½ inches behind the centerline of the bottom bracket. Look at the "i" dimension in Figure 3-7. If you dropped a plumb line from the saddle nose, it should fall 2 to 2½ inches behind the centerline of the bottom-bracket axle (spindle).

So loosen the saddle-clamp binder bolt or the Campy-type adjustment bolts, both of them (Fig. 3-6), and slide the saddle back or forward until you find the approximate nose-to-bottom-centerline distance as shown. Leave the binder bolt or Campy bolts loose. Put your elbow on the nose of the saddle and your fingertips on the edge of the handlebars. If you picked the right size frame and the saddle is the right distance behind the bottom-bracket centerline, your fingers should just touch the bars. If your fingers are no more than a half inch or so ahead or behind the bars, move the saddle forward or backward until your elbow is on the saddle nose and your fingertips are on the edge of the handlebars. This is the so-called cubit adjustment.

If you can't combine the correct basic location of the saddle behind the bottom-bracket centerline with your "cubit" adjustment, either you have picked the wrong size frame or the manufacturer has put in too long or too short a stem, or your arms are too long or short for your height or inseam measurement or your fingers are too long or short for your arm length and height. There are now two more solutions available. But remember, it is important that you be able to reach the bars without strain or discomfort. Before we take further drastic steps, let's make one more check of this saddle horizontal location.

With someone holding the bicycle upright, sit on the saddle in a comfortable, slightly forward position. Put one hand on top of the handlebars. Swing the other arm over your shoulder, keeping it relaxed, and let this arm fall naturally onto the bars. The hands should just be able to curl around the top of the bars comfortably. If you feel strain, and the saddle can't move you far enough to or from the handlebars without moving it too far away or too far over the bottom-bracket centerline (remember, the 2- or 2½-inch saddle-nose location behind the bottom-bracket centerline lets you pedal more efficiently than if the saddle nose is right over the bottom bracket or too far behind it—within the 2-to-2½-inch range is a location right for you) then you have two more alternatives. You can twist the seat-post saddle clamp around so the clamp is forward on the seat post. This you can do by removing the clamp from the saddle and turning it so it faces forward. Or on a Campy-type seat post (Fig. 3-6) loosen both adjustment bolts, remove the saddle, loosen

Fig. 3-7: Important frame measurements are (A) frame size, (B) saddle height, (C) handlebar angle, (D) bottom-bracket road clearance, (E) handlebar throw, (F) stem length, (G) pedal-to-ground clearance, (H) handlebar height, (I) saddle position behind bottom-bracket centerline, (J) crank length.

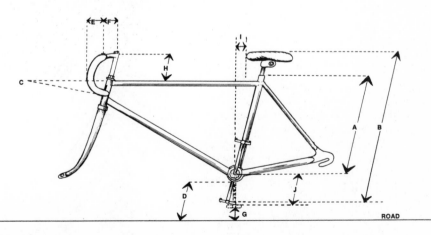

the seat-post binder bolt, twist the entire seat post around until the saddle-clamp section faces forward, retighten saddle-post binder bolt, reinstall the saddle and readjust saddle tilt and height. (I mark my saddle height by scratching a tiny line on the seat post so I can bring it back to the laboriously worked out correct saddle height for me, should I have to remove the saddle or post for any reason.) By reversing the direction of the saddle clamp or Campy seat post you can pick up about one extra inch of saddle movement.

A better way to adjust saddle distance from the handlebars is to replace the stock stem with a shorter or longer stem as necessary, or borrow an adjustable stem from the dealer for a week or two until you find a stem of the correct length. Figure 3-8 shows a variety of stem lengths, and at top left, an adjustable stem.

Most saddles will eventually stretch, thus altering the saddle-nose-tip-to-handlebar adjustment. The better saddles have a stretch adjustment that will restore the original saddle tension. The location of the saddle-tension adjustment is shown at the left of Figure 3-6. When you take slack out of the saddle you should readjust the saddle location horizontally, as shown.

Sometimes a leather, or even a plastic saddle will stretch and so become swaybacked, and the saddle will have a lot of bounce, sometimes so much that you will hit the saddle supports. In that case, the better

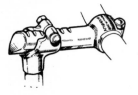

Fig. 3-8: A shorter or longer stem can be used to adjust the distance of the saddle from the handlebars. Seven stems of different lengths are shown and, at top left, an adjustable stem.

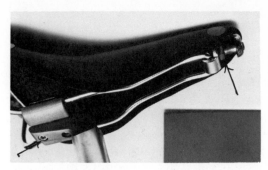

Fig. 3-9: Better saddles have a stretch adjustment (arrow).

saddles have an adjustment in the nose bolt that takes out this stretch. Figure 3-9 shows the stretch adjustment on my well-broken-in Brooks Pro saddle, arrow. The other arrow shows the saddle-tilt adjustment.

Saddle Frame Construction

If you have an older bicycle, I suggest, before buying a new saddle, that you check the width of your seat-post mounting, whether that seat post is the more deluxe design (Fig. 3-10) or the el cheapo in Figure 3-11, the clamp type. Most saddles these days come with the wire frame about 48 millimeters as measured on the outside of the frame members, and so most seat posts, such as the one in Figure 3-10, will accommodate this width. But if you have an older bike, say one made around 1974 or earlier, better check the width of the seat-post clamp to make sure a new saddle will fit it. And vice versa with a new saddle.

Fig. 3-10: Measure a new seat post where shown to make sure a new saddle cradle will fit it. Most saddles today have 48-millimeter-wide cradles, or close to that dimension. This is an Avocet seat post.

Fig. 3-11: An "el cheapo" seat-post clamp design.

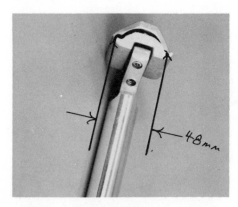

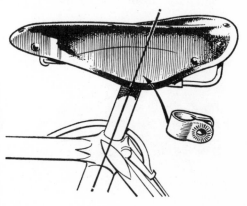

THE SELECTION OF SEAT POSTS

First, the mechanics of seat-post sizing. There's an incredible array of tubing used by bike manufacturers worldwide. The inside diameter can range anywhere between 26.2 and 27.2 millimeters, in 2-millimeter increments. If you try to stuff a 26.8-millimeter seat post down the throat of a 26.4- or 26.2-millimeter seat tube, you will have nothing but trouble. You'll get it down maybe one inch, just past the seat-tube binder-bolt slot, and then the post will jam and you won't be able to back it out without cutting it in pieces with a special hacksaw—a tedious process, indeed. Not to mention the possibility of cutting into the seat tube itself. *So don't guess*, especially if you order by mail. Know the inside diameter of your seat tube by measuring it. Sometimes you will find the seat-post diameter stamped on the post, and if you are changing posts and your old one fits, that's the new size to order.

If your bike was made in England, chances are the seat tube will be 27, 27.2, 26.2 or 26.8 millimeters. If the bike is from Italy, the seat tube I.D. can be 26.2, 26.8, 27 or 27.2. If from France, the seat tube will most likely be either 26.2, 26.6., 26.8 or 26.4. Good luck and measure accurately!

Until fairly recently, the best seat posts were made by Campagnolo, and even these seat posts were a real nuisance to adjust, even though the adjustments were micro-tilt. The reason? You had to reach up under the saddle (Fig. 3-12) and with a 10-millimeter wrench adjust the fore and aft bolts to put the saddle at the distance desired from the handlebars and the saddle at the tilt you wanted. Figure 3-13 shows another view of this adjustment. The bolts were very hard to reach, and if you had a tough leather saddle, pushing the side of the saddle away was not

Fig. 3-12: On older Campagnolo seat-post binder bolts microadjustments are hard to make because bolts are located under the saddle.

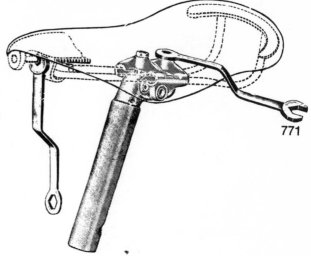

Fig. 3-13: Campy seat-post micro-tilt adjuster bolts, another view. Note saddle stretch bolt in nose of saddle.

771

easy. Today Campagnolo has come out with a beautiful fluted seat post with an Allen binder bolt you can easily reach from under the seat-post mounting bracket (Fig. 3-14), which weighs only 8½ ounces (241 grams) versus 11.5 ounces (326 grams) for the old version (Fig. 3-12). As Figure 3-14 shows, the tilt and lock binder bolt is readily accessible, with a 13-millimeter wrench. One reason, fluting and bracket aside, for the lighter weight is the thinner gauge of the post tube, as shown in Figure 3-15. The old post is on the left.

Fig. 3-14: New Campagnolo Super Record seat-post tilt can be adjusted with a conveniently located, easy-to-reach adjustment bolt under the seat-post head (arrow).

Fig. 3-15: Old Campy seat-post tube, left, is thicker walled, heavier. New Super Record seat post is thinner, lighter, as shown at right.

Table 3-1   Standard Seat-Post Diameters

Metric	Inches (decimal)	Inches Fraction (approx.)
25	.98437	$63/64$
25.8	1.01562	$1\frac{1}{64}$
26	1.03125	$1\frac{1}{32}$
26.2	1.03911	$1\frac{1}{32}$
26.4	1.04687	$1\frac{3}{64}$
26.6	1.05473	$1\frac{3}{64}$
26.8	1.06250	$1\frac{1}{16}$
27	1.07036	$1\frac{1}{16}$
27.2	1.07812	$1\frac{5}{64}$
27.4	1.08598	$1\frac{5}{64}$

CHOOSING HANDLEBARS

There are many configurations of handlebars and design, and they all have their devotees. For example, many tourists swear by Randonneur shaped handlebars (left, Fig. 3-16), which have a slight upward bend toward the sides. The theory is that the upsweep gives you more places to put your hands, which varies the pressure points on the hands. During the course of a long day's cycle, the ulnar nerve, which is somewhere in the middle of the palm of your hand, can hurt, a lot, if pressure is constant on it. If you can move your hand around so as to relieve the pressure at one point on the ulnar nerve, you will have a lot less pain and, in fact, little or none if you shift hands around. There are old, experienced cyclists who would never tour on anything but Randonneurs. For me, I prefer the flatter bar because I find the rise at the ends somehow contorts my shoulders, and I just don't like the shifting effect on my skeleton and muscles, such as they are, of the Randonneur. I would never suggest you not try a Randonneur, however, particularly if you have pain in the palm of your hands as you ride. For you, Randonneur design bars could be the answer. We are all built so differently, with such widely varying bone structures, that I hesitate to offer steel engraved recommendations about handlebars. Going on from the Randonneur, we have the bars with flat tops, the various trade names meaning little because they all come out pretty much the same. I really see little difference, other than drop and reach and width, between makes of the same basic design. This may be heresy, but so be it. Then we have the track handlebars, such as the one at the right of Figure 3-16, with radical sweeping bend from the stem to the drops. Definitely not for touring, track bars have a long "reach" (see Fig. 3-17 for a description of "reach," "width" and "drop"). How radical the bend of the track bar is is a function of the track racer's fancy, or need. Bikecology, in their catalog, shows a track bar with a very radical bend, with just about two inches of flat on either side of the ferrule. The ferrule is the thicker flat part in the center of the top of the handlebar (Fig. 3-17). Figure 3-18 shows a variety of bends, all pretty much the same, except for variances

Fig. 3-16: Three basic handlebar shapes: at left, a Randonneur bar with the top bar rising slightly at the outer section, favored by touring cyclists; center, the more conventional dropped bar with flat top tube; and right, track bars with more area for that bent-over, streamlined position and a bigger drop.

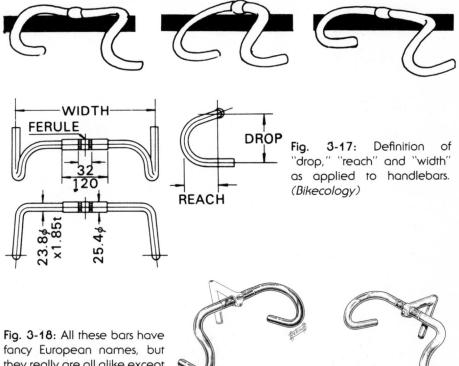

Fig. 3-17: Definition of "drop," "reach" and "width" as applied to handlebars. *(Bikecology)*

Fig. 3-18: All these bars have fancy European names, but they really are all alike except for the reach, width and drop. For example, the bar at upper right has much less drop and reach than the bar at lower left.

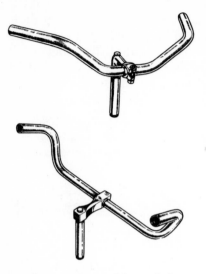

Fig. 3-19: Top, gently rising bars and, below, a more extreme version, tend to force you to sit up straighter than do downturned bars. The upright position compresses spinal segments and is harder on the back when you hit bumps. Downturned bars let you bend over a bit so that the cartilage between spinal segments expands and acts as a shock absorber. Also, bent-over position lets you absorb more road shock with your arms.

in the reach, width and drop. Figure 3-19 shows two types of more or less flat bars, which I would hope you would not use. We need the downturned bars to throw more weight forward and to stretch the spine, to absorb road shock, and to let you bend forward a little bit to ease wind resistance. The sit-up-straight school is hell on the spine, because road shock travels straight up from the saddle. Also the downturned bars let you use your arms and shoulder and chest muscles to transmit torque to the pedals, along with legs. On steep hills you can literally almost pull yourself along by grabbing farther down on the drops of the bars and "honking" up hill. So whether you call conventional downturned bars Campione Del Mondo, Giro d'Italia, Maes, or whatever, these fancy, racy European names are nothing more than the manufacturers' designations for the same bar but with different width, drop and reach. Unless, of course, you're talking about track bars, which are another design entirely.

Now, you quite properly ask, bars of which reach, drop and width should I use? The width should be about the same as the width of your shoulders, so that if you have shoulders 15 inches across (38.1 cm.) you should use handlebars of about that width. The better handlebars come in widths from 38 to 40 centimeters, and the model 66 Cinelli comes in a 42-centimeter width. (The conversion factor to translate centimeters to inches is .3937; and to convert inches to centimeters multiply by 2.54.)

If you have big hands you need a longer reach and possibly a deeper drop. If you have long arms you will need a longer reach, particularly if you like to ride on the drops. Most touring cyclists seldom seem to use the drops anyway (the bottom part of the handlebar) except perhaps going downhill when it is necessary to steady the bike steering. You also

Table 3-2 Compatibility Table

Stem	Bar	Fits
ttt	ttt (all)	Good
	Cinelli	Good
SR	SR (all)	Good
Cinelli	ttt (all)	Good
	Cinelli	Good
	SR (all)	Good
SR	ttt (all)	No
	Cinelli	No
	SR Randonneur	Good
Gran Compe	ttt (all)	No
	Cinelli	No
	SR Randonneur	OK

need a greater drop if you have a wide hand. I realize you can't buy a lot of handlebars to determine which one you should have—thus these general guidelines, which will at least steer you in the right direction.

There is one further dimension to be aware of on handlebars, and that is the outside diameter of the ferrule (Fig. 3-17). There is little uniformity between makes of stems and the overall dimensions of bar ferrules, and unless you are careful you could wind up with a stem you can't tighten down enough to grip the handlebars, so they don't turn in the stem, or so small you can't get the bar ferrule through it without almost spreading the stem expander section apart so far you are in danger of breaking off part of the stem, and of having to use a longer binder bolt. I am indebted to Bikecology for Table 3-2, which lists good, indifferent and no-go fits between stems and handlebars.

Adjusting the Handlebars

The handlebars, whether flat or down turned, should be set so they are about as high as the saddle. If you have a frame too small for you, the saddle should be set as high as possible while still leaving 2½ inches of the seat post inside the seat post, as noted above. In this case you can't raise the handlebars as high as the saddle because you must have at least 2 inches of the stem inside the seat tube, as shown in Figure 3-20. The 2 inches must be above the stem's split skirt, shown at the bottom of Figure 3-20.

To raise or lower the handlebars, loosen the stem bolt (Fig. 3-21). The stem-expander bolt is beveled and is inside the stem. As you tighten the bolt, the beveled bolt expands the stem in the split-skirt area and holds the stem in place inside the head tube (Fig. 3-21). In some stems, when

Fig. 3-20: To prevent handlebar stem from breaking under stress, always have two inches of the stem above the split skirt, as shown below, inside the head tube below the head set locknut.

you loosen the expander bolt (either with an Allen wrench or spanner, depending on the stem) the stem is still tight. In that case, tap the expander bolt with a plastic mallet to push the bolt down. The problem is that the bolt bevel is still tight inside the stem.

STEMS

The stem is that "L"-shaped component, one leg of which goes into the steering tube, the other end of which holds the handlebars. Stems come in a variety of lengths to suit different body, arm and torso sizes.

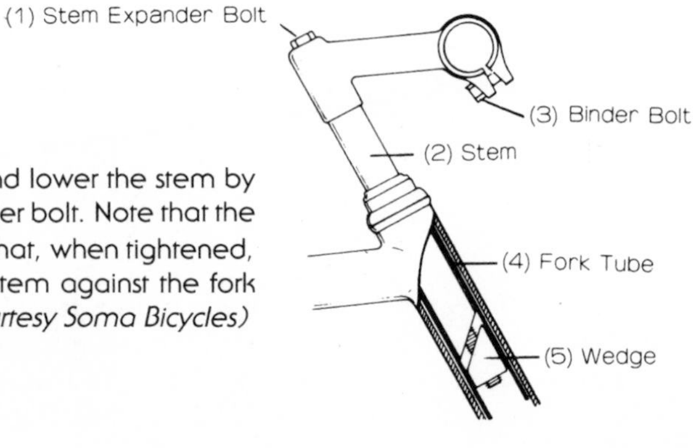

(1) Stem Expander Bolt

(3) Binder Bolt

(2) Stem

Fig. 3-21: You can raise and lower the stem by loosening the stem expander bolt. Note that the expander bolt is a wedge that, when tightened, forces the split skirt of the stem against the fork (head) tube. *(Drawing courtesy Soma Bicycles)*

(4) Fork Tube

(5) Wedge

Fig. 3-22: Cinelli stem. Note the location of binder bolt at handlebar end.

Fig. 3-23: Cinelli stem, showing binder-bolt wedge that fits into stem head.

The cheaper stems have bolts with protruding bolt heads that usually take a 10-millimeter wrench; and the market has been flooded in recent years with inexpensive imitations of high-quality European stems with recessed Allen bolts. So the mere presence of an Allen bolt does not necessarily guarantee that the stem is a high-quality, strong forged alloy one. Some cheaper stems are made of steel and are, of course, a lot heavier than alloy stems. The relatively new *Cinelli road stem,* Model 1/Record (Fig. 3-22) has a hidden expanding binder bolt arrangement that grips the handlebars via an internal expansion sleeve. Figure 3-23 is a front view of this stem. Note the slotted skirt, bottom. Both the hidden and the top binder bolts take a 6-millimeter Allen wrench. This stem comes in lengths of 10, 11, 12, 13 and 14 centimeters (smaller sizes not available because the internal expansion sleeve would interfere). To find inches, multiply the centimeter figure by the conversion factor .3937. Figure 3-24 shows a cross-section drawing of this stem. This stem weighs 287 grams in the 10-centimeter size, slightly more in longer

Fig. 3-24: Cross section of Cinelli stem. One drawing shows binder bolt loose, and internal expanding wedge drawn back from handlebar. Other drawing shows binder bolt tight, expanding wedge firmly tight against handlebar.

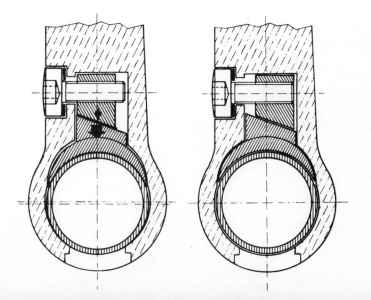

sizes, and costs $29.50. The 1/Record comes in a 22-millimeter diameter, which will fit steering tubes with a 22-millimeter inside diameter.

Before you order any stem, you should measure the inside diameter of your steering tube. Most English and Italian bikes take a 22.2-millimeter stem, French bikes a 21.9-millimeter stem and Japanese bikes a 21.15-millimeter stem. The difference between the 22.2- and 21.15-millimeter stems is 1.05 millimeters, which is about 1/16th of an inch, which is just too much slop to deal with for the tightly fitting stem you should have. After all, you don't want suddenly to wrench the handlebar one way and to find the bike does not respond though the bars turn. The difference of .2 millimeters between 22 and 22.2 millimeters is only around 8 thousandths of an inch, so the 22-millimeter stem would probably work in a 22.2 millimeter but not the other way around. I prefer a stem that fits exactly.

TAPING HANDLEBARS

The conventional canvas or cotton tape is okay, if you don't mind a fairly hard gripping surface that can hurt your ulnar nerve. Certainly racing cyclists need that kind of firm, unyielding gripping surface. The rest of us could surely use a more comfortable grip, and some suppliers have tried to bring us just that. For example, the Grab-On people have come up with a sponge type of bar cover that works well for me. To mount it you have to remove *all* the old tape and *all* the old tape-glue residue on the handlebars. I removed my old glue stuff with paint remover, being careful, of course, not to drop any on the frame finish. To slide the Grab-Ons on, it helps to whip up a soapy mixture of liquid dish detergent and water and pour some inside the Grab-On and put some on the handlebars. You also have to remove the brake levers. Figure 3-25 shows the finished job. For flat bars, you can replace the rubber grips with Grab-

Fig. 3-25: Any kind of padding, such as the Grab-On sponge type, helps alleviate or prevent ulnar-nerve pain in the palm of your hand.

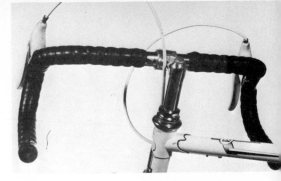

Fig. 3-26: This type of padding, by Grab-On, fits on end of flat bars.

Fig. 3-27: Or you can use Bailey II tape over sponge-rubber segments.

Ons, as shown in Figure 3-26. You can also buy a tape something like the leather tape used on tennis rackets, which is elegant, expensive, sweat absorbing, good gripping but not very spongy. On my own favorite Alex Singer touring bike I wound thin sections of sponge rubber around the bars, and held them in place with rubber cement, while I wrapped overlapping rubber tape with raised middle sections (Fig. 3-27), available in bike stores. Another less expensive solution to softer bars is to go down to your hardware store and buy the kind of pipe insulation used to keep basement pipes from dripping. It installs and looks and feels much like Grab-On. Measure the overall dimension of your bars to make sure you get the insulation tape that will slide over; not too big so it slides around; not too small so it won't fit on.

If you prefer conventional tape, start at the top, work down and tape around the brake levers as shown in Figure 3-28 (which does not show brake-lever rubber covers, but you can raise the skirts of these enough to get the tape under them as shown) and leave an inch or so extra and tuck that extra into the ends of the drops, and push in the bar-end plugs over the tape, as shown in the rear drop in this illustration. If you use bar-end shift levers, though, start taping from the bottom, just behind the levers, using tape with adhesive backing, and wind up at the ferrule. It's not considered good form to cover the ferrule, especially if it has fancy engraving, as do Cinelli bars, for example. The bumpy kind of rubber tape mentioned and shown in Figure 3-27 is made by Bailey.

Fig. 3-28: Conventional canvas tape goes on as shown. Brake-lever rubbers are removed to show how tape goes around lever body. You can lift the rubber cover to get the same effect. End of tape is tucked into bar-end plugs.

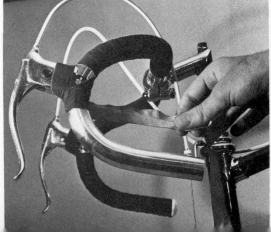

Chapter Four

DERAILLEURS

Derailleurs are fairly simple mechanisms designed to nudge the chain off one gear or cog or chainwheel and onto the next smaller or bigger one. Like all mechanical components of a bicycle, they do get out of order and require either replacement or adjustment. You may also wish to replace your derailleur, either because it is worn out, bent or otherwise damaged, or simply to upgrade your bicycle. Or, you may have changed from a low or intermediate gear ratio setup to a wide ratio gearing by changing, let's say, your freewheel cluster from a 13 to 24 or 26 or 28-tooth set of cogs over to a 14 to 34-tooth set of cogs.

DERAILLEUR ADJUSTMENT TROUBLESHOOTING

Before we get into details on troubleshooting, you might take a look at Figures 4-1, a close-up view of a Shimano DuraAce rear derailleur, 4-2, the same for a DuraAce front derailleur, and 4-3, downtube shifters. Figure 4-4 shows in detail a Campagnolo second line derailleur, the Gran Sport.

1. PROBLEM: Gear changes while riding.
   CAUSE: Gear-shift control lever too loose.
   SOLUTION: Tighten gear-control-lever thumbscrew (wing nut), or use a screwdriver on nut type. Caution: Tighten just enough so lever feels slightly tight. Do not tighten so hard that shifting becomes difficult.

2. PROBLEM: Difficulty in shifting to front high-gear chainwheel.
   CAUSE: Front-derailleur right-hand control stop needs readjusting.
   SOLUTION: Readjust so front-derailleur cage can travel far enough to the right to lift chain up onto front high-gear chainwheel.

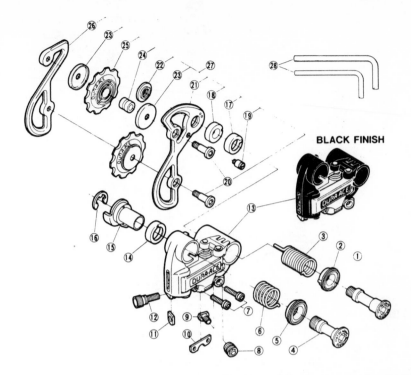

Fig. 4-1: Shimano DuraAce rear derailleur. Parts are: (1) plate-mounting bolt; (2) plate-mounting collar; (3) P-tension spring; (4) adapter-mounting bolt; (5) adapter-mounting collar; (6) B-tension spring; (7) adjusting screw; (8) cable-fixing nut; (9) cable-fixing bolt; (10) adjusting plate; (11) cable-adjusting plate; (12) cable-adjusting barrel; (13) mechanism assembly; (14) adapter-mounting sleeve; (15) adapter bushing assembly; (16) stop ring; (17) plate-mounting sleeve; (18) plate bushing; (19) stopper pin; (20) pulley bolt; (21) inner cage plate; (22) plate-mounting nut; (23) pulley cap; (24) pulley bushing; (25) pulley; (26) outer cage plate; (27) pulley plate assembly; (28) hex wrench keys, 3 mm. and 6 mm. (⅛" and ¼").

CAUSE: Bottom-bracket spindle too long. For example, you may have changed to a longer spindle when installing a new bottom-bracket set. Just one or two millimeters too long a spindle will do it. SOLUTION: Install a spindle of the correct length for your bottom-bracket shell width. See discussion of bottom-bracket dimensions later on in this chapter.

3. PROBLEM: Gear changes erratically, slowly and noisily. CAUSE: Derailleur jockey and tension sprockets are not lined up in the same plane as rear gears. SOLUTION: Turn bike upside down. (Note: I prefer to hang the bicycle from the ceiling by hooks attached to the saddle and handlebars, which puts all parts at eye level or close to it; or I use a bike stand.) Sight along a vertical line to check that tension and jockey

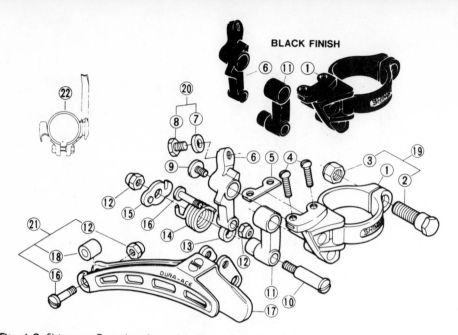

Fig. 4-2: Shimano DuraAce front derailleur. Parts are: (1) clamp assembly; (2) clamp bolt; (3) clamp nut; (4) stroke-adjusting screw; (5) stroke-adjusting plate; (6) outer link; (7) cable-fixing plate; (8) cable-fixing bolt; (9) fixing screw; (10) axle screw B; (11) inner link; (12) nut; (13) spring collar; (14) return spring; (15) spring plate; (16) screw A; (17) chain guide assembly; (18) roller; (19) clamp bolt and nut; (20) cable-fixing plate and bolt; (21) roller fixing screw assembly; (22) cable guide.

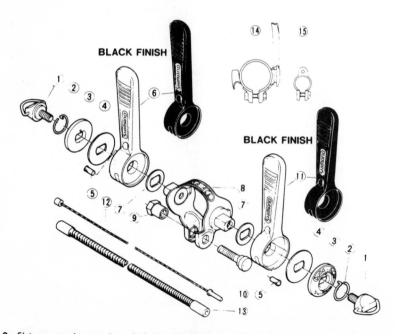

Fig. 4-3: Shimano downtube shift levers. Parts are: (1) lever fixing bolt; (2) clutch spring; (3) cap; (4) spring washer; (5) stopper pin; (6) front shifter lever; (7) washer; (8) lever clamp, goes on downtube; (9) clamp nut; (10) clamp bolt; (11) rear-derailleur lever; (12) inner cable (2); (13) cable housing (2); (14) cable guide; (15) outer stopper.

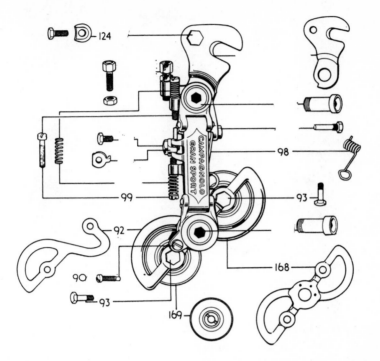

Fig. 4-4: Typical derailleur mechanism, in this case the Campagnolo "Gran Sport" unit. Parts are as follows (major ones only); (90) peg stop; (92) inner roller plate; (93) bolt to jockey roller; (98) traverse spring; (99) limit stop adjuster bolts (top bolt is for low or larger gear limit travel, lower bolt is for high or smaller gear limit travel); (124) chainstay bolt; (168) outer roller plate; (169) tension roller.

wheels are parallel to rear hub gears, as discussed earlier in this chapter.

A good reason for having everything in correct alignment on derailleur mechanisms, aside from the noise and extra wear and tear caused by misalignment, is that a good deal of energy-wasting friction can also result from such misalignment.

4. PROBLEM: Chain keeps riding up on the rear low-gear sprocket (the largest rear gear). This can cause the chain to bind in the spokes, with disastrous results.
CAUSE: The low-gear derailleur adjustment screw needs readjustment (Fig. 4-5).
SOLUTION: Make this adjustment.

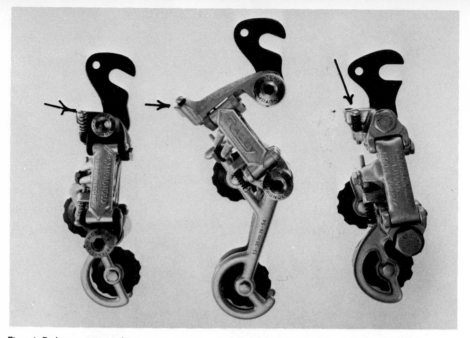

Fig. 4-5: Low-gear adjustment screws on three popular Campagnolo rear derailleurs (arrows). Left to right: Super Record; Rally (wide ratio); Gran Sport (bargain basement).

5. PROBLEM: Chain runs off high-gear (small) sprocket.
   CAUSE: High-gear adjusting screw is moved out of place because of vibration.
   SOLUTION: Readjust the high-gear adjusting screw. Turn wheel so that the chain is on the large front chainwheel and small rear gear. If the chain has jammed between seat stay and gear, be careful that in pulling it out you don't bend it or the derailleur. If necessary, loosen the quick-release skewer or axle nuts and push the wheel forward, or rotate it gently backward. Turn the high-gear adjusting screw until the chain will not slip off high gear. On Huret Allvit derailleurs, the high-gear adjusting screw is the small screw about two-thirds of the way down the outside face of the main housing bracket, recessed into a small hole in the bracket. On Campagnolo derailleurs, the high-gear adjusting screw is located about halfway down, at the rear of the main housing casting, and points toward the bottom. And on the Shimano "Skylark," it is at the bottom of the two Phillips-head screws at the center rear of the derailleur.

Note: Every time your bicycle is knocked over on the derailleur side, you should check high- and low-gear stops on the rear derailleur. If you've parked (and locked) your bicycle where people can get at it, curious passersby may have played with the gear shifters. If this is the case, look at the position of the gear-shift handle, move it back about where it was when you parked, and start off by pedaling very gently, while, at the same time, adjusting the gear-shift levers. Otherwise, if you take off with the chain on one gear and the lever in position for another, you can catch the chain between gears and damage the derailleur. This goes for the front (chainwheel) derailleur too.

If you've had your bicycle for some time (six months or so), or you've ridden on sandy or dusty roads, sand or dirt can get into the derailleur linkage arms and clog up the derailleur. It is a good idea to clean the mechanism about every hundred miles, and relubricate pivot points and linkage with light oil.

6. PROBLEM: Chain skips while pedaling, usually in high gear.
   CAUSE: Insufficient chain tension.
   SOLUTION: Varies with type of derailleur.

HURET ALLVIT DERAILLEUR: Move the chain tension spring back a notch.

SIMPLEX DERAILLEUR: For more spring tension on a Simplex derailleur, remove the screw and dust cap from the bottom pivot bolt, and insert a metric Allen wrench in the hole you'll now see. Then, while you hold the locknut between the pivot bolt and the cage (the bracket with two half-moons holding the two small derailleur wheels), with a wrench (metric), turn the Allen wrench toward the rear of the bicycle for more chain tension, or toward the front for less tension. (Note: Use as little tension as possible to reduce drag, wear and tear, and make pedaling easier. This applies to all derailleurs.)

CAMPAGNOLO DERAILLEUR: To increase chain tension on a Campagnolo rear derailleur, remove the chain cage stop-bolt (the thin bolt with a small round head that looks like a water tower lying on the ground, and that keeps the cage from rotating too far clockwise). Let the cage unwind until no more spring tension can be felt. Then, with an Allen wrench, remove the cage pivot bolt (the bolt that holds cage to derailleur), located at the bottom of the derailleur, and remove the cage from the spring end. Turn the cage slightly forward until the end of the spring fits into the next of the three holes. Replace the pivot bolt and cage assembly and tighten the pivot bolt. Wind the cage assembly counterclockwise one-half to one-and-a-half turns, hold it in this position and reinstall the cage stop-bolt. (Make sure the cage assembly is right side up by checking that the top roller is the one that has the inner side exposed. The bottom roller has the cage on both sides of the wheel, the top wheel has the cage on the outer side only.)

Replace the chain (with wheel in place) and check the shifting while pedaling. (Always check the bicycle on the road, not hanging from the ceiling.) Be sure to check high- and low-gear adjustment screws.

CAUSE: Burrs on teeth of freewheel gear.
SOLUTION: File or grind burrs off.

CAUSE: A chain link too tight or binding.
SOLUTION: If you've removed and reinstalled the chain, check the link involved. Or check *all* the chain links. If a link binds or is tight (when you move it up and down), twist the chain gently from side to side. Of course, if your chain is rusty, don't bother with this procedure; simply install a new chain.

CAUSE: Excessive wear in chain or gears.
SOLUTION: Chains and gears do wear, and old chains stretch as a result of wear. Always replace worn, loose chains (an old chain always breaks when you're miles from a bike shop). Do not replace an old chain and leave worn gears. Replace both at the same time. Old gears are identifiable by a slight hook on the inner lip of the gear teeth, which can catch the chain and make it "skip." Check the most-used gears first, using your fingernail. Hooks can be filed or ground off. Removing a gear from the freewheel is not difficult, but you will need a special tool. Therefore, I will not describe this procedure here.

CHECK CHAINWHEEL TEETH: Chainwheel teeth can also wear. They show this wear on the "lands" of the teeth; that is, by wearing away the face of the curvature of the gear teeth on the side toward the rear of the bicycle, away from the direction of rotation of the chainwheel. If the chainwheel is worn this much, it should be discarded and replaced with a new one, to avoid rough pedaling and erratic drive. Also, a worn chainwheel will soon wear out a new chain. If you're in doubt about chainwheel wear, check the chainwheel as follows: wrap a chain around the chainwheel and pull the chain down into the teeth by holding the ends of the chain snugly together. If the chain links fit tightly into the chainwheel teeth and cannot be picked away from the wheel at any gear, the wheel is in good shape. But if the chain climbs up on the teeth without being lifted up by you, mark this point of climb. Then try a new chain and repeat the procedure. If the new chain comes up at the same point, the gear is worn and should be replaced; however, if the new chain fits nicely, the old chain is shot and should be replaced.

Remember that a chain doesn't actually "stretch," but because the parts wear and "give," it acts as though it *has* stretched. It takes only a few thousandths of an inch of wear on each of the rivets to make the chain stretch a half inch. (This is why frequent cleaning and lubrication are important in chain maintenance.)

Another check for the chainwheel and chain fit is to put the chain you intend to use on the chainwheel, already installed on the bicycle, and watch how the chain flows over the chainwheel teeth. There should be no "lifting" or sticking of the chain to the chainwheel teeth. Hang the bike for this test and hand-turn the pedals.

CAUSE: Chain is too long.
SOLUTION: Remove extra links.

7. PROBLEM: Gear won't shift all the way into low (onto rear, large sprocket).
CAUSE: Low-gear adjusting screw is out of adjustment.
SOLUTION: Readjust as per instructions in this chapter.

CAUSE: Cable has stretched, or has slipped in the cable pivot bolt (where it is fastened to derailleur).
SOLUTION: Shift derailleur into high gear while turning pedals. Cable should have small amount of slack. If too loose, take up slack by turning the adjusting barrel on the derailleur, or, if there is no barrel on your machine (many good bicycles don't have one), put shift lever in high-gear position, all the way toward the front of the bicycle, loosen the cable pivot bolt-nut, pull some of the cable slack through, and retighten.

If the gear-shift cable breaks while you are on a trip, you can at least avoid having to pedal all the way home in high gear by adjusting the high-gear stop screw to keep the chain on the first or second gear up from the highest (small-sprocket) gear.

8. PROBLEM: Chain slips off small front chainwheel sprocket.
CAUSE: Low-gear limit screw is out of adjustment.
SOLUTION: Turn pedals and shift front derailleur to small chainwheel. Readjust low-gear limit screw. On most front derailleurs, the low-gear adjusting screw is the inner (closest to seat tube) screw, just forward of the cable anchor screw. Remember, the function of the chain guard is to derail or move the chain from one chainwheel sprocket to the other. There is no tension adjustment to the front derailleur; this is taken care of by the rear derailleur.

9. PROBLEM: Chain won't stay on large chainwheel (front derailleur).
CAUSE: High-gear adjusting screw is out of adjustment.
SOLUTION: Because there are only two adjusting screws on front derailleurs (chainwheels), and we have already told you where the low-gear adjustment screw is on all popular front derailleurs, all you need do is shift the front derailleur lever to the high position (toward the rear of the bicycle), while turning the pedals, and adjust the chain guide over the large chainwheel with the high-gear adjusting screw. If shifting from small to large chainwheel after this adjustment is hard, bend the upper front corner of the inner part of the chain guide (cage) slightly inward, toward the chainwheel. If, however, the chain tends to jump off the chainwheel toward the outside (away from the bicycle), bend the upper front corner of the outer chain guide slightly toward the chainwheel. To find the exact spot where you bend the chainwheel guide, turn the pedals (cranks) by hand while the bicycle is off the ground and move the front shift lever until the chain just starts to lift off the chainwheel teeth. The part of the chain guide (cage) to be bent is touching the chain at this point.

10. PROBLEM: Chain won't shift onto large front chainwheel.
CAUSE: High-gear adjusting screw is out of adjustment.
SOLUTION: Readjust screw so chain guide will push chain up onto large front chainwheel.

CAUSE: Cable has stretched.
SOLUTION: Push front-derailleur control lever all the way forward while turning pedals (cranks). Cable should be nearly tight. If it is loose, move shift lever all the way forward, unscrew cable bolt (the bolt that holds the cable to the front-derailleur shifting mechanism), pull cable through and retighten cable bolt.

11. PROBLEM: Front-derailleur chain cage rubs on chain. Chain rattles.
CAUSE: Low- or high-gear adjustment screws have vibrated out of adjustment.
SOLUTION: Readjust screws.

CAUSE: Front-derailleur mechanism not aligned so chain cage is parallel with chainwheel.
SOLUTION: Loosen the two bolts that hold the front-derailleur mechanism to seat tube (frame) and turn the derailleur mechanism left or right to align the chain cage parallel to the chainwheel. While you've got the mechanism loose, make sure it is as close (low) to the

chainwheel as possible, so that the outer plate of the chain cage just clears the teeth of the large chainwheel.

CAUSE: Crooked or wavy chainwheel. Chain rattles.
SOLUTION: Straighten chainwheel by prying it back into position with a long, square-shanked screwdriver. To avoid bending the chainwheel more than you want to, use as fulcrum (levering) points the bottom-bracket cup (holding chainwheel axle in frame bottom), inside the right crank and chain-ring mounting bolts, with chain on large chainwheel. To judge which way to bend the chainwheel, sight through the front-derailleur chain cage, and use the inside plane of the chain cage as a guide.

Another good way to straighten a chainwheel is to use the rear stay as a guide, turn the chainwheel and mark the high and low spots (near and far distances from chainstay) on the chainwheel with a china marking pencil or a piece of chalk. If a high and low spot are opposite each other (directly across the chainwheel), using adjustable wrenches and pulling on the low point and pushing on the high point will usually bring the chainwheel back into true.

To protect chrome plating or finish on the chainwheel, use a piece of rag between the jaws of the wrench. Take it easy as you push—don't overdo it. It is far better to make too slight a push than to give it all you've got and shove the chainwheel out of true in the other direction.

If, however, there are two high points opposite each other, and two low points opposite each other, all you need do is push the two high points inward toward the frame simultaneously.

If the chainwheel is wavy, the straightening job is going to be tougher. Use an adjustable wrench at the point where the wave peaks or bottoms out and press gently in the required direction. Move around the wheel and adjust all waves or bends in this manner. If you can't bring the wheel back into true, you'd better buy and install a new chainwheel. Find out what kind of rough treatment bent the chainwheel in the first place so this problem won't arise again. (If you have to install a new chainwheel, see Chapter 6 for instructions on removing and installing chainwheels.)

12. PROBLEM: Pedals turn, crank turns, chain turns, freewheel turns, but the wheel doesn't turn.
   CAUSE: Pawls inside the freewheel mechanism are stuck open by a piece of dirt or by the use of too heavy a lubricating oil in the freewheel.

SOLUTION: Remove the freewheel and soak it in kerosene to remove dirt and/or heavy oil. Oil again with a light oil such as No. 5 SAE.

Note: If the spacing washers in the rear wheel on the freewheel side are too narrow or too wide, the freewheel gears will not be aligned correctly with the chainwheel and you will have chain rub front or rear, as well as loss of power due to rub. Please see section on alignment, this chapter and Chapters 6 and 11.

It is also important to know that if the chain is on the small front chainwheel and on the large rear gear, as you start to shift the chain down from the largest to the smallest rear gear the chain will assume a sharp angle. Try it—put the chain on the small front chainwheel and on the small rear gear and notice that the chain is at an extreme angle and, in fact, is rubbing on the inside of the front-derailleur cage. You can avoid this type of rub if you will shift the front cage slightly to the left as you shift down, and slightly to the right as you shift up to the high-gear cogs.

13. PROBLEM: Chain won't shift to combination of largest front chainwheel and next-to-largest and largest rear gears.
    CAUSE: Chain is too short.
    SOLUTION: Add one or two links. See instructions earlier in this chapter for finding correct chain length.

14. PROBLEM: Chain won't shift to small rear gear, or rubs on chainstay when in this position.
    CAUSE: Too little clearance between small gear and chainstay.
    SOLUTION: Add clearance by removing washer from left side of axle and adding one or two washers to right side of axle under locknut. This will move freewheel far enough to the left to allow chain clearance.

    CAUSE: You have too long a bolt head holding the carrier onto the frame. Replace with a shorter bolt or file the bolt head flat so it projects as little as possible on the inside of the seat stays, and clears the chain.

To help you locate the high- and low-gear and cable-clamp bolts on some of the popular makes of front and rear derailleurs, Figures 4-6 through 4-13 show these locations. You will note that in every case the *low*-gear adjustment screw is located closest to the nearest frame tube. In the front derailleurs, the low-gear adjuster is closest to the seat tube; in rear derailleurs, the low-gear adjuster is closest to the dropout or chainstay.

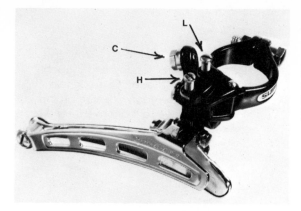

Fig. 4-6: Shimano DuraAce derailleur: (C) cable clamp; (L) low-gear adjustment; (H) high-gear adjustment.

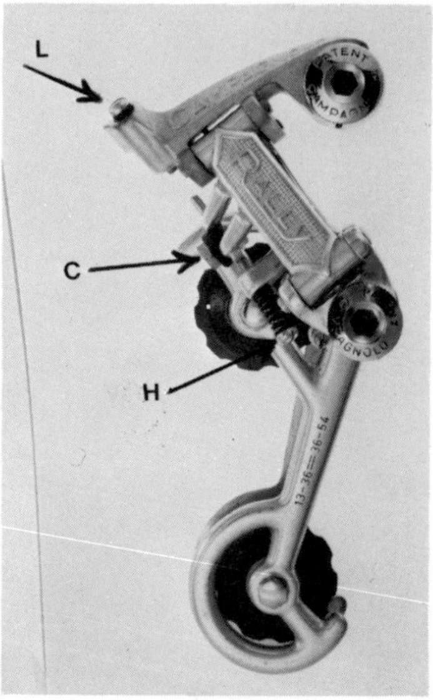

Fig. 4-7: Another view of the Campy Rally derailleur: (L) low gear; (H) high gear; (C) cable clamp.

Fig. 4-8: A closer view of the Campy Gran Sport, with a very good view of the derailleur travel stops. The low-gear stop (L) prevents the derailleur from overtraveling the chain so it jams between the low gear and spokes. High-gear adjustment stops derailleur from pushing chain off high gear so it jams between high-gear cog and chainstay. (C) is the cable clamp.

Fig. 4-9: The old standby and probably the best derailleur made. Campagnolo Super Record has low-gear adjuster at top (L); high-gear adjuster at bottom (H); and cable stop center (C).

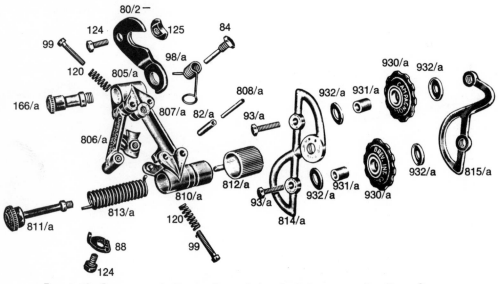

Fig. 4-10: Campagnolo Nuovo Record detailed view, rear derailleur. Parts are:

80/2	**Gear** fixing plate		806/a	**Front** arm
82/a	**Body** ferrule		807/a	**Inner** arm
84	**Spring** screw		808/a	**Spindle**
88	**Clamp** washer		810/a	**Spring** cage
93	**Sprocket** bolt		811/a	**Gear** spring bolt
98/a	**Gear** return spring		812/a	**Spring** cage cover
99	**Gear** adjusting screw		813/a	**Tension** spring
120	**Safety** spring		814/a	**Outer** cage plate
124	**Fixing** screw		815/a	**Inner** cage plate
125	**Clamp** nut		930/a	**Roller**
166/a	**Upper** pivot bolt		931/a	**Roller** bush
805/a	**Rear** body		932/a	**Roller** dust cover

Fig. 4-11: Shimano Crane close ratio derailleur. Low-gear stop (L) is nearest dropout fixing bolt. High-gear stop (H) is outboard of (L) and (C) is cable clamp.

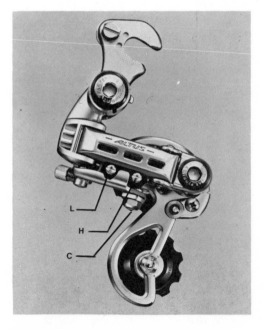

Fig. 4-12: Shimano Altus is on less expensive bikes: (L) low-gear adjustment; (H) high gear; (C) cable stop.

Fig. 4-13: Adjustments are in slightly different locations on different makes of derailleurs. Here's a Triplex with low-speed adjustment (L) at left and high-gear adjustment at right. You can clearly see where adjustment screws hit travel stops, as at bottom or left side of screw (H).

CHAIN OVERSHIFTING

One other derailleur problem I should mention is that of chain overshift or overshooting the gear you select. You may, for example, be shifting up from a low to a higher gear and instead of the chain landing on the next higher gear, as you want it to, it goes over an extra gear, so you are pedaling harder and slower than you, or your knees, want to. The major cause of overshift is either the wrong derailleur or the derailleur's not being at the correct angle. If, for example, you have a close-ratio free-wheel, say a 26-tooth low cog, and you have a wide-range derailleur such as the Campagnolo Rally, SunTour Cyclone GT or the Shimano Crane GS (Fig. 4-14) then the jockey wheel is going to be so far from the cog that it will shift at a smaller angle than if it were closer. Figure 4-15 illustrates my point.

In Figure 4-15 you will note that the derailleur at the left is closer to the cog "C" than the long-cage derailleur at the right is to cog "CC." As the jockey wheel "J" attempts to move the chain from cog "C" to cog "D" it assumes the characteristic angle best suited to crisp shifting. Now

Fig. 4-14: Shimano Crane wide-range derailleur, with longer cage, has adjustments in same place as the close-ratio model.

look at cog "CC." You will notice that the jockey wheel "JJ" of the rear long-cage derailleur is at a narrower angle than chain "E." In other words, at the same point, chain "E" is at a greater angle that chain "EE." Thus chain "EE" shifts less precisely and is more likely to overshoot than chain "E" because it is the greater angle of chain attack by the jockey wheel that contributes to precise shifting.

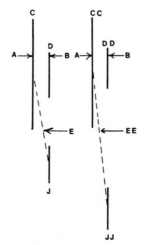

Fig. 4-15: Which derailleur, the one with jockey wheel "J" or "JJ," will give you the snappiest, most accurate shifting? "J" will because the acuter angle between "J" and the cog "C" moves chain faster and more accurately.

THE PROBLEM OF CHAIN RUB, FRONT DERAILLEUR

The novice ten-speed cyclist will wonder why, with all parts properly adjusted as instructed so far, the chain makes an annoying sound as it rubs on the inside of the front-derailleur cage when you shift from one rear cog to another. What you have to get used to is making minor adjustments of the front-derailleur shift lever so as to move the front-derailleur cage slightly one way or the other, depending on whether you are shifting up or down on the rear cogs.

For example, take a look at Figure 4-16. Here is the gear setup that most of you will have—a simple five-speed freewheel rear and a double chainwheel up front. In this drawing, the chain "A" is on the smaller chainwheel. Now you shift down to the low gear (the one with the most teeth) on the freewheel. You will see that the chain "B" has assumed an angle that brings it so close to the left side of the front-derailleur cage that it rubs, making a metallic sound as you pedal. To correct this rub, you now have to reshift the front lever, moving it forward so that the cage moves slightly to the left. If you have adjusted the cage so it can't move far enough to the left for chain clearance with the cage with the chain in this position, now is the time to readjust the front-derailleur stop so it can move over more to the left. Now you have climbed the hill that caused you to shift to the low rear cog, and you are on a slight downgrade, so you can shift over to the high rear cog (the one with the smallest teeth). As you can see from Figure 4-16, the chain "C" position is such that the opposite angle from chain "A" is taken; and if you have moved the cage left to compensate for chain angle in position "A" you will surely have rub in position "C" and so must again make a minor adjustment of the front-derailleur cage, pulling the shift lever slightly upward. Don't worry, after a few hundred miles this minor reshifting will become automatic, and you will instinctively reach for the front lever right after shifting a rear cog, to make this slight adjustment.

Now if you have become a cycle-touring enthusiast you will perhaps want a triple chainwheel so you can have a super low "Granny" gear for those steep 10- and 15-percent grades, without sacrificing an intermediate chainwheel. The Granny gear can be 30 or 34 teeth, the intermediate 40 teeth, the high-gear chainwheel 48 teeth. You may also want a wider gear spread, so you have gone to a six- or seven-speed freewheel. The extreme would be a triple chainset with a seven-speed rear cluster (Fig. 4-17). Now you will have chain rub for sure as you shift through the various gear combinations, and to keep the chain from rubbing on the derailleur cage up front you will need to make these slight adjustments with the front-derailleur shift lever. You won't have chain rub in all gear

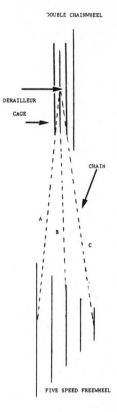

Fig. 4-16: As you shift from one rear cog to the other but don't shift to another front chainwheel, the chain assumes an ever-increasing angle. Here, with the chain on the low front gear it begins to rub on the front derailleur cage as it approaches the low rear cog. And with chain in the "C" position the chain again rubs on the derailleur cage. All this means is that you need to readjust the front derailleur slightly so the chain won't rub on its cage as you shift from one gear to another. In the "B" position the chain will not rub on the front cage.

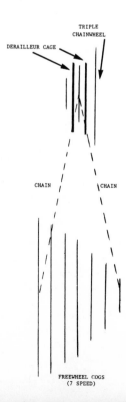

Fig. 4-17: Chain rub can be especially acute with a seven-speed freewheel and triple chainwheel.

combinations, of course, but as the chain approaches extreme angles, your ears will tell you that the front-derailleur cage and the chain are in pain.

The new Shimano front derailleurs have a wider cage than other makes, as noted in Table 4-2. For example, the 600 model has a cage width of 14.6 millimeters, 3 millimeters wider than the Campagnolo Nuovo Record. The wider cage minimizes but does not eliminate all problems of chain rub up front. You will also note from Table 4-1 that front-derailleur capacity is a function of the difference in the number of teeth between the smallest and the largest chainwheel. My Alex Singer has a 30 small and 48 large chainwheel, a difference of 18 teeth. Campy does not give capacity but it handles this range nicely. The DuraAce should also handle this range, although Shimano rates it at 16 teeth. With the wider cage you would think that you would have to shift through a great lateral movement to get the chain to move from one chainwheel to another. Shimano seems to have solved this problem by incorporating a trapezoidal motion (Fig. 4-18) which they claim lifts the chain up and deposits it squarely on the chainwheel teeth, providing a shorter-stroke cage movement, and permitting the wider cage. Looking at other front-derailleur movements, they all seem about the same to me; but the Shimano design does work well, and that's what counts.

Even with a short-cage derailleur, the jockey wheel can be too far away from the cog for precise shifting if the chain is too long. As noted

Table 4-1 Specifications, Selected Rear Derailleurs

Make and Model	Distance of Travel (mm)*	Cage Length (mm)†	Capacity‡	Weight (grams)	Cost
Campagnolo Super Record	47.9	45.5	28T	214.33	$61.98
Campagnolo Nuovo Record	47.9	45.5	28T	242.51	37.98
Campagnolo Nuovo Gran Sport	47.9	45.5	28T	258.00	24.50
Campagnolo Rally	34.2	74.3	34T	286.34	28.50
SunTour Cyclone	42.2	65.9	34T	190.00	20.98
Shimano DuraAce	45.3	45.0	26T	175.00	NA
Shimano Crane GS	36.7	75.2	34T	226.80	NA
SunTour VX (Wide Range)	52.0	67.6	34T	243.80	11.50
SunTour VX-S	49.0	61.5	28T	243.80	10.98
Shimano 600 EX	45.3	45.0	28T	190.00	NA
Shimano Altus	45.3	45.0	30T	262.00	NA

* Distance between inner and outer stops, with both stops wide open.
† As measured between centerline of the jockey and tension wheels.
‡ Number of teeth in largest rear sprocket (cog) derailleur will handle.

Table 4-2   Specifications, Front Derailleurs

Make and Model	Travel* (Milli-meters)	Weight (Grams)	Capacity † (No. Teeth)	Cage Width ‡ (Milli-meters)	Cage Length § (Milli-meters)
SunTour Cyclone	21.0	99.23	NA	12.5	118.5
SunTour NSL	17.3	113.4	NA	12.5	95.0
SunTour VX	23.0	116.24	NA	11.7	104.0
Campagnolo Nuovo Record	24.0	99.24	NA	11.6	104.5
Shimano 600	18.5	113.40	14 or less	14.6	107.8
Shimano DuraAce	18.5	108.00	16 or less	14.6	107.8
Shimano Altus	21.0	127.60	14 or less	14.9	108.0

* Maximum cage travel with high and low stops wide open.

† Difference between number of teeth on both chainwheels, or largest and smallest chainwheel. For example, small chainwheel has 36 teeth, big one has 52 teeth. Difference is 16 teeth.

‡ Measured from center width of inner surface of cage plates.

§ A measure of longest (right) cage plate from tip to tip.

earlier in this chapter, the derailleur body should be at about a 45-degree angle, when the chain is on the low-gear cog in the rear and the high-gear chainwheel up front. If necessary, remove links from the chain but not so many that there is "play" or upward movement left in the derailleur body.

Only one maker of derailleurs, at this writing, provides a fine adjustment for tuning derailleur angle, and that is the SunTour Cyclone, both

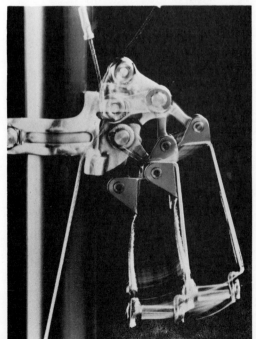

Fig. 4-18: Shimano's new front derailleur has a wider cage which minimizes the need for adjustment as you shift, and the trapeze swing movement helps smooth shifting.

the short- and the long-cage (GT) models. Figure 4-19 shows this adjustment, which is very convenient when you are off only a half link in chain length. Another point. Look again at Figure 4-15. You will note that to get jockey wheel "JJ" to assume the same angle as jockey wheel "J," you will have to move the derailleur farther. This can contribute to chain overshoot also. That is, to get the chain at a steep enough angle to move it, the derailleur with jockey wheel farthest from the cog has to move farther.

Another way to adjust chain tension to move the jockey wheel closer to the cogs is to move the rear wheel in the dropout slot (provided of course you do not have vertical dropouts, which are a rarity).

CHAINLINE ALIGNMENT

To keep the chain from assuming too great an angle, and to divide the chain angles that do occur as evenly as possible between the gears, the bottom bracket and, therefore, the chainwheels and, to some extent, the freewheel cluster, should be aligned as follows:

Single chainwheel and five-speed freewheel (five-speed setup) should have the chainwheel in line with the third freewheel gear, as shown in Figure 4-20.

Double chainwheel, five-speed rear cluster should have the centerline *between* the chainwheels in line with the third rear gear, as shown in Figure 4-21.

Triple chainwheel and five-speed freewheel should have the center chainwheel in line with the center (third) rear cog (Fig. 4-22).

Double chainwheel and six-speed freewheel. Here the centerline *between* the chainwheels should be in line with the centerline *between* the third and fourth rear cogs (Fig. 4-23).

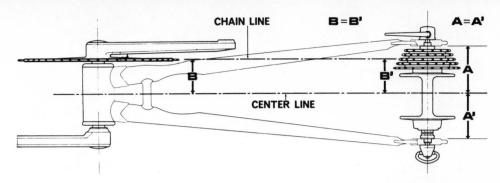

Fig. 4-20: Chainline adjustment for a single chainwheel and five-speed freewheel. Chain should line up with third-rear cog.

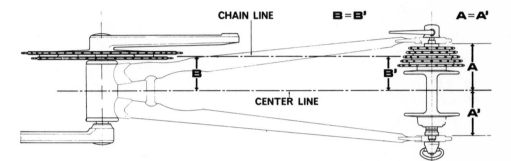

Fig. 4-21: For double chainwheel and five-speed freewheel, chain should line up between chainwheels and on third rear cog.

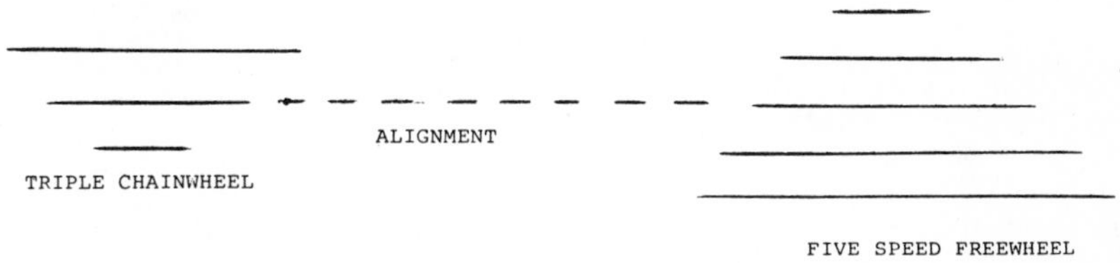

ALIGNMENT

TRIPLE CHAINWHEEL

FIVE SPEED FREEWHEEL

Fig. 4-22: With a triple chainwheel and five-speed freewheel, chain should line up with center freewheel and third rear cog.

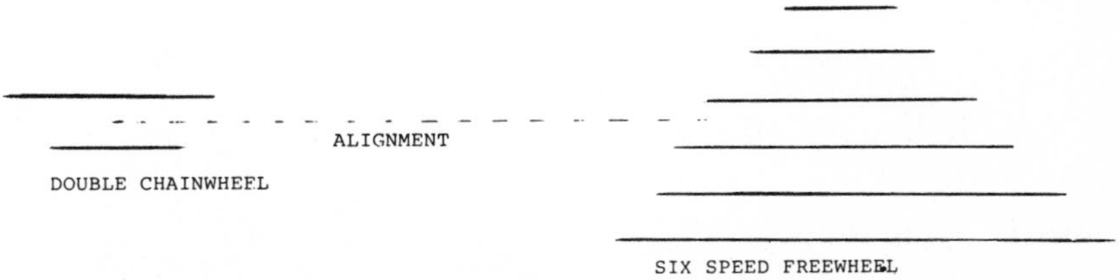

ALIGNMENT

DOUBLE CHAINWHEEL

SIX SPEED FREEWHEEL

Fig. 4-23: With a double chainwheel and six-speed freewheel, chain should line up centered between chainwheels and between third and fourth cogs.

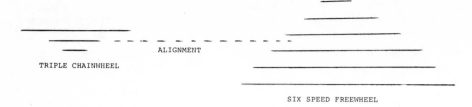

Fig. 4-24: With a triple chainwheel and six-speed freewheel, line up chain on center chainwheel and between third and fourth cogs.

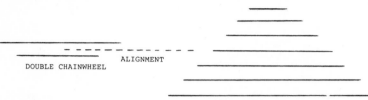

Fig. 4-25: With a double chainwheel and seven-speed freewheel, center chain between chainwheels and on fourth cog.

Fig. 4-26: With a triple chainwheel and seven-speed freewheel, line up chain on center chainwheel and fourth cog.

Triple chainwheel and six-speed freewheel should have the center chainwheel in line *between* the third and fourth rear cogs (Fig. 4-24).

Double chainwheel and seven-speed freewheel should have the center-line *between* the chainwheels in line with the fourth rear cog (Fig. 4-25).

Triple chainwheel and seven-speed freewheel should have the center chainwheel in line with the fourth rear cog (Fig. 4-26).

Alignment Adjustments

Adding or removing spacers on the rear hub. This is most practical with the Durham Bullseye hub. The wheel should be re-dished in this case. See Chapter 5.

Using a shorter or longer bottom-bracket axle (spindle). There is a limit to how short the axle can be to avoid chainwheel rub on the chainstay.

Adjusting a Phil Wood bottom bracket. As you will see when we discuss bottom brackets, it is possible to make a small adjustment on these units which would move the chainwheel laterally a few millimeters.

Adjusting a Durham Bullseye bottom bracket. There is considerably more adjustment possible with this bottom-bracket spindle set than with the Phil Wood or any other kind of bottom-bracket arrangement. You can move the spindle until the cranks rub—in either direction. For more details, see Chapter 6.

REMOVING THE REAR DERAILLEUR

Hanging a derailleur on the rear dropout is a fairly simple procedure. First, let's remove the old one:

STEP ONE: Unless you have a derailleur with a two-piece cage on the left side, such as the SunTour Cyclone (Fig. 4-27) or the Shimano 600 EX (Fig. 4-28), you will need to "break" the chain with a rivet remover. In Chapter 6 you will see that there are derailleur chains that can be "broken" without tools, or with a simple Allen wrench. If you have, or think you have, that kind of chain, I suggest you refer to Chapter 6 before proceeding further.

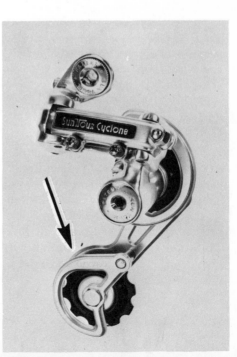

Fig. 4-27: This SunTour topline derailleur has a left-side cage in two pieces, which permits removal of the derailleur without having to "break" the chain with a rivet remover.

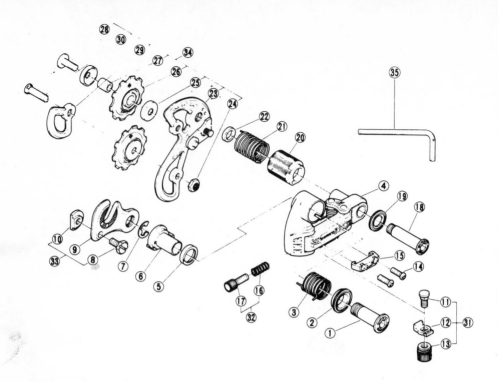

Fig. 4-28: Detailed view of a typical rear derailleur, the Shimano 600EX second-line model. Parts are: (1) adapter-mounting bolt; (2) adapter-mounting collar (bolt will also fit into threaded "ear" of Campagnolo dropout); (3) B-tension spring; (4) mechanism assembly; (5) sleeve; (6) adapter bushing; (7) stop ring; (8) adapter screw; (9) adapter (all this adapter stuff is for cheaper bikes without a threaded "ear" on the dropout to receive the derailleur. I will never understand the economics of this); (10) adapter nut; (11) cable-fixing bolt; (12) cable-fixing washer; (13) cable-fixing nut; (14) adjusting screw; (15) adjusting plate; (16) cable-adjusting spring; (17) cable-adjusting barrel; (18) plate-mounting bolt; (19) plate-mounting collar; (20) spring cover; (21) P-tension spring; (22) plate bushing; (23) inner cage plate (note that most of us call it an **outer** cage plate because it faces toward the outer, or right, side of the bike. Just so you don't get confused); (24) pulley nut; (25) pulley cap; (26) pulley (also known as wheel); (27) pulley bushing; (28) pulley bolt; (29) outer cage plate; (30) pulley bolt; (31) cable fixing bolt assembly; (32) cable adjusting barrel and spring; (33) adapter screw and nut; (34) pulley plate assembly; (35) hex wrench key, 6 mm.

STEP TWO: With the chain removed or slipped over the two-piece inner cage plate, unscrew the cable stop bolt ("A" in Fig. 4-29) and pull the cable through and away from the derailleur.

STEP THREE: Most derailleur bolts take a 6-millimeter Allen wrench. The Campagnolo derailleur shown in Figure 4-28 is no exception. With the Allen wrench, turn the fixing bolt, "B" in Figure 4-29, counterclockwise and remove the derailleur.

Fig. 4-29: Campagnolo Nuovo Record derailleur. Basic parts are: (A) cable-fixing bolt; (B) attaching bolt (screws into threaded dropout "ear," none of this adapter-plate monkey business; (C) high-gear limit stop (keeps derailleur from going off the high end, pushing chain too far to the right so it jams between chainstay (CG) and freewheel); (D) low-gear travel limit stop (adjusts to keep the derailleur from kicking the chain too far to the left where it can jam between freewheel low gear and spokes); (E) flimsy screw that is supposed to keep wheel aligned accurately in dropouts (soon bends and breaks off unless you are very careful); (F) freewheel; (HH) cable stop brazed on chain-stay.

INSTALLING A NEW REAR DERAILLEUR

STEP ONE: Figure 4-29 shows a derailleur installed in a threaded "ear," which is part of the dropout. Less expensive bicycles do not have such an "ear" but use a mounting bracket ("A" in Fig. 4-30) that is bolted into the dropout itself and through which the hub axle fits. If your new derailleur does not have one supplied with it, you can buy a mounting bracket from the bike store. Screw the derailleur fixing bolt either into the dropout "ear" or the mounting bracket, turning the fixing bolt clockwise. Make sure the limit stop on the derailleur body fits into the matching limit stop on the dropout "ear" or mounting brackets (Fig. 4-31). Some derailleurs, such as the SunTour Cyclone, have an adjustable stop (Fig. 4-32). Figure 4-33 shows the derailleur fixing or mounting bolt being tightened.

Fig. 4-30: Campagnolo Rally wide-range derailleur for those low, low gears. "A" points to adapter plate, which enables you to mount this derailleur (or any other) onto less expensive bikes without a threaded "ear" on dropout.

Fig. 4-31: Looking at a derailleur as it would appear if you were standing on the left side of the bike, if you had X-ray vision and could see through the hub and freewheel. I took this picture to show that there is a stop machined onto all derailleurs where they mount on the dropout threaded ear or the adapter plate. The stop keeps the derailleur from rotating so it loses spring tension that keeps the chain under constant tension regardless of which gear the chain is in. If you have a French bicycle you may not be able to use anything but a French derailleur, particularly if the dropout is a Simplex, designed for a Simplex derailleur.

Fig. 4-32: SunTour has a better idea, an adjustable stop so you can adjust the derailleur to keep its wheels (pulleys) as close to the freewheel as possible, without jamming them, for snappier, more accurate shifting. Arrow points to adjusting screw.

Fig. 4-33: In case you are wondering where the low-gear and high-gear adjustments are on a derailleur, keep this rule of thumb in mind. The low-gear adjustment is always the one closest to the freewheel. "A°" shows the derailleur angle adjuster on this SunTour top-line derailleur. Note that the left-side cage is in two pieces so chain can be lifted off without being taken apart.

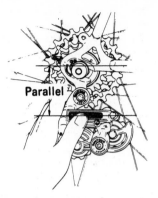

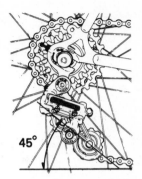

Fig. 4-34: The derailleur body should be adjusted so it is parallel to the chainstays, as shown. *(SunTour)*

Fig. 4-35: Derailleur wheels at the proper 45-degree angle to keep chain tension in all gears. *(SunTour)*

STEP TWO: Ideally, the derailleur body should be parallel to the chainstay. The chainstay is the frame tube marked "G-G" in Figure 4-29. If the derailleur has an adjustable stop, adjust it until the derailleur body is at the correct angle (Fig. 4-34).

STEP THREE: If you have installed new gears, say a low gear with more teeth, as in going from a 28-tooth rear cog to a 34-tooth rear cog, you will now need a longer chain. If you went to a smaller rear cog, say from a 28- to a 23-tooth low gear, you will need less chain. In either case, put the chain on the low (biggest) rear cog and high (biggest chainwheel) front gear. Add or remove chain links as necessary to bring the tension pulley to around a 45-degree angle to the ground (Fig. 4-35). If after shifting to the two high gears, you find you do not have enough chain tension to keep the chain engaged and the chain tends to jump off the gear, particularly the rear gear, try removing another chain link so that with the chain on the low-gear rear and high-gear front, the derailleur pulleys are at the angle shown in Figure 4-36, parallel and in line with

Fig. 4-36: This is the angle the derailleur should assume when the chain is on the low gear in the rear and on the high gear in the front. With all tension the chain will not jump off the cogs in higher gears in the rear. The idea is to keep the chain under as much tension as possible when it is on the two biggest gears, so that as you shift up to higher gears in the rear or down to a smaller chainwheel, the chain will be kept under enough tension so it won't jump off the cog.

Fig. 4-37: To check for chain tension when the chain is on the big cog rear and big chainwheel up front, give it the "pinch" test by seeing if you can squeeze two links together, as shown. If you can, all should be well.

the chain. Another way to check for correct chain length is to pinch together two links (Fig. 4-37). If you can't do that, the chain is too short and you need to add one or two more links. Please also note that there are differences between brands of derailleurs. For example, the Campagnolo Nuovo Record short-cage derailleur should have the cage and pulleys parallel or close to parallel to the chain when the chain is on the two largest (most number of teeth) gears. SunTour and most long-cage derailleurs should, with the chain in this position, be at around a 45-degree angle to the ground. None of these instructions are really absolute but are intended as a guide to correct chain length. But you will get pretty close to accurate chain-length fit with these instructions. Although you probably will never (and I would add, *should not*) use the low-gear and high-front gears together, if you have enough chain wrap-around to do so and in this position can pinch two chain links together, you should still have enough chain tension (from the derailleur) to keep the chain on the high-rear and low-front gears without chain jump.

STEP FOUR: Put the chain on the low-rear gear (biggest cog) and adjust the low-gear travel stop on the derailleur until the derailleur pulleys are in line with the cog. Figure 4-29 shows the low-gear travel stop on a Campagnolo derailleur, "D." The low-gear stop is always the stop closest to the freewheel, on any derailleur I know of. You should move the chain by hand, because we have yet to install the cable. Move the chain to the high gear (smallest freewheel cog) and adjust the high-gear stop so the derailleur pulleys are in line with this gear (Fig. 4-38). Figure 4-39 shows derailleur pulleys lined up with both high and low gears.

STEP FIVE: With the chain on either the biggest or the smallest rear cog, check to make sure the derailleur pulleys are not only centered on the freewheel cog but also that they are in line laterally with the cog. Some-

Fig. 4-38: When installing a new derailleur, even before you attach the cable, move the chain over by hand to the high-gear rear cog and adjust that stop so the derailleur wheels are in line with that cog, as shown.

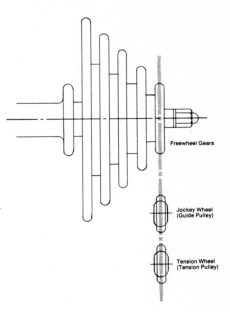

Freewheel Gears

Jockey Wheel
(Guide Pulley)

Tension Wheel
(Tension Pulley)

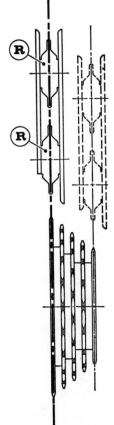

Fig. 4-39: The derailleur wheels should also line up with the low-gear cog.

times, when the derailleur body is bent, as from an accident, the dropout "ear" is bent or the dropout is bent slightly out of line, so that the derailleur is slightly cockeyed with respect to the freewheel cogs. You should be able to eyeball this alignment. If the derailleur itself is twisted, move it back in position by using an adjustable crescent wrench on the derailleur body. If you suspect the problem lies with alignment of dropouts, please stop right here and go to Chapter 11 where you will find instructions on how to check for dropout alignment. If the dropout is out of line it can be twisted back to true with the adjustable wrench. Do this adjustment slowly and carefully. If you are installing a new high-quality derailleur, such as a Campagnolo Nuovo Record, SunTour Cyclone or Shimano DuraAce, I really do not advise you to twist the derailleur body to realign, because it is highly unlikely that the alignment problem lies with the derailleur. All I want you to note is that the derailleur pulleys can be centered on the cog by adjustment, but that the pulleys and cogs must also line up laterally or you will have chain jump, an annoying unscheduled shift from one gear to another as you pedal. Remember also that both the cable and the chain will stretch with use. Chain stretch is not much of a problem unless the stretch is such that the chain is worn. But cable stretch can mean that you will have to readjust the cable tension, a procedure we will discuss in installing the cable.

STEP SIX: I am going to assume that you want a new cable, either because the old one has become frayed, so that you can't thread the end through the spaghetti tubing, or you are going on a trip and quite correctly want a new cable for breakdown insurance. Installing a cable on a rear derailleur is fairly straightforward. If you install a new cable I also recommend new spaghetti tubing. Thread the cable into the shift lever, making sure the lead ball is seated all the way in the lever. Figure 4-40 shows the cable end correctly seated, Figure 4-41 shows the other side of the levers, with cable under the guide in the correct location.

Fig. 4-40: Arrow shows proper insertion of cable.

Fig. 4-41: Derailleur cable threads under guide (arrow).

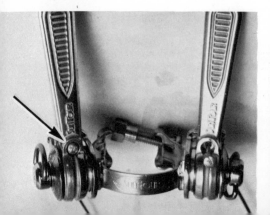
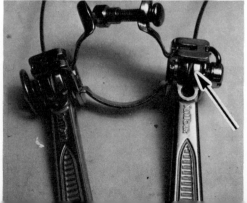

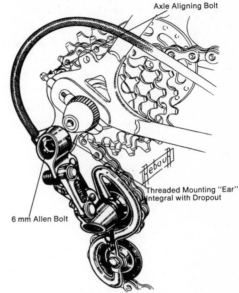

Fig. 4-42: Huret derailleur threaded on dropout integral "ear," hallmark of a higher-quality bicycle.

STEP SEVEN: Cut off enough length of derailleur-cable spaghetti tubing so that you have the kind of curve shown in Figures 4-27 and 4-42. The length of the tubing will depend on the make of derailleur. In measuring tubing, the chain should be on the low-rear cog so the derailleur is at its maximum travel. When cutting tubing, check ends to make sure they are not partially cut, leaving a piece that either obstructs the tubing exits or has sharp edges at this location. I grind off the ends on a bench grinder to eliminate burrs that would hamper cable travel and possibly cut the cable strands. Thread the cable through the cable guides brazed or clamped onto the frame. Brazed-on cable guides are shown in Figures 4-29(HH) and 4-43.

Fig. 4-43: Some custom-built bikes have cable guides underneath the bottom bracket (arrows).

STEP EIGHT: For the correct initial cable adjustment push the shift lever all the way forward, with the chain on the high-gear cog (smallest freewheel cog). Put the end of the cable through the derailleur cable clamp, pull the cable tight and tighten the cable clamp bolt ("A" in Fig. 4-29). If you're lucky, the clamp bolt is just that—a clamp, and not a bolt with a hole through it into which the cable must go, like threading a needle. If the cable end frays just one strand, it means a new cable if you have to remove the derailleur later on, and the cable clamp bolt is the kind with a hole in it. If it's the clamp type, no problem, so long as the cable end is not too badly frayed. I am assuming at this point, though, that you are installing a new cable which has its free end dipped in solder to prevent fraying. Lightly sand the cable from a location about one to two inches from the derailleur and apply solder along this one-inch section. When the solder cools, you can cut and trim off extra cable length, cutting in the middle of your solder area. I use an electrician's wire trimmer, which has holes of various sizes. The hole marked 4–40 nicely trims off the derailleur cable (and brake cables, too).

STEP NINE: Now hang the bike from pipes in the basement. (I prefer hanging the bike, using coated "U" hooks, to standing it. Bike workstands that clamp good tubing and mar the finish are not for me. Besides, you can make two coated hooks for practically nothing; a bike workstand costs upwards of $50 or more.) Twiddle the pedals, move the rear derailleur lever so the derailleur goes through all its gears and make sure it shifts smoothly, without chain override on the high or low gears. At this juncture I would like to add that I *hate* those metal pie plates that are supposed to keep the chain from tangling in the spokes on the high-gear side. If you keep the derailleur properly adjusted, the chain will never jump over the gear and land between it and the spokes. Pie plates are ugly and add unnecessary weight; I suggest you remove the freewheel (see Chapter 9) and pull off that hunk of metal. I don't even like plastic pie plates. I know Uncle Sam has in his infinite wisdom decreed them. But if I want to take one off my very own bike, by golly, I am going to.

If you added a new freewheel that's wider, say from a five- to a seven-speed freewheel, you may need to add a spacer on the freewheel side of the hub axle so the chain won't rub or jam on the seat stay when it's on the high-gear cog. Chapter 9 has details on axle length. You may also have to re-dish the wheel (see Chapter 10).

INSTALLING A FRONT DERAILLEUR

In selecting a front derailleur, make sure it will handle whatever gears you have up front. Table 4-2 gives front-derailleur specifications and capacities, where this data is available from the manufacturer. For ex-

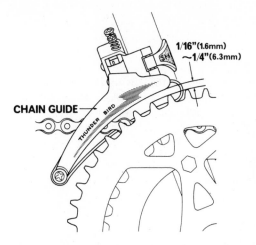

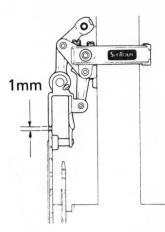

Fig. 4-44: Align front derailleur cage with chainwheel and about ¹⁄₁₆ to ¼ inch above outer (high-gear) chainwheel.

Fig. 4-45: Chainwheel cage should be in line with chainwheels. *(SunTour)*

ample, and here I am assuming you have a bottom-bracket spindle of the correct length and not one that's too long (see discussion of bottom brackets later on in this chapter), so the chainwheel is not too far away from the seat tube for the front derailleur to be able to move the chain to the biggest chainwheel. If you have a triple chainwheel you need a derailleur with a wide travel, such as the SunTour Cyclone which will move through 21 millimeters, or the Campagnolo Nuovo Record which will go through 24 millimeters. I have the most success and satisfaction with the Campagnolo front derailleur, which handles my triple chainset nicely. To install a front derailleur, follow these fairly uncomplicated steps:

STEP ONE: Assuming the old derailleur has been removed, clamp the new one around the seat tube so that the cage is parallel to and about ¹⁄₁₆th inch above the biggest chainwheel (Figs. 4-44 and 4-45).

STEP TWO: The spring action of most front derailleurs is such that the cage is always at the left when the shift lever is all the way forward. Adjust the left, or smallest, chainwheel derailleur travel stop screw so that the cage is centered over the small chainwheel (left chainwheel). In front derailleurs where the spring action pulls the cage to the right, over the largest chainwheel, adjust the high-gear stop, at right, so the

Fig. 4-46: Low- and high-gear stops on a front derailleur. Note that low-gear adjustment stop is closest to seat tube, which is where most of the low-gear stops are located on front derailleurs.

chainwheel is centered in the derailleur chain cage. Figure 4-46 shows the gear stops. The low-gear stop, which limits how far the derailleur cage will move to the left, is always located closest to the seat tube. The front derailleur where spring action keeps the cage at the right is typified by the SunTour Model NSL.

STEP THREE: Insert the cable through the shift lever (Figs. 4-40 and 4-41) and through the cable guides, and fasten the end to the cable clamp of the derailleur, with the shift lever all the way forward, in the low-gear position. Pull the cable taut to remove cable slack, tighten cable clamp bolt. There is very little uniformity among derailleurs, in terms of bolt and nut sizes. For example, the excellent SunTour front derailleur is clamped to the seat tube with a 4-millimeter Allen bolt, its cable clamp is an 8-millimeter bolt and the adjusting screws (travel stops) are Phillips head which can take, however, a standard screwdriver. Campy uses 8-millimeter bolts for the tube and cable clamps. Shimano uses, on the 600 EX, 6-millimeter bolts on tube and cable clamps. In installing the cable, remember that you may need spaghetti tubing between the cable guide and the derailleur so that the cable will not rub on the downtube.

STEP FOUR: Move the shift lever back as you twirl the pedals (with bike suspended from the ceiling, on a stand or upside down) to get the chain onto the largest front chainwheel. Adjust the high-gear stop so the derailleur cage is centered over the chainwheel, with the chain on the middle rear freewheel cog. Now run the gears through all speeds. You will note that as you shift from one freewheel cog to another, without changing adjustment of the chainwheel shift lever, that the chain will tend to rub on the cage as it assumes steeper angles going up and down the gears of the freewheel.

LOCATING THE SHIFT LEVERS

Less expensive bicycles often come with shift levers mounted on the handlebar stem (Fig. 4-47). You should not have shift levers in this location. If you were to hit something, such as a bad bump, or a rut, or get the front wheel caught in a bridge expansion joint, as I have, you will go flying over the handlebars. With shift levers in the location shown in Figure 4-47, men are in fair danger of getting hurt in a testicular spot, and women can also get gouged. I would move the shift levers to some other place.

The more common location is on the downtube (Fig. 4-48). Better bikes have a small "pip" brazed on the downtube that keeps the shifters from sliding down the tube. Clamping shift levers onto the tube will usually hold them, but sometimes vibration works them loose, and the pull of both front- and rear-derailleur springs on the cables can pull the shift levers downward. When this happens all the derailleur adjustments, front and rear, go out the window, at least in the higher-gear front and lower-gear rear, because the cable will be too slack to pull the derailleurs over.

The only other problem with downtube shifters is that the shift lever

Fig. 4-47: Shift levers mounted on stem should at least have lever tops below handlebars. This photo shows levers above handlebars, where you could get hurt in an accident. Sudden bike stops almost always mean you are propelled over the handlebars. I prefer shift levers on the downtube or handlebar ends.

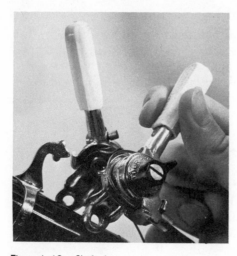 

Fig. 4-48: Shift levers can clamp on downtube. To keep them from moving or sliding down the tube, better bikes have a "pip" brazed on the downtube against which the shift-lever clamp can seat.

Fig. 4-49: Better shift levers have a turn grip so you can tighten the shift-lever mounting bolts, which will work loose eventually. Other makes may require a screwdriver, or a dime. If gears shift by themselves check this adjustment.

lock bolt works loose under constant shifting. That's why the better shift levers, like the one shown in Figure 4-49, have a wire grip on the bolt so you can bend over as you cycle to tighten the lever down. You can tell when your lever bolt has worked loose because the gears shift by themselves. There are other causes for this phenomenon, such as a worn chain or cog or too long a chain causing low tension and chain jump. But your first check should be the shift lever bolt. In fact, you should make a habit of twisting this bolt every day if you ride a lot. Less expensive downtube shifters require a screwdriver but sometimes a dime will work. Even the best of levers will have loosened retaining bolts eventually.

My favorite place to put the shift lever is at the tip end of the handlebars. We have already discussed the safety aspects of stem-mounted shift levers. As for downtube shifters, the problem here is that you have to bend down slightly to reach them, which can be a safety hazard because you are momentarily unbalanced, and because you have to remove one hand from the handlebars to use the lever. With the shifters located at the ends of the handlebar, you can shift with both hands on the bars, without having to lean over sideways, or without having to take your eyes off the road ahead; however, bar-end shifters (Fig 4-50) are a

Fig. 4-50: Bar-end shifters, located at handlebar ends, as shown here, are a lot safer than levers located anywhere else because you can shift without removing your hands from the bars.

separate piece of equipment from downtube shifters and are not interchangeable. You can also use both hands to shift as you go through the gears, without taking your hands off the bars. As I have mentioned before and will bring up again, you need to readjust the front derailleur slightly to compensate for changing chain angle as you shift through the gears, in order to keep the chain from rubbing on the inside of the front derailleur cage. With downtube-mounted shift levers you can only use one hand at a time, so you will find yourself reaching down with the right hand to move to a different rear spocket, then bringing that hand back to the bars while you bend over the left side and reach down with the left hand to readjust the front derailleur. The bar-end shifters are *much* more convenient.

Here is a pictorial step-by-step method for changing to handlebar shift levers. First, though, a word about which lever system to change to. Handlebar shifters are made by Campagnolo, Shimano, SunTour, Huret, and Simplex, among others. I prefer the Shimano (Fig. 4-51) levers because they have internal spring tension, which compensates for derail-

Fig. 4-51: Detailed view of Shimano bar-end controls. (1) anchor bolt; (2) plastic washer; (3) tapered washer; (4) segment assembly with spring; (5) body; (6) lever assembly with lever cap; (7) lever cap; (8) spring washer; (9) lever fixing bolt; (10) front inner cable, rear inner cable; (11) lever-end outer casing, front derailleur outer casing, rear derailleur outer casing.

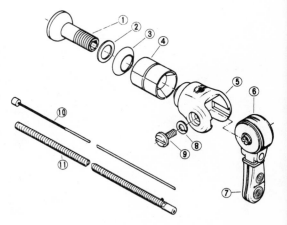

leur spring tension, making shifting easier. Next I prefer the SunTour, which has a ratchet mechanism to hold the gear where you shifted. I don't like the Campagnolo bar levers because they are hard to shift and won't stay in place; it's easy for the rear gear to shift by itself. Construction details among the various makes of handlebar shifters vary slightly, but basic principles are the same. If you can master one, you can install any of them. Tools and materials you will need are: Campagnolo "T" wrench or 6-millimeter Allen wrench; medium-sized screwdriver; new handlebar tape, preferably the cloth type; extra-long derailleur cables for handlebar-end shifters (if yours did not come with them); ⅛-inch or 3/16-inch inside-diameter clear plastic tubing (from a chemical supply or hobby store, to keep cable tubing from rubbing on head tube); 6- or 8-millimeter socket wrench or adjustable wrench to remove old cable and install new cable on derailleurs.

STEP ONE: Become acquainted with the basic parts of handlebar shifters. (A) shift lever-axle bolt; (B) housing barrel; (C) lever housing; (D) cable (extra long); (E) lever; (F) lever-axle nut; (G) lever-axle locknut. (H) is not a part of the shifters; it is the 6-millimeter Allen wrench you will need to tighten the barrel in the handlebar end (Fig. 4-52).

STEP TWO: Remove cable from front derailleur (Fig. 4-53).

STEP THREE: Remove derailleur shift levers and cable, and remove handlebar tape and end plugs. If tape can be reused, remove only as far as brake-lever body (Fig. 4-54).

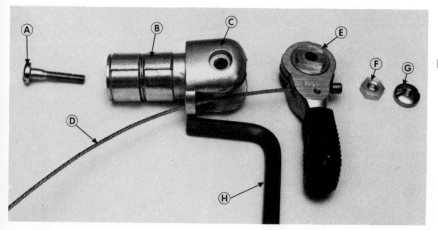

Fig. 4-52:
Step One

Fig. 4-53: Step Two

STEP FOUR: Insert handlebar shift barrel into handlebar end, with cable partially installed as shown (Figure 4-55).

STEP FIVE: Insert 6-millimeter Allen wrench into barrel and tighten counterclockwise, making sure axle holes are level as shown (Fig. 4-56).

STEP SIX: Slide shift lever into milled section of housing. Note that flat lever flange fits into milled section of housing (Fig. 4-57).

STEP SEVEN: Insert lever-axle bolt into round countersunk hole in lever housing (*not* into square shank hole; see Step Eight) (Fig. 4-58).

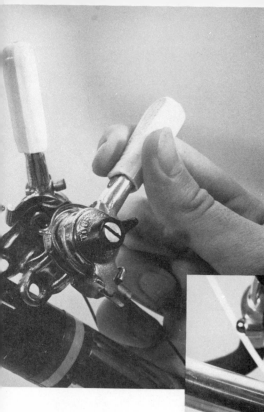

Fig. 4-54: Step Three

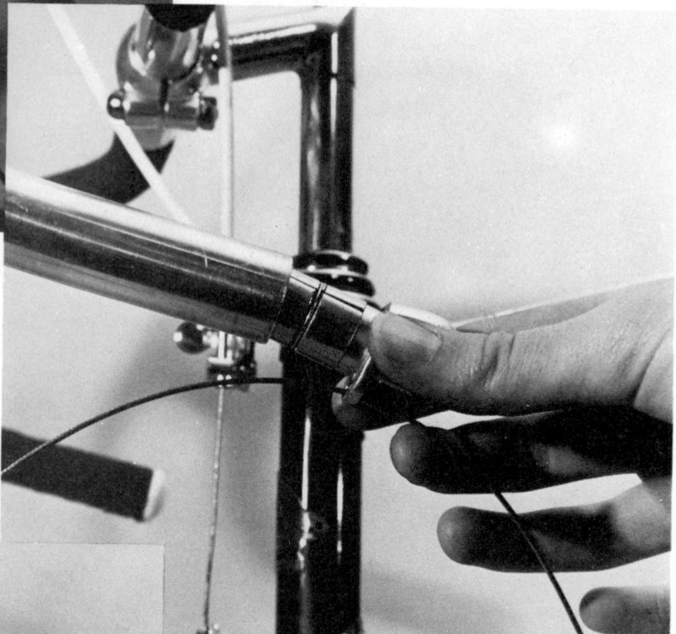

Fig. 4-55: Step Four

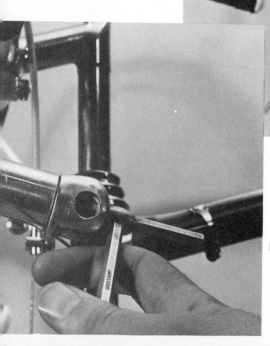

Fig. 4-56: Step Five

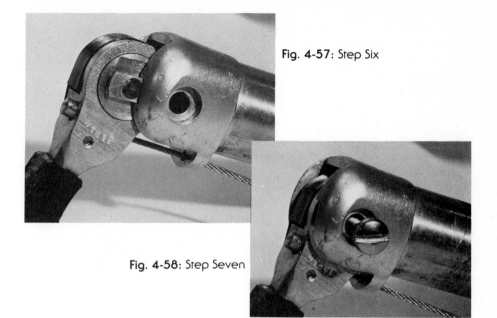

Fig. 4-57: Step Six

Fig. 4-58: Step Seven

STEP EIGHT: Insert lever-axle nut on axle and thread down into octago-nal-shaped hole that holds this bolt in place. Tighten lever-axle-nut from other side with screwdriver (Fig. 4-59).

STEP NINE: Thread on and tighten lever-axle locknut, using screwdriver. Slide steel tubing sheath over cables, and enough ⅛- or ³⁄₁₆-inch clear plastic tubing over sheath so that sheath won't rub on head tube (Fig. 4-60). Fish tank air pump tubing works fine.

STEP TEN: Install cable sheath stop on downtube. Leave enough cable out so handlebars can turn unimpeded. Bring cable through metal sheath and cable stop, and install ends in front and rear derailleurs (Fig. 4-61). Check adjustment of derailleurs.

STEP ELEVEN: Retape handlebars. You can either stop tape over derail-leur cable sheathing just before you reach brake levers and let sheathing flop loose at this point, continuing beyond levers to top of bar without going over cable sheathing; or continue over cable sheathing until cable is covered up to near end of bars near stem. The latter method keeps cables from flopping around and looks a lot neater, but makes it difficult or impossible to remove handlebars when you take your bike on an airplane, as some airlines request.

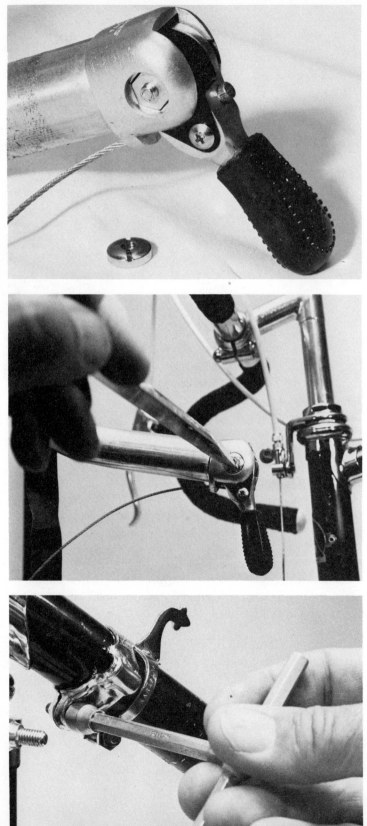

Fig. 4-59:
Step Eight

Fig. 4-60:
Step Nine

Fig. 4-61:
Step Ten

SEALED-BEARING DERAILLEUR WHEELS

None of the rear derailleurs I have dissected recently has ball bearing idler and jockey wheels. Earlier Campy models had them but in recent years Campy has gone to the sintered bronze solid bushing or axle, upon which the wheels turn. Naturally there is more friction generated with this type of loading than with ball bearings. The difference may be hard to detect, of course, given the small amount of rolling resistance even in the cheapest, most recalcitrant of derailleur wheel bearings. But rolling resistance isn't the whole story. Derailleurs are right down there where the dirt is, are very vulnerable to being coated with gunk, sand, all sorts of road debris that can wear out the metal and add friction. So it is with some enthusiasm that I, a sealed-bearing buff, welcome Roger Durham's brainchild: sealed-bearing rear derailleur wheels (Fig. 4-62). Here you will see one of his wheels with a bearing seal removed. Compare it with the plain shaft bushing of the average derailleur wheel. Roger sells his wheels for $14.50 a pair, and guarantees they will fit any derailleur; they come with adapters for many makes of derailleurs. The price is a bit steep, but the piece of mind on a long tour is worth it. Roger sells through bike stores or directly. (Durham Bicycles, Los Angeles, California 90029 (213/664-4534).

There is just one trick about removing the seal on any sealed bearing, and I learned it the hard way, by bending up a seal. First of all, remember that the seal is a very, very thin brass sheet covered with a thin layer of nylon or some other plastic. If you dab at it with a screwdriver you are going to dent the thin seal metal and will have a tough time restoring it to something resembling the original. The seal also fits into a tiny groove inside the bearing shell. It sort of *snaps* back in place, and you

Fig. 4-62: Top row, Durham sealed-ball-bearing derailleur wheels. Left to right, top row: (A) wheel with seal in place; (B) wheel with seal removed to show bearings; and (C) seal. Bottom row, Campagnolo pulley, left to right; (D) cap seal; (F) bolt; (G) sleeve or journal bushing; (E) wheel. Durham wheels will fit any derailleur.

can feel it pop back in as you press gently with your finger all around the edges until it is seated. But to remove it, I have the best success with the end of a sharp penknife blade or an X-acto knife. I slip it carefully but firmly straight down between the outer edge of the seal and the bearing housing, and once the tip of the knife has gone past the seal, I pry upward, gently. I might repeat the process in another location if the seal does not pop out at the first try. There's no secret to it, but you do have to go gently to avoid damaging the seal. You should remove the wheels from the derailleur if you are going to grease them, and here I refer to Durham sealed bearings only. Other derailleurs need only a dab of the same lubricant you use on the chain, applied as often as you spray the chain. As you spray, it's important to keep lubricant off the tires; many lubricants have solvents that can eat away your tires and weaken side walls. This applies in double spades and aces to tubular tires, especially hand-sewn silks. We have already covered lubrication of brake pivot points in Chapter 1.

A WORD ABOUT DERAILLEUR CAPACITY

To determine derailleur capacity, you subtract the number of teeth in the high-gear rear cog from the number of teeth in the low-gear rear cog —subtract the number of teeth in the low-gear front chainwheel from the number of teeth in the high-gear front chainwheel and add up the two numbers. For example, my Alex Singer touring bike has (as of now) a 14–32 rear cluster and a 30–48 front chainwheel. Well, actually, the front chainwheel is 30–38–48 at the moment. Subtracting the rear cogs: 32 minus 14 = 18. From the front, 48 minus 30 = 18. That the two numbers are the same is pure coincidence and entirely irrelevant. So we have 18 plus 18 = 36 teeth. One of these days I am going to change to a 26-tooth front low gear and a 34-tooth rear gear, so I will need a rear derailleur with a capacity of 48 − 26 + 34 − 14 = 42T. Then I'll really be able to see just how far these wide-range derailleurs will stretch. I can predict the results. I 'won't be able to use the combination of both high-rear, low-front and low-rear and high-front, but boy, will I have a super duper "Granny" gear for that mean old 15-percent climb into Vermont's Calvin Coolidge State Park and other roads of that disposition.

I think there's an awful lot of undue mysticism about derailleur capacity anyhow. Look at Table 4-1, for example. You will note that most of the derailleurs have a maximum extension or travel (the average lateral distance the jockey wheel will move) of 45.1 millimeters. The widest travel is the SunTour VX wide range with 52 millimeters, smallest is the

Campagnolo Rally wide range at 34.2 millimeters. I would agree that these measurements may be somewhat unrealistic in that with the low-gear stop wide open you might have the cage enmeshed in the spokes. But allowing 10 full millimeters to keep the cage away from the spokes, you would still have 35 to 39 millimeters of useful travel. The new $200 Regina Titall aluminum/titanium seven-speed freewheel has a maximum tooth-to-tooth width between high and low gears of 32 millimeters, so I would certainly expect any rear derailleur with a useful travel of 39 millimeters to handle it easily. You need a derailleur that will swing the width of the freewheel and then some, that will maintain correct chain tension through all gears for snappy, precision gear changes and that will resist wear and tear at least for five or six thousand miles.

Frankly, I like the Campagnolo derailleurs for high-quality construction. I think the ultimate, as Campy calls it, in close-ratio (up to 28 teeth) rear derailleurs is their Super Record. It has a prelubed titanium pivot bolt (spring loaded), inner and outer arms of hot-forged aluminum alloy, replaceable brass bushing on body arms (replaceable, sure, but did you ever try to buy a tiny Campy derailleur part in a bike store?), removable stop so you can take the lower pivot joint apart for maintenance and spring-tension adjustment. The lower pivot spring is adjustable, which is necessary because the spring will lose tension as time goes on. Cage plates, the sea horse-shaped pieces that hold the jockey and idler wheels, are of cold forged alloy that resists flex when shifting, and these wheels roll on a sintered bronze bushing.

A shorter caged rear derailleur that shifted nicely when your biggest low-gear rear cog was 28 teeth simply won't hack it with a 34-tooth cog. What happens is this: if the chain is long enough to handle the new gear setup with the short-cage derailleur, the derailleur cage will be too short when the chain is on the two high gears, with the rear cog at, let's say, 14 teeth and the chainwheel up front with 36 teeth. There will be too much chain slack and the chain will jump off the gears due to lack of proper tension exerted on the chain by the rear derailleur.

From Table 4-1 you will note that some derailleurs have longer cage lengths (column 2 in table) than others. For example, the Campagnolo Rally, SunTour Cyclone, SunTour VX wide range, all have long cages and will handle up to 34 teeth on the freewheel. The other derailleurs have shorter cages and can handle only up to 28 teeth on the freewheel, except the Shimano Altus, which goes to 30 teeth. So if you're replacing your rear derailleur, be sure to select one that will handle the chain wraparound you need and at the same time maintain chain tension in all gear ratios.

Super wide range "Granny" gears are going to have to be a compromise. If you want a rear cog with 36 teeth and a chainwheel up front with 26 teeth, then you're very likely to find that you can't use the low-gear rear cog and the high-gear or big chainwheel, for two reasons. First I'm assuming that you don't want to drop from a 52- to a 26-tooth chainwheel, that there's a triple chainset involved, which there should be. So the wider chainset, with three chainwheels, means that when the chain is on the far-left big cog in the rear and on the far-right chainwheel up front, the chain is going to be at an extreme angle. It's possible that the new Shimano DuraAce front derailleur with a cage width of 14.6 millimeters will handle this extreme angle without chain rub on the wider front-derailleur cage, and without having to move the front derailleur so as to avoid chain rub. I have this combination and it works for me. But if the chain is long enough for wrapping around these big cogs, then the chain will be too long when you're going in the opposite direction, let's say when the chain is on the high-gear cog (smallest) and low-gear chainwheel (smallest). Now even the widest-range rear derailleur is going to have trouble winding up far enough to maintain sufficient chain tension to keep the chain from jumping off the cog or chainwheel. So if you want a super "Granny" gear like mine, you're going to find, as I have, that two of the gear combinations are not really usable or practical —that is, combinations of the two largest and two smallest cogs and freewheels. I have recently switched to a SunTour six-speed freewheel on my Alex Singer, keeping the 30, 40 and 48 triple chainset up front. Theoretically I now have (6 × 3) an 18-speed setup. In practice, I have at best a 16-speed setup. I prefer this arrangement for two reasons. I don't mind sacrificing the two combinations noted above so long as I wind up with my good old "Granny" hill-climbing low low gear. Second, jumps between gear ratios are reasonable, so I am not constantly changing gears. At any rate I am happy, and that's what counts. You may want bigger gaps between gears, or smaller gaps, depending on your physical condition and the type of riding you do.

TO SWING OR NOT TO SWING

Some derailleurs, such as the SunTour, pivot freely on the mounting bolt that threads into the rear dropout or into the adapter bracket. This permits you to pull the derailleur back out of the way when removing the rear wheel. Without a spring in the mounting bolt, or rather attached to it, it's easier to pull the derailleur body back out of the way. Some rear derailleurs, such as the Campagnolo and some of the Shimano models, have the mounting bolt spring-loaded, so this spring tension helps the main spring in the derailleur body maintain chain tension, which in turn helps keep the chain on the gear you have selected, and

Fig. 4-63: Derailleur at left has no spring in mounting bolt; the one at right does.

makes for somewhat snappier changes. You can tell whether or not the mounting pivot bolt is spring loaded simply by looking at the thickness of the derailleur body through which the mounting bolt goes. Figure 4-63 shows the difference.

Which works the best, the spring-loaded or non-spring-loaded pivot bolt? There are advantages and disadvantages both ways. Obviously the spring-loaded pivot-bolt design, which also has a main spring in the body pivot point (as shown in Fig. 4-64) puts more tension on the chain. My experience has been that the double-spring models have a wider range and greater capacity than single-spring models (no spring on the pivot bolt) of equal cage length. The disadvantage of the spring-loaded

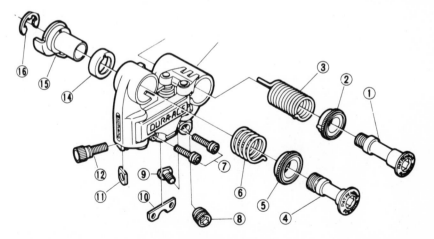

Fig. 4-64: Derailleur with spring-loaded mounting bolt—the Shimano DuraAce. We are concerned here only with part No. 6, the spring that keeps the derailleur on back pressure to aid in control of chain tension.

pivot-bolt design is that this spring pulls the derailleur back at all times. Thus, as you shift up to smaller cogs, the spring-loaded pivot-bolt model takes up the chain tension nicely, but in the process, pulls back so far that there is less chain wraparound on the smaller (higher gear) cogs. Figure 4-64 shows the free pivoting bolt at left and the spring-loaded pivot bolt at right. This is not an actual working demo, just a setup on my workbench table to help you get the point. On balance, I opt for the spring-loaded pivot bolt.

Speaking of the necessity of keeping the jockey wheel as close as possible to the rear cogs for precise, snappy gear shifting (you do remember, don't you, about Figure 4-15? If not, please check it out), a few years ago Huret introduced a derailleur that pretty well solves this problem. The Huret Duopar uses an interesting variation on the normal parallelogram. The Duopar actually has *two* parallelogram movements, one is lateral travel movement normal to all derailleurs. The other is a front-to-rear parallelogram action. As you shift, both actions work together, one to move laterally, side to side—the other to keep the jockey wheel as close as possible to whatever rear cog you have shifted to. The Duopar comes in a short cage, close-ratio version, which weighs around 10 ounces, and a long-cage, wide-ratio version that is said to have a capacity of a fantastic 50 teeth. My own test of this unit showed that it performed with flying colors. I tried shifting too late, on a hard uphill climb. Most derailleurs would have refused to shift at all, or would have overshifted or even mangled the derailleur. Not so with the Duopar; it shifted even under this rather severe, stressful torque. Both models are made of aluminum and titanium. They look like no other derailleur you have ever seen, but they sure do work well.

Chapter Five

Hubs

Hubs are right down there near the ground. Dirt, dust or sand are thrown up at them pretty much all the time, and when it rains it pours all over the hubs. Tires kick up dirt and pick up water. In connection with hubs, I well remember one bicycle camping trip in Vermont. We had pulled into Calvin Coolidge State Park, off that notorious 15-percent grade backbreaker off Route 101A. I felt, subconsciously, that something was amiss with my rear hub. When we settled in and got the tents up and the panniers unpacked, I pulled off the rear wheel and twirled the axle between thumb and forefinger. There it was. I could *feel* as well as *hear* the grains of sand wearing down my expensive Campagnolo hub bearings and beautifully ground and precision-polished and honed cones and races. Fortunately I had a pair of hub wrenches along for this very eventuality, along with a small tube of grease. I cleaned out hub and bearings and repacked with Lubriplate grease. Took about fifteen minutes all told.

CONVENTIONAL HUB MAINTENANCE

You should remove the wheel every six months or so, spin the axle between thumb and forefinger and feel and listen for signs of roughness and dirt. Once a year you should disassemble hubs (Fig. 5-1) clean out old grease, repack with fresh light grease and readjust hub cones. Here's how to do it:

STEP ONE: Remove wheel from bike. Remove freewheel. You will need a freewheel remover that fits your freewheel. If you have a freewheel that takes a splined tool (Fig. 5-2) you're lucky, because all you need do

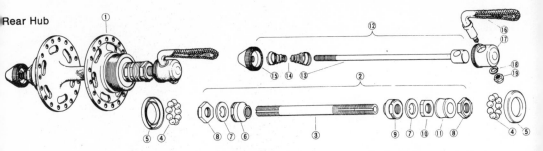

Fig. 5-1: Detailed view of a typical good-to-excellent conventional rear high-flange aluminum alloy hub. Parts are: (1) complete hub; (2) complete axle; (3) axle; (4) ¼-in. steel balls; (5) dust cap; (6) cone nut; (7) keyed washer; (8) locknut; (9) cone nut; (10) locknut (two on freewheel side on this particular hub); (11) spacer; (12) complete quick-release skewer assembly; (13) skewer axle (mounting stud); (14) volute springs; (15) nut for mounting stud; (16) quick-release lever; (17) lever body; (18) spring washer; (19) cap nut on lever.

is remove the quick-release skewer or axle bolt, insert the freewheel remover in the freewheel, turn the wheel over, holding the tool in place, and clamp the tool in a vise. Then just twist the wheel counterclockwise. The freewheel will be very tight, so you will need a little muscle, both hands on the tire. If the freewheel tool won't fit over the locknut, then remove it. You might also have to remove any washers and spacers under the locknut. If you do not have the multi-splined kind of freewheel, but one with two female splines, you will need a freewheel-removing tool like that in Figure 5-3.

STEP TWO: With one cone wrench (Fig. 5-4) on the inner cone, holding it so it can't turn, loosen the left locknut. Figure 5-1 shows a close-up of a rear-wheel hub. One cone wrench should hold the cone, number 6 in Figure 5-1, the other cone wrench should turn the locknut, part number

Fig. 5-2: Freewheel remover for splined Normandy freewheel. (*Bicycle Research*)

Fig. 5-3: Freewheel remover for Regina BRP freewheels

8. If the hub has never been apart, the locknut may be pretty tight due to factory assembly. If this is the case, you can put two pieces of hard wood in the jaws of a vise and the freewheel side locknut in between the wood, and clamp down on that locknut. You will still need to hold the cone nut on the left side as you put leverage on its locknut with the cone wrench.

STEP THREE: With the locknut loose, you should be able to back it off the axle by hand. If not, use the cone wrench. Remove the locknut. Now stop and make a note about the location of the washer and the spacer, if any. You will see next to the locknut a washer with a tiny raised portion on the inside circumference, which fits into a slot machined in the axle. This is part 7 in Figure 5-1. The reason for this washer is to keep the spacer and the cone nut from turning as you tighten up the locknut. This doesn't always work and you will need to hold the cone with the cone wrench to keep it from turning. Now remove the spacer if there is one. At this point, put the wheel and hub on the workbench, so the freewheel side of the axle is resting on the bench. This is so the axle won't fall out when you remove the cone nut.

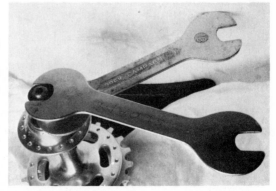

Fig. 5-4: Thin cone wrenches are needed to disassemble hub. One, bottom, holds cone nut so that it does not turn while the upper wrench loosens locknut.

STEP FOUR: Remove the cone nut from the left side of the hub (you've just removed the locknut, washer and spacer) and pop out the grease seal (number 5 in Fig. 5-1). The axle, with its freewheel end resting on the bench, will stay in the hub when the cone is removed. A rag should be under the hub to catch balls as they fall out of the hub. We all have different ways of preventing hub balls from dropping on the floor. Mine is to try to remove as many balls as I can reach from the top, then lift the wheel, remove the axle slowly from underneath to keep the balls from dropping out, and put the hub, with axle removed, back down on the bench over a rag. Then, with a small screwdriver, I push the top set of balls, those that have rolled down the shaft of the hub axle, out the other side and lift the others out of the race by hand or with the edge of the small screwdriver. Usually there's enough grease left in the hub to hold the balls in the race—but don't count on it. Now turn the hub over carefully, with a hand all ready on the other side, to catch any balls that will fall out at this point. With the·hub turned over, remove the rest of the balls, and the grease seal.

STEP FIVE: Clean out all old grease and dirt with kerosene (don't get kerosene on the tire!), clean balls and cones and axle. This is also a good time to clean the outside of the hub and the spokes and to polish the rim of the wheel.

STEP SIX: With cones and balls now clean, inspect them for damage. Look for a galled spot, an area around the hub cone that's obviously different from the other polished surfaces of the cone. If the galled spot (caused by excessive pressure from cone and locknuts that are screwed too tight) is so deep you can feel it with your fingernail, I would suggest you need a new hub. Check the cone for the same condition. You may only need a new set of cone nuts. Your dealer will need to know the make of your hub or, better, that plus the old cone nut, for a replacement. Do not mix other makes of cone nuts with your own, because the radii may be different, and you can wind up with a ruined hub! Further, some hubs use $7/32$-inch balls, and to use a cone machined for $1/4$-inch balls is going to concentrate wear points and lead to early cone failure. A word at this point about nomenclature: I think I've been remiss in using the word "race" too freely, and you may have the impression that a "race" is one thing and a cone another. Actually the part inside the hub into which the balls fit and around which they turn is more properly called a "cup" and it is in fact cup shaped. The cone is the threaded part with a highly machined surface, which threads on the shaft or axle and fits on the outside of the balls. The "race" is that part of both the cup and the cone against which the balls rotate. When I mention galled spots

I refer specifically to rough sections of the races, either or both on the cup or cone race.

STEP SEVEN: Now that the races are okay and the balls look good, devoid of any cracks, rust or galled spots, or have been replaced, let's reassemble the hub. First, put a dab of grease on a rag and roll the clean, shiny balls around in the grease. This makes the balls much easier to pick up. Put a layer of grease in the cup and on the cone race surfaces. To make ball placement easier, put the axle back through the hub, ignoring the fact that there are no balls in place. You may have the right-side cone, assorted spacers and washer and locknut also in place on the axle. Now slide the axle in from the freewheel side. Then drop the balls in place on the left side, around the axle, and tamp some grease on top of the balls. They should now stay in place while you withdraw the axle and reverse it in the hub, and follow the same procedure as above. Then reverse the axle again and insert it through the hub. Another way is simply to lay the balls carefully in the freewheel side of the cup and depend on the grease to hold them in place; then put the axle back in the hub. Now comes the tricky part.

STEP EIGHT: Here is where all your good work can go down the drain unless you are very careful. Hub-cone adjustment is a fine art, almost. Every brand of hub has just slightly different slop in the threads cut into the cone nut and axle. You can't depend on generalizations such as "take up the cone until it is finger tight, then tighten down the locknut," because with those instructions you could wind up with a hub that will wear out in nothing flat if you have too much side pressure on the cones and balls and races. Try this procedure. Take up or tighten the cone nut by hand, until it's snug, and won't turn anymore. Back it off a half turn. Holding the cone nut with the cone wrench, tighten the locknut (having, of course, replaced the spacer, if any, and the washer). Then spin the axle by hand. There should be no feeling of tightness, the axle should spin silky free and smooth. Then move the axle from side to side. There may be just a bit of sideplay. Very little. Very, very little. Put the wheel in the dropout, install the quick-release skewer and tighten it. Now put the wheel so the valve is at two o'clock and let it go. The wheel should move by the weight of the valve alone, and swing past the six-o'clock position. The valve should oscillate back and forth over the six-o'clock position at least fifteen or twenty times, moving more slowly all the time with each oscillation. If your wheel has a reflector, put it at the two-o'clock position because it's a lot heavier than the valve. Now, with your fingertips, check the wheel for sideplay by trying to move the tire from side to side. There should be no sideplay, if you're lucky, or very experienced, or, indeed, both. And the initial adjustment on the cone nut that will work for some will not work on others. You need a bit of sideplay at first, and this you get by backing off the cone nut from the initial finger snug position about a half turn. Of course, thread slop may call for a full turn, or a quarter turn. The important fact to remember is that getting the wheel to spin freely *before* you clamp down on the quick-release lever is not the final criterion of a correctly adjusted set of hub bearings. The final judgment depends on what happens *after* you tighten down the quick-release or axle bolts, and that's what a lot of people do not realize.

MAINTENANCE OF THE SHIMANO FREEHUB

The Shimano Freehub, in both DuraAce, the next lower priced 600 EX, and the Altus models in the lower price range, incorporates the freewheel as part of the hub. In weighing the Shimano freewheel, with six-speed cogs installed and quick-release skewer in place, I came up on my scales with a weight of 666.5 grams (23.5 ounces). Weighing a Campagnolo hub with a much bigger freewheel, also six speeds but with larger cogs, I came up with a weight of 694.5 grams (24.5 ounces), only a 4 percent difference in weight between the two. With a Regina Titall seven-speed freewheel, the Campy rear hub with quick-release weighed only 567 grams (20 ounces).

However, the freehub does offer advantages, other than weight savings, over conventional hubs with separate freewheel. First, the freewheel cogs come in a cassette (Fig. 5-5) held together by three 4-millimeter bolts. In Figure 5-5 the bolts are painted white so you can see them. It is possible to make up different gear combinations (see Table 5-1) and carry them along with you on tour. To change gears, all

Fig. 5-5: Shimano freewheel cassette for the Freehub. Cassette slides into the splined Freehub body and is tightened by the last (high-gear) cog using the cog tool (Fig. 5-6). Arrow points to 4-mm. cassette bolt. There are three. To change individual cogs, remove all three bolts.

Table 5-1 Shimano Freehubs*

Model No.	Speeds	Flange	Weight* (grams)	Locknut-to-Locknut Dimensions (mm)†	High-Gear Selections (threaded cog)	Low-Gear Selections	Cost‡
DuraAce EX							
HF-100	6	Low	398	120	11,12,13,14	12,13,14,15,16,17,18,19,20,21, 22,23,24	$42.50
Same	6	Low	403	126	Same	Same	45.00
HF-110	5	Low	393	120	Same	Same	41.50
600 EX §							
HF 350	6	Low	403	120	12,13,14,15	13,14,15,16,17,18,19,20,21,22, 23,24,28	27.00
HF 360	5	Low	395	120	Same	Combinations of above in five speeds	25.00
HF 370	6	High	405	120	Same	Same in six-speed selection	28.00
HF 380	5	High	413	120	Same	Same in five-speed selection	25.00

* Weight is less cogs.
† Combination freewheel and hub in one unit. Use only with EX derailleur.
‡ Costs are approximate and subject to change without notice. Dealers have different markups; shop around.
§ Also available in 124- and 126-millimeter locknut-to-locknut widths. Weights will be a bit greater.

you do is unscrew the high-gear cog, the one farthest on the right, remove it and pull off the remaining four or five teeth (depending on whether you use five or six gears). Shimano says you can switch from five to six gears without re-dishing the wheel or changing the bike frame, but in their literature I notice that whereas zero dish (see Chapter 10) is required for the 110-millimeter locknut-to-locknut hub, 2.95 millimeters are required for the five-speed 120-millimeter hub and 7.8 millimeters of dish are required for the six-speed 120-millimeter rear hub, so some re-dishing will be necessary in switching from the five- to the six-speed combination. As of this writing, you can only get up to a low gear of 26 teeth on the DuraAce freehub, which is not enough for your author, who likes a "Granny" gear combination of 32 or 34 teeth plus a 24- or 26-tooth chainwheel for a low, low, low hill-climbing gear. You could walk up the hill faster, but riding is easier and more elegant. But the Shimano people tell me that they are working on a wider gear range for the freewheel hub. Back to the cassette system. I suppose this would appeal to you if you were a real fanatic and wanted just that perfect combination of gears for each and every flat or hill and didn't mind stopping every few miles to change the cassette. To do this, though, you

Fig. 5-6: Cog remover (and tightener). Tool is shown on a Shimano cassette. But use this tool the same way on any freewheel to remove cogs, always taking off the high-gear cog first. You can hold freewheel gears in a special holder that grips them without damage, or put the freewheel between two pieces of wood in the jaws of a vise, or if the freewheel is on a hub, put the opposite-side locknut in a vise. In all cases, turn the cog remover **clockwise** to remove a cog. In reassembling cogs, hold the low-gear cog in a freewheel and with the cog tool, tighten the cog down lightly. Pedal action will take care of the rest. Just make sure that the cogs are seated as far as they can go before you pedal away.

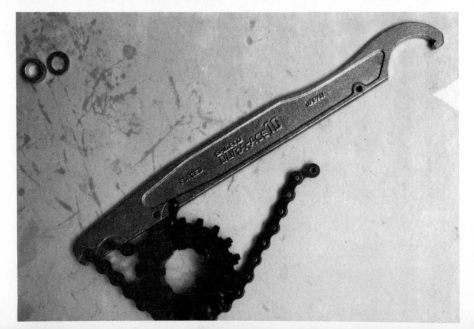

Fig. 5-7: Freewheel remover for splined Atom freewheel. *(Bicycle Research)*

would need to carry along a fairly heavy tool (Fig. 5-6) that weighs nearly one pound (around 440 grams), not a terribly practical touring tool to lug around. If you race, have a sagwagon on the road and it's a long, long stage race, you would find the cassette sprocket interchange system handy, though. You can also tear down individual freewheels, with the tool shown in Figure 5-6, and swap cogs around, although the freewheel cassette system is more convenient. If you leave out the cassette bolts (Fig. 5-5) and forget about the cogs as a cassette, you can carry individual cogs and change them with the cog-removal tool.

If, with a freehub, you break a spoke on the freewheel side, you will have to remove the cogs so you can install a new spoke. This also applies to the conventional hub and separate freewheel system, except that in this case all you need do is remove the entire freewheel with a freewheel removal tool, which is a lot lighter and smaller than the cog remover in Figure 5-6. Figures 5-7 and 5-2 show a number of these tools, and you will note that they are different, so on tour be sure to carry the one that fits your freewheel. The splined freewheel and matching tool are the easier combination to use. Figure 5-8 shows a Shimano Altus

Fig. 5-8: Shimano Altus freehub. Freewheel is an integral part of the hub. Cogs fit on splines, except high-gear cog, which threads on.

Fig. 5-9: With Shimano freehubs, you can only use a derailleur with the top inner case, or most of it, missing. Otherwise the full cage would rub on the low-gear cogs. Arrow points to area where inner cage has been eliminated except for small guide. In this design, the chain can also be lifted off so derailleur can be removed without "breaking" chain.

freehub with cassette gear cluster removed. The Shimano DuraAce, or 600 EX series freehubs, *must* be used with an EX series rear derailleur. This is the type of derailleur that has an open cage on the inner or left side (Fig. 5-9). This type of derailleur must be used because the freewheel unit is so close to the right-hub flange that it would run against the flange when the chain is shifted onto the low gear. There's nothing new about this type of "broken" cage derailleur; SunTour has had them for years. They do offer the additional advantage of being able to lift the chain out of the freewheel entirely, without having to use a rivet remover to take the chain apart. This is handy when all you want to do is remove the derailleur for cleaning. Of course, if you really need to clean the derailleur, the chain undoubtedly needs cleaning too and should be removed, cleaned and relubed as explained in Chapter 6. The type of derailleur shown in Figure 5-10 cannot be used with the freehub be-

Fig. 5-10: This is the kind of derailleur you **cannot** use with a Shimano freehub. Arrow points to inner cage that would rub on low-gear cogs.

cause here, as shown, the cage is not "broken" and extends around the derailleur cage and would run on the Shimano Freehub right flange when in the low gear. This explains in part why the freehub only goes to 26 teeth—because the Shimano Crane GS wide-range derailleur with extra-long cage, similar to the one in Figure 5-10, does not have a "broken" cage and so a cog with more than 28 teeth requiring a wide-range derailleur could not be used. This poses no terrible technical problem and I expect to see it solved fairly soon, probably by the time this book is off the press.

Let's look now at problems involved with the Shimano DuraAce freehub and similar Shimano freehub designs. To take the DuraAce version apart you need a 14-millimeter cone wrench for the cone nut and a 13-millimeter cone wrench for the locknut over the cone. You also need a special Shimano tool to remove the freewheel unit, (indicated with an asterisk in Fig 5-11, which also shows the entire freehub dismantled).

Dismantle following these steps:

STEP ONE: Remove quick-release skewer by holding the lever in one hand and unscrewing the skewer nut at the other end. Be careful to catch the two small springs as you pull the skewer through the hollow

Fig. 5-11: Shimano DuraAce Freehub dissected. Arrow points to threading on the freewheel body that fits into matching threads inside the hub itself. Asterisk is next to special freewheel remover.

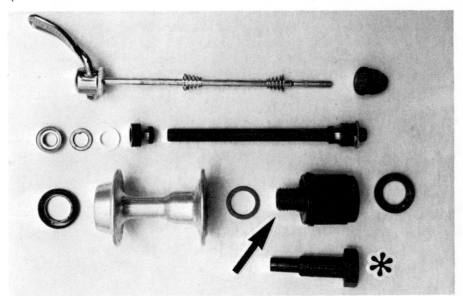

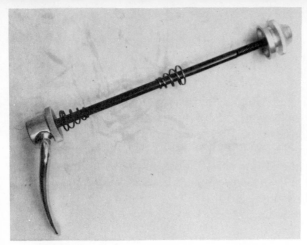

Fig. 5-12: Typical quick-release skewer. Note correct position of springs, small end facing toward hub. As you remove skewer from hub, be ready to catch the spring, because if you drop it on the floor it will bounce right to a terrific hiding place. I must have a dozen such lurking around my basement, destined never to be found.

axle. Figure 5-12 shows a skewer. Note that the smaller part of each spring always faces toward the hub.

STEP TWO: With a 14-millimeter cone wrench holding the cone, loosen the locknut on the left side (facing forward) of the hub. Remove splined washer and spacer. Remove the cone. Now carefully pull the axle out through the freewheel side, catching all loose balls (and they will be loose) in a rag on the workbench or table. If you drop a ball on the floor, you may never find it, as I noted earlier in this chapter. If you lose a ball, don't worry about measuring another one. Just take one of the remaining balls to the bike shop where they can find you a duplicate. The freehub uses nine quarter-inch (6.35-mm.) balls per side.

STEP THREE: Insert the special freehub removal tool (arrow, Fig. 5-11) and turn it counterclockwise. The freehub threads out of the hub shell, and if you look closely at Figure 5-13 you will see the threads. Note that there is a washer or spacer between the freehub and the hub shell which must be replaced when you reassemble the freehub. The round black things at both sides of the freehub are plastic dust seals.

Fig. 5-13: Avocet sealed-bearing hubs, showing one of the bearings removed. Left is the rear hub.

Fig. 5-14: This is the part of the hub where the freewheel (Shimano DuraAce hub) fits. Arrow points to threads inside hub body where freewheel threads. Note layer of grease in outer hub flange, where end of freewheel rotates. There is a spacer that must be used between the freewheel and the hub, shown above. Freewheel must not be overtightened or it will bind and rub on hub body.

There is a layer of grease between the freewheel and the hub. Figure 5-14 shows the bored-out hole into which the freehub is threaded, and you can see deeper inside the hub some of the threads for the freehub.

STEP FOUR: Clean out all old grease and dirt, repack with grease and reassemble, reversing the above instructions. As you begin to adjust the left-side hub cone, however, be very careful about taking up on it. Leave just a smidgen of sideplay so that when you tighten the locknut the freewheel turns freely. I have found that just a touch too tight an adjustment on the cone and locknut will cause the freewheel to rub and bind against the hub. You can have acceptable smoothness in axle rotation but still have tightness in the freewheel rotation. As you tighten the quick-release, again check to make sure *both* axle and freewheel turn freely and that there is no sideplay in the axle.

I do not recommend taking the freewheel apart. There are about fifteen million tiny little ball bearings plus springs and ratchets. Everything you need to do will be covered later on in Chapter 9, in more detail, and I will disassemble a typical freewheel and lay the parts out on a table and show you what you will be faced with. Then, if you're brave, go ahead. You may have a broken ratchet, or a stuck one in your good freewheel, or want to replace worn cogs and save the freewheel body, and we'll get into that later.

SEALED-BEARING VERSUS CONVENTIONAL HUBS

For touring, the obvious advantages of maintenance-free sealed bearings are the major selling point for their use in hubs. I like the idea that I can take off and never have to worry about dirt, fine sand or, in a

Fig. 5-15: Durham hub dissected. Note that the seal at top left is slightly damaged and will have to be carefully straightened before installation so that it won't rub on bearing. This is the only sealed-bearing hub on the market that you can easily disassemble yourself. All it takes is the tiny Allen wrench furnished with the hub. Bolts are furnished if you do not wish to use a quick-release skewer. I prefer the bolts. They save a lot of weight and provide greater security and peace of mind. Internal spacer is at top of photo.

downpour, water getting into my hub bearings and abrading polished cone surfaces, or water washing grease away. It's a happy feeling to leave a campsite on a lovely morning with the certain knowledge that all is well with my hubs. I might also point out here that I like sealed-bearing everything, including pedals, bottom brackets and headset; these we will review later on in other chapters. If there were such a thing as a sealed-bearing chain, you can bet I'd have one on my touring bike.

The non-sealed-bearing hubs such as Campagnolo, DuraAce and SunTour Superbe are easy to disassemble, clean and put back together, as I did on my Vermont tour. You would need to take these hubs apart, clean out all old grease and dirt, repack and reassemble about once a year, depending on how much you bicycle.

The sealed-bearing hubs, such as Phil Wood, Avocet Models II and III and Durham, will go for years without requiring disassembly, cleaning and repacking with grease. I have been riding on Phil Wood hubs for about four years and they show absolutely no sign of needing lubricant or of being infiltrated with any abrasive substance such as fine sand. Occasionally, during shore rides along an ocean or Lake Michigan, I will ride over fine sand blown upon the bike trail from the beach. It's unavoidable as long as I am out on the trail; there will always be a thin, virtually invisible layer of beach sand on the bike trail near any beach. So far, the Phil Woods are doing fine.

Sealed-bearing hubs are just that. They use a set of precision bearings fitted with neoprene or similar material (capillary or labyrinth shields, which are effective dirt and water stoppers). Figure 5-15 shows a Durham hub dissected, with parts laid out. At the left is a complete, intact sealed bearing; also at the left, a sealed bearing with seal removed. Later on we will show how to take one of these hubs apart, step by step, and reassemble it. For now, in terms of maintenance, the Durham is the only one of the three that can be so maintained without special tools. In fact,

Phil Wood has designed his hubs so you *can't* take them apart because he would prefer to do that himself. In over five years of making many thousands of these hubs, Phil reports that only a handful have been returned for bearing work. The Avocet hubs you can take apart as far as the bearing by removing the two locknuts on one end and pulling the shaft out. But then there is no place to grip the bearings to pull them out, and you can only get at one side of the bearing to remove the seal for relube. But if it's only a matter of having to replace the grease, which, although it may last for five years, will ultimately need to be replaced, I don't see this as any great drawback. The sealed bearings are not sealed between sides. There is room between the balls in their races to force grease through to the other side, so even though you can't get at the other seal, on the inside of the bearing, you can still get some grease through by pushing it into the openings around the balls. In fact, you can easily lift off the outside grease seal on any of these sealed-bearing hubs, dunk the entire hub in a grease-removing solvent such as Carbo-Chlor (1,1,1-Trichloroethane) available in your hardware store, and re-pack from one side only. Now this is not the method I would recommend. It's much better to remove the entire bearing, both seals and repack that way. But if you are about to go on a trip and your sealed bearings are dry, or you think they are, just pry off the outer seal and inspect. If they need lubricant, add a dab, force through and replace the seal.

Sealed-Bearing Adjustment

There are no cone nuts, as such, on sealed bearings. But there are flat nuts followed by locknuts on the Avocet hubs (Fig. 5-13). If these are taken up too tightly, excess side load is placed on the sealed bearings and they will bind, turn tightly. Figure 5-16 shows the axle removed from an Avocet Model II sealed bearing. Figure 5-17 shows a seal removed from one of the bearings. When (or if) you remove the axle and look inside the Avocet hub you will notice two long spacers inside the hub itself. There's about a quarter-inch space between the outer edge of the spacers and the inner edge of the bearing, room enough for a small driver to be placed and an attempt made to carefully punch out the bearing at the opposite end. No go. The bearing is in the hub in a very tight press fit. I don't recommend any attempt at replacing these bearings. Send any bad hubs back to Avocet; they will be glad to replace them. For subsequent lubrication, if ever needed, prying off the outer seal should enable you to force enough light grease into the bearing for another 5,000 miles or so. As Figure 5-17 shows—and this is a factory-fresh hub—there isn't much grease in a new hub anyway, and what there is is almost the consistency of oil. In prying off the seal, the best

Fig. 5-16: This is as far as you can go in disassembling the Avocet hub without special tools to remove the bearing. But you can remove the axle, should it need replacing if it gets bent. The bearing outer seal can also be removed, and one of them is shown at bottom left. This is a thin brass and neoprene seal, easily damaged; so if you remove it, be careful not to force or bend it. See text for details.

way, and this applies to all such seals, is to insert the point of a small knife blade behind the outer edge of the seal, and carefully pry upward and outward. The seal should lift off easily, and be as easily replaced by two fingers. It sort of snaps back into a groove just below the rim of the bearing.

I felt that the lubrication in Avocet hubs was so light that this in part accounted for the ease with which the axle could be spun between thumb and forefinger. I also feel that this very light grease or oil is not adequate lubrication for the stresses of a loaded-down bicycle on a long camping tour, although I am sure that the factory supplied the bearings to Avocet this way. I removed seals from both bearings and packed them with Lubriplate. Now the axle does not spin so freely. In fact, it does not spin nearly as freely as a properly adjusted non-sealed-bearing Campagnolo hub, packed with the same grease. Sealed bearings in the Durham hub are packed with a grease similar to the viscosity of Lubriplate, yet

Fig. 5-17: The Avocet hub with seal removed. Note that you can force grease through the bearings into the other side; but go easy so that you don't push off the seal on the inside where you can't get at it. But sealed bearings are easy to regrease because the seal comes off so readily.

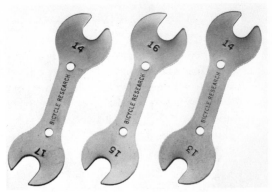

Fig. 5-18: To do any hub maintenance you will need these thin but strong hub-cone wrenches. I recommend two of each, because you will need to hold the cone while you tighten the locknut. Any bike shop will have them.

the axle spins very freely.[1] To remove locknuts from the Avocet hubs you will need two thin cone wrenches (spanners), (Fig. 5-18) as for all hubs, available from your local bike shop for about $3 each. The Avocet takes two 13-millimeter cone wrenches, one to hold the inner nut, one to turn the outer nut while you hold the inner nut from turning.

Grease is more viscous, heavier, than oil and will of course reduce rolling resistance. That's why racing cyclists use oil in bearings, and why on Campy hubs there's an oil hole in the hub, covered by a black clip. But unless you are a racing cyclist, oil instead of grease on a tour will lead to disaster, to prematurely aged bearings.

The dust cap on Campy hubs is pretty good (arrows in Fig. 5-19), fits

[1] To be fair to Avocet, I may have overpacked the bearings, in turn causing friction between the grease and the seals.

Fig. 5-19: Campagnolo Record hub dissected. This hub, like all rear Campy hubs, takes a total of sixteen ¼-inch balls, eight to a side. The two grease seals are shown at top left and at right. (Campy does not make this hi-lo combination at this time.)

closely against the axle but is not as good a seal as on sealed precision-bearing sets. Some fine dust can still get into conventional loose ball and cup hubs. Spoke holes on Avocet hubs are not generously radiused. That is, they don't cup outward enough, in my opinion, to support spokes at this crucial location. The point where spokes bend through flange holes is an area of high stress where spokes are most likely to break.

Phil Wood Sealed-Bearing Hubs

The most popular sealed-bearing hub in this country is the one that's made here and has been around the longest, the Phil Wood hub (Fig. 5-20). There are a number of excellent features designed into this hub. First, I have never been able to get it to bind, no matter how tightly I squeeze the quick-release lever. Hubs always run freely. So there's no problem in excessive side loading. The flanges angle in slightly, instead of being straight up and down as in conventional hubs, including the Campagnolo front hub in Figure 5-21. Figure 5-20 does not show this slight angle, but it's enough to lead spokes at a less stressful angle, which, combined with the generous radiusing or cupping of flange spoke holes which *is* shown in Figure 5-20, leads to longer spoke life and less likelihood of spoke breakage. The hub in Figure 5-20 happens to be a bolt-on, with more convenient Allen nuts. You will also note the serrated end of the spacer, which helps hold the hub where you want it.

The axle is hollow, so you can use a quick-release if you wish. And here is as good a place as any to take a breather and talk for a moment about bolt-on versus quick-release hubs.

Fig. 5-20: This hub, made by Phil Wood, has sealed bearings that last for thousands of miles without requiring maintenance. Note that you can use a quick-release skewer, or bolt the hub on with the Allen bolts furnished and shown on the hub. Spacer also has serrated detents which help hold it where you put it.

Fig. 5-21: Here is a conventional, loose-ball-bearing hub, and a very fine one at that, made by Campagnolo. This is a low-flange Record front hub. Arrow points to quick-release skewer.

To Bolt or Not to Bolt

If you understand the genesis, the development of the high-performance touring bicycle we Americans love so well, you can understand how it came to pass that we see most of these machines with quick-release hubs. The modern high-performance touring bicycle is descended from the high-performance road-racing bicycle popular in Europe. When the bike boom hit America in the late 1960s and early 1970s, the only decent bikes were actually modified road-racing bikes with, for the most part, minor concessions to touring, such as fenders and conventional tires. But the best bikes most of us bought were short-wheelbase, short-fork-rake racing machines, with tubular tires and high-flange hubs with quick-release skewers. The quick-release is a fairly heavy device. The quick-release in Figure 5-12 weighs 70.875 grams (around 2.5 oz.) and that's the shorter front-hub unit. A longer, heavier rear-wheel quick-release skewer weighs 87.885 grams or a tad over 3 ounces. Compare these measurements, a combined weight of 158.76 grams, with the 57.7 grams (2 oz.) of the axle bolts of the Durham hubs, or about the same weight for axle nuts, and you will see there is a considerable savings in weight when you bolt the axle and do not use a quick-release. *Per wheel.* Remember, an ounce off the wheel is worth two off the frame.

The only reason for the quick-release is to be able to change wheels in a hurry. That's why quick-releases are universally used by road-racing cyclists, both professionals and amateurs. But tourists are not road racers, and you don't need to be able to tear a wheel from a bike and stick on a new one in seconds. You have time, if you get a flat, to leisurely sit down and curse out the situation, then repair the puncture, in most instances without even removing the wheel. Quick-release skewers can be accidentally loosened, so that when you hit a bump, the wheel can pop out of the dropouts and cause an accident. Or, if you push hard on the pedals, you can pull the rear wheel to one side so it rubs on the stay. If you bolt the wheels on, however, they are in place to stay, and you need not worry that leaning the bike against a tree or bumping into something as you wheel the bike has loosened the skewer lever. And bolted-on wheels are a bit harder to steal. A quick-release invites wheel theft. True, bolted-on wheels are the hallmark of cheap bikes, with heavy threaded solid axles. But anyone who can't tell your good bike from an el cheapo, with or without quick releases, is not someone you need to impress anyhow.

On tour, take along one lightweight wrench that will fit hub nuts so you can remove the wheel from the bike if you have to. If you are touring with friends, only one of you need carry a tool kit if you include enough sizes to fit everybody's bike. You don't need ten sets of tools for ten bikes. Just make sure that any odd-size Allen wrenches, for instance, are in the tool kit.

Durham Sealed-Bearing Hubs

You can buy the more popular Phil Wood hubs in most bike stores, but you may have to order Durham hubs from the manufacturer because these are so new. Major specifications and prices are in Table 5-2. The Durham people are: Durham Bicycles, 3944 Marathon Street, Los Angeles, California 90029. Phone: 213/664-4534.

The Durham sealed-bearing hubs are the only ones of this type that you can easily and quickly take apart, including removal of the bearings. This is a convenience because you don't need to return hubs to the factory if, after 5,000 miles or whenever, the bearing develops roughness. Any roughness in a sealed precision bearing means that it should be replaced. This is unlike a conventional loose-ball hub, since these can develop some roughness which usually only indicates the presence of dirt. A quick disassembly, cleaning, repacking with grease, readjusting of cones and you're on your way. Durham uses Conrad type of bearings, as do all sealed-bearing hubs, which, when properly greased and seated, have substantially less friction than loose-ball hubs, sometimes as much as 30 percent less.

I have tried to side-load a Durham hub with both axle nuts and quick-releases, and it just can't be done, because bearings have end clearance between them and the internal spacer. The Durham hubs use NTN #6001-LLB bearings, available from bearing supply houses. A cross-reference check will discover other makes of bearings that will fit.

Table 5-2 Comparative Specifications of Hubs

Make and Model	Front	Rear	Flange	Speed	Locknut to Locknut (mm)	Spoke Holes	Weight* (grams)	Threading†	Cost (Per Hub)‡
Campagnolo Hubs									
Record 1034/A Road	x		Low	—	100	24,28,32,36,40	227	—	$35.00
Record 1034/B Road		x	Low	5	120	Same	291	A,B,C	40.00
Record 1034/P Road		x	Low	6	125	Same	299	Same	43.00
Record 1035/A Road	x		High	—	100	Same	263	—	45.00
Record 1035/P		x	Same	5	120	Same	326	Same	51.00
Record 1035/P		x	Same	6	125	Same	331	Same	53.00
Record 1036/A Track	x		High	—	100	24,28,32,36	226	—	45.00
Record 1036/P Track		x	High	—	120	Same	336	Same	51.00
Nuovo Tipo 1264 Road	x		Low	—	100	Same	227	—	23.00
Nuovo Tipo 1265 Road		x	Low	5	120	Same	291	Same	26.00
Nuovo Tipo 1266 Road	x		High	—	100	Same	251	—	27.00
Nuovo Tipo 1267 Road		x	High	5	120	Same	326	Same	29.00
Shimano Road Hubs									
DuraAce HA100	x		Low	—	100	28,32,36	220	A,B	31.00
Same		x	Low	5	120	Same	305	Same	35.00
Same		x	Low	6	125	Same	310	Same	38.00
DuraAce HA200	x		High	—	100	Same	260	Same	30.00
Same		x	High	5	120	Same	330	Same	33.00
Same		x	High	6	125	Same	335	Same	37.00
600 HB100	x		High	—	100	36	275	—	23.00
Same		x	High	5	120	36	350	A	25.00
Same		x	High	6	125	36	355	A	26.00
600 HB200	x		Low	—	100	36	235	—	22.00
Same		x	Low	5	120	36	340	A	24.00
Same		x	Low	6	125	36	355	A	25.00

(*See Table 5-1 for Shimano Freehub specifications*)

Table 5-2 Comparative Specifications of Hubs

Make and Model	Front	Rear	Flange	Speed	Locknut to Locknut (mm)	Spoke Holes	Weight* (grams)	Threading†	Cost (Per Hub)‡
Shimano Track Hubs									
DuraAce HA310	x		High	—	100	28,32,36	225	—	28.50
DuraAce HA310		x	High	—	110 or 120	Same	295	—	32.50
DuraAce HA300	x		High	—	100	Same	240	—	21.00
DuraAce HA300		x	High	—	110 or 120	Same	313	—	23.50
Hi-E Road Hubs									
201	x		High	—	100	28,32,36,40	170	—	34.50
2282 (Tandem)	x		High	—	110	Same	210	—	28.50
232		x	Low	5	120	Same	227	A	26.00
233 (Heavy Duty)		x	Low	5	120	Same	245	A	28.00
Normandy Road Hubs									
H3F Sport	x		High	—	100	36	270	—	7.00
H3R		x	High	5	120	36	355	A	8.00
Sanshin Road Hubs									
HPA 101	x		Low	—	100	36	241	—	15.00
HPA 102		x	Low	5	120	36	327	A	16.00
HPA 103	x		High	—	100	36	270	—	16.00
HPA 104		x	High	5	120	36	344	A	17.00
SunTour Road Hubs (Maeda)									
Superbe RH 2000	x		High	—	100	28,32,36	236	—	25.00
Superbe RH 2000		x	High	5	120	Same	341	A	27.00
Superbe RH 2000		x	High	6	125	Same	346	A	29.00
Superbe RH 1000	x		Low	—	100	Same	278	—	23.00
Superbe RH 1000		x	Low	5	120	Same	354	A	25.00
Superbe RH 1000		x	Low	6	125	Same	362	A	26.00

Make and Model	Front	Rear	Flange	Speed	Locknut to Locknut (mm)	Spoke Holes	Weight* (grams)	Threading†	Cost (Per Hub)‡
Phil Wood Hubs (1)									
Standard (Road)	x		Med.	—	90,100 or 108	20 to 48	170	—	26.00
Standard (Road)		x	Med.	5 or 6	120 or 127	Same	225	A	35.00
Brake Hub	x		Med.	—	90,100 or 108	Same	210	—	35.00
Brake Hub§		x	Med.	5 or 6	120,125,130, 135,140	Same	354 to 378	A	48.00
Track§	x		Med.	—	100,105,110	Same	170	—	35.00
Track§		x	Med.	—	115 or 120	Same	265	—	42.00
BMX Motocross	x		Med.	—	90 or 100	Same	170	—	26.00
BMX Motocross		x	Med.	—	100,105,110, 115,120	Same	225	—	35.00
Zeus Road Hubs §									
81	x		Low	—	NA	24,28,30,32,36,40	230	—	NA
81		x	Low	5	NA	Same	305	A,B,C	NA
81		x	Low	6	NA	Same	321	A,B,C	NA
81	x		High	—	NA	Same	241	—	NA
81		x	High	5	NA	Same	340	A,B,C	NA
81		x	High	6	NA	Same	353	A,B,C	NA
Zeus Criterium 80-1	x		Low	—	NA	Same	210	—	NA
80-1		x	Low	5	NA	Same	310	A,B,C	NA
80-1		x	Low	6	NA	Same	353	A,B,C	NA
Road Titanium	x		Low	—	NA	Same	180	—	NA
Road Titanium		x	Low	5	NA	Same	290	A,B,C	NA
Avocet Road Hubs									
Model I	x		Low	—	100	36	202	—	16.50
Same		x	Low	5	120	36	310	A	23.50
Same		x	Low	6	125	36	319	A	25.00
Model I	x		High	—	100	36	212	—	18.50
Same		x	High	5	120	36	346	A	25.50
Same		x	High	6	125	36	351	A	27.50

Make and Model	Front	Rear	Flange	Speed	Locknut to Locknut (mm)	Spoke Holes	Weight* (grams)	Threading†	Cost (Per Hub)‡
Model II	x		Low	—	100	28,32,36	198	—	21.50
Same		x	Low	5	120	Same	252	A	28.00
Same		x	Low	6	125	Same	258	A	31.50
Same	x		High	—	100	Same	205	—	23.50
Same		x	High	5	120	Same	295	A	31.50
Same		x	High	6	125	Same	310	A	34.50
Model III	x		Low	—	100	Same	110	—	53.50
Same		x	Low	5	120	Same	285	A	72.00
Same		x	Low	6	125	Same	295	A	76.00
Durham Hubs									
Bullseye	x		Low	—	110	28,32,36,40	170	—	34.50
Same		x	Low	5	120	Same	230	A	40.50
Same		x	Low	6	125	Same	242	A	42.50

* Less skewers but with dropout locknuts where provided.

† A = English (1.370 inch x 24 TPI [threads per inch] BSC). B = French or metric (34.70mm x 1mm). C = Italian (35mm x 24 TPI).

‡ Pairs of hubs will be priced slightly less than single hubs. Zeus prices and components sizes about the same as Campagnolo, but varies considerably from dealer to dealer. Shop around.

§ Bolt on only. Bolt on road axles available at slight extra cost.

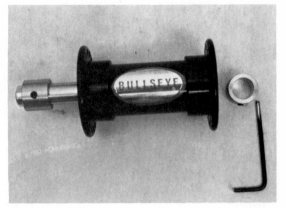

Fig. 5-22: Durham sealed-bearing hub. Spacer comes with Allen bolt and Allen wrench to fit.

To disassemble Durham hubs:

STEP ONE: Loosen Allen bolt with small Allen wrench provided with hub (Fig. 5-22).

STEP TWO: Pull axle out through one of the bearings (Fig. 5-22).

STEP THREE: Look inside, through one of the bearings. You will see a central spacer that has dropped off to one side, like the Leaning Tower of Pisa. With the end of the axle, push lightly and the bearing at the other end will drop out. Bearings are held in the hub by a hand-pressure fit, snug but not very tight. This takes accurate machining, because you want just enough tightness to keep the outer circumference of the bearing from spinning under a load but enough looseness so bearings can be removed without special tools, and replaced the same way.

STEP FOUR: Remove the other bearing, following Step 3.

STEP FIVE: With the sharp edge of a knife, press down at the edge of the seal and slightly outward, lifting the seal carefully out of the bearing. The seal has a thin brass shell that's easily dented and, once dented, difficult to straighten. If not straightened, though, the seal can rub internally on the bearing and cause a slight amount of drag—enough to bother you, or at least me. Figure 5-15 shows a bent seal arrow (the one at the top).

STEP SIX: Clean and repack bearings, both sides, with a light grease such as Lubriplate or the grease Phil Wood sells through bike shops in tubes.

STEP SEVEN: Replace seals, being careful to get them into the groove around the inner edge of the bearing, pressing all around until well seated.

STEP EIGHT: Replace center spacer. Push in both bearings with the palm of your hand. If they do not go in easily, push around the edges. Try to seat them in evenly so they don't get cocked to one side as you insert them.

STEP NINE: Replace end bushings (spacers) and tighten Allen bolts.

NOTE: The rear hub has two one-millimeter spacers on the left side and one on the right, or freewheel, side. If you use a freewheel that is so wide that the high gear is too close to the chainstay, so the chain binds on the stay, you need to move the hub to the left. On the Durham, you just use the old Allen wrench, remove both spacers, and move a washer (Fig. 5-23) from the left to the right side. So you can calculate the amount of "dish" you will need when lacing up the hub and rim (see Chapter 10), it's a good idea to screw the freewheel onto the hub and put it into the rear dropout, making sure there is enough room for the chain between the small high gear and the chainstay (please refer to Appendix for an illustrated glossary of bicycle terms). Do not use washers on the right unless you have to, to keep "dishing" at a minimum. The greater the dish, the weaker the wheel construction. We'll talk more about wheel dishing in Chapter 10, and when we discuss the new Shimano Freehubs later on in this chapter.

Internally generated friction is low in Durham hubs. One reason for this is the noncontact labyrinth seals, which seal without touching inner races. If you plan to ride in rough, open country where you will meet a

Fig. 5-23: Durham rear hub. Note longer spacers. Arrow points to washers that can be moved from one side of hub to the other to improve chainline.

lot of dust and dirt, Durham can provide heavy-duty contact seals, but expect greater friction.

Durham, in their literature, claims that a wheel used for six months with their hub was released, with valve stem around the 2-o'clock position, and the wheel oscillated back and forth sixty-four times before stopping! I tried it on my own bike, and although not exactly hitting that world's record, I did pretty well at fifty-one small oscillations, on a hub with about ten miles on it. By oscillations I mean the valve moving back and forth past the six-o'clock mark. I know I've given Durham hubs a lot more space in this book than any other hub. This does not imply that good sealed-bearing hubs such as the Phil Wood or Avocet are any worse . . . or better, but simply that Roger Durham, the engineer who designs and builds those hubs, is a very verbal type who loves to furnish scads of detailed data, a small part of which I have used.

A few more points. Durham bearings can carry 885 pounds each, a total of 3,540 pounds, which is a bit more than I recommend you carry on a bike touring trip! But you can peak out at a fairly hefty load if you hit a pothole, and cheap hubs bend axles fairly easily under such conditions. Durham axles are machined flat where they fit onto dropouts (Fig. 5-24), which is a more efficient way to transmit the wheel load to the frame. The load is spread over a wider area in the flattened axle than on the smaller area of the conventional rounded axle. Also, if you totally strip the alloy threads of the freewheel boss, you can have it replaced at the factory, so you can salvage the hub. The Phil Wood hubs are great, but because you can't remove the bearings except at the factory, something of a mystery. That they work and are durable cannot be denied.

Fig. 5-24: Durham hub has flats on axle (arrows) which distribute the load to the axle more efficiently than if the axle were round, as on other hubs.

I've traveled thousands of miles on them. Durham hubs are newer. I've traveled hundreds, not thousands, of miles on them and like them as well as the Phil Woods. And I feel a bit more independent knowing that I can take the Durhams apart and fix them myself with no more tools than a fifty-cent Allen wrench that comes with the hubs.

Hi-E Sealed-Bearing Hubs

There's one more make of sealed-bearing hub on the market, made and designed by that innovative aircraft engineer and bicycle racer, Harlan Byrne, president of Hi-E Engineering, Inc. Harlan sells most of his products by mail and can be reached at 1247 School Lane, Nashville, Tennessee 37217, 615/361-1312.

Harlan makes road and track hubs (Fig. 5-25), and some of these are the lightest in the world (see Table 5-2). I can testify to the strength of these hubs, paper light as they are, because in my own inimitable fashion I put the front hub, traditionally the weaker of the two hubs because it's smaller, to the total-destruct test. I hit the expansion crack in a long bridge at about 30 miles per hour. (The going was downhill, the wind was at my back. I normally travel at a more sedate speed with a loaded bike.) The bike broke in half at the steering head tube. I nearly died but the hub stood up fine and I use it to this day on my lightest frame, which is handy when impressing bike novices about how light a bike can get (this one is around eighteen pounds but strictly for day touring. I don't

Fig. 5-25: Lightweight Hi-E Engineering, Inc., sealed-bearing hub weighs only 3.1 ounces, can go around 1,500 miles before requiring hub maintenance.

race and to tour on this super lightweight would be not only a travesty of use but would probably hurt this poor light baby).

Hi-E hubs, like all such, use precision-sealed bearings. They're rated as ABEC-1 in the Hi-E hub, which means they are very high precision. You can't remove these bearings without special tools, and Harlan asks you to return them if they get rough. You also have to be careful not to overtighten the quick-release so as to prevent undue sideload on the bearings. Harlan goes for lightness and low rolling friction in his designs, as witnessed in probably the world's lightest front hub, his Number 202 time-trial hub which weighs in at a flyweight 114 grams (4 ounces). The Hi-E heavy-duty front hub is what you should tour on, though, and this weighs 156 grams, or 5.5 ounces, still among the world's lightest, although Zeus's titanium front hub reaches down there at 180 grams (Table 5-2).

Hi-E bearings can only be replaced at the factory unless you have a machine shop with arbor press and are careful to pack up the hub area to prevent damage. Harlan uses Santotrac HT-2 grease to repack his hubs. This is an excellent waterproof, light-viscosity grease which should be obtainable at your local bearing supply house. Repacking should include replacing bearing capillary seals.

CHOOSING A NEW HUB

High Flange Versus Low Flange

Back in the early 1970s when the bike boom began and a lot of European bikes were imported to fill the demand in this country, most of them had high-flange hubs because they looked sporty and racy. In fact, with high-flange hubs you use shorter spokes. Shorter spokes make for a more rigid wheel, which is fine for a road-racing cyclist who wants maximum efficiency in getting his energy into forward movement. But for a touring cyclist, the less resilient high-flange wheel offers a harder ride.

That's why I prefer low-flange hubs for touring. The wheels are more resilient. If, however, you have a problem with spokes breaking, due to your size and strength, you might want to go to a 40- or a 44-spoke wheel, in which case, I would recommend a high-flange hub, because all those holes drilled in the flange of a small-flange hub are awfully close together and weaken the hub. This would be particularly true in a tandem. See Table 5-2 for hubs with these drillings.

Checking for Width. Dropout distances (distance between the inner surface of both dropouts) on both fork and rear dropouts come in different

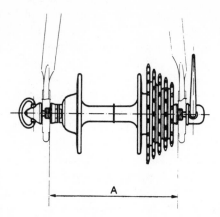

Fig. 5-26: Hubs come with varying locknut-to-locknut widths, as do the spacings between the inner surface of front and rear dropouts. To make sure a new hub will fit in your bicycle, measure distance (A) between dropouts and the same distance between inner surface of dropouts. Both measurements should be the same, or at least within one millimeter of each other. Add or remove thin spacers if necessary. But before buying a new set of hubs, specify correct locknut-to-locknut distance.

widths, so you should measure these widths and select a hub with correct width to fit. For example, front dropouts, measured from the inside surface, (Fig. 5-26) can be 90, 100 or 110 millimeters (3.937 in. or 4.3307 in.). Rear-dropout distances can be 120, 125, 126 or 127 millimeters. The wider distances are designed for six- or seven-speed freewheel clearances. Tables 5-3 and 5-4 recap these dimensions.

The better non-sealed-bearing hubs have, as noted, beautifully finished cones and races. The cheaper hubs have bearing races machined out of the same steel of which the hub is made, and you know *that* steel is not going to be anything like the inserts of polished alloy steel metal

Table 5-3 Front Dropout Standard Dimensions*
(Measured from inner surfaces of dropouts)

Inches	Millimeters
3.5433	90
3.937	100
4.13385	105
4.252	108
4.3307	110

* There may be differences of plus or minus one or two millimeters but these are negligible. See also Figure 5-27 for measuring hub size to fit the dimensions in this table.

Fig. 5-27: A high-quality hub race, showing the ground, lapped, honed and polished race surface. This cup is a high-quality steel insert in the aluminum-alloy hub body.

Fig. 5-28: This is an inexpensive steel hub, showing the race (arrow). The race is actually machined right out of the hub metal, and is not an insert, so the cup and race are not of high-quality steel. Arrow points to slight defect.

used in aluminum alloy hubs. For example, Figure 5-27 shows the ground, lapped and polished bearing race of a Campagnolo hub. Figure 5-28 shows the roughly machined race of a cheap steel hub. The Campy hub has a steel insert for the race, but the cheap steel hub race is made out of the same steel used for the entire hub. These two photos do not really do justice to the enormous differences between the two hubs, but you will get the picture. The arrow in Figure 5-28 points to a corroded spot in the cheap hub.

Table 5-4 Rear Dropout Standard Dimensions*
(Measured from inner surfaces of dropouts)

Number of Freewheel Cogs	Inches	Millimeters
5	4.7244	120
6	4.9125	125
6	4.9999	127 †
6 or 7	5.1181	130 †
6 or 7	5.31495	135 †
6 or 7	5.5118	140 †

* There may be differences of plus or minus one or two millimeters, but these are negligible. Use spacing washers. See also Figure 5-27 for measuring hub size to fit dimensions in this table.
† This size hub available from Phil Wood.

Another fairly major problem with cheap hubs is, as I stated earlier, the roughness of axle, cone and locknut thread cutting. There's so much slop in these that you have to be really careful in reassembling them. As you will note later on, when I get into more detail on hub assembly in Chapter 12, in tightening cone nuts you do it until you feel tightness (tightening by hand, never by wrench). As the cone snugs up to the bearings, back the cone off a half turn. Then insert any spacers and the locknut, and tighten the locknut. You should have a barely perceptible amount of sideplay in the hub axle. Now, if you tighten the quick-release skewer (arrow in Figure 5-21) on a cheap hub, slop in threads will force the cone tightly against the hub balls and, in short order, will score and gall the balls and races and make a poor hub even worse. Even on a fine hub, as in Figure 5-21, you have to be really careful in hub-cone adjustment. Due to machining variations, no two hubs are really *exactly* alike, so you have to judge for yourself how tight the cone nut should be, how much play to leave in the hub, before tightening down on the locknut. Remember, the play or looseness between cone-race surface and balls will be taken up to some extent as you tighten down on the locknut, and to an additional extent as you tighten down on the quick-release lever or axle nuts. *Ideally there should be no sideplay in the hub after tightening the quick-release skewer or axle bolts, yet the wheel should spin freely.* How free is free? One way to tell if the wheel hub is binding is to spin the axle between thumb and forefinger before inserting the wheel into the dropout (end of fork or rear stays). You can tell right away if there is any roughness. The axle should rotate with a feeling of silky softness, like mist sliding over the land on a damp morning. When the wheel is back in the dropouts, tighten down on the quick-release skewer or axle bolts and turn the wheel until the valve is at the one-o'clock position and stop the rim at this point. As you let go, the wheel should turn by itself; the weight of the valve should pull it down. A properly adjusted hub will, if started at one o'clock, continue to spin on past six o'clock to about nine o'clock, back to four o'clock and oscillate more slowly back to between five and seven o'clock, with axle quick-release or axle bolts tightened. If the wheel does not show this degree of freeness, with *no* sideplay, you are putting way too much pressure on cones, balls, and races and will have a fairly short-lived hub. Eventually·you will notice a wear spot, galling, around the hub race where excess pressures are forcing balls into the race metal.

Chapter Six

CHAINS, BOTTOM BRACKETS AND CRANKS

In this chapter we will discuss chain maintenance—how to tell when to install a new chain and how to do it. Since your bike may not have the wide range of gears you want (or the close-ratio gears you need for commuting on the flats or for racing) you will want to be able to change freewheels and chainwheels. We have already discussed removing and installing freewheels in Chapter 5 and will deal with this subject again in Chapter 9. In this chapter we will also cover chainwheel selection and installation, including conversions from two-speed to three-speed chainwheel combinations (dual to triple chainwheel sets). And we will attempt to settle, once and for all, the controversy about extra-long cranks. Finally, we will give you the latest information about elliptical chainwheels. Now, let's start with chains, your link between legs and wheels.

CHAINS

If you have changed to wide-ratio gears and installed a long cage derailleur to handle these gears, you will need to install a longer chain—or vice versa if you switched to close-ratio gears. Tips on choosing the correct chain length are given in Chapter 4, Installing a New Rear Derailleur, Step Three. I suggest you review this data before installing a new chain.

First, chain stretch. Eventually, like all things, chains wear out. Most of the wear is detected by stretch. A chain can stretch as much as 1 inch, and when it does you will have the chain jumping from one gear to the next inadvertently, or "skipping" over gears, which means chain side plates are hanging up on the cog teeth, creating a feeling of chain roughness as you pedal. A stretched chain should be junked and replaced immediately, because it can cause undue wear on cog teeth, particularly on the softer aluminum alloy teeth of chainwheels (unless chainwheels are steel, of course, and on the small freewheel cog).

At least once a year, more often if you ride a lot, and certainly before the start of each new spring riding season, check chain stretch. With the chain on the bicycle and with a ruler, measure exactly twenty-four chain links, from center of rivet to center of rivet, or from edge of outer plate to edge of outer plate. If either distance is more than 1/16th inch over 12 inches, you have a worn chain which should be replaced. In fact, don't keep it around—dump it; because you might forget later on and use some of the worn links with a newer chain.

To remove the chain, you will need a rivet remover or, as some call it, a "chain breaker," a name akin to a baggage smasher at airports. I prefer the more genteel name of "rivet remover." To use the rivet remover (Fig. 6-1) you need first to take some precautions to avoid damage to the chain side plate. First, check the tool point, the part that pushes the rivet out of the chain. The point must be absolutely straight. If others have been using the tool, the point could be slightly bent. If you screw this crooked point into the rivet it won't go in straight and part of it will hit the side plate, enlarging the rivet hole. Figure 6-2 shows such a damaged plate. If you put this chain back together the chain will come apart, usually when you are miles from nowhere and you have forgotten your rivet tool. This happened to me once, in the wilds of central Wis-

Fig. 6-1: Chain rivet remover. To use, line up tool point with chain rivet, turn handle five times to leave a bit of rivet still in chain side plate for easier reassembly.

Fig. 6-2: Damaged side plate caused by improper use of chain rivet remover tool. Tool point was not accurately lined up with rivet. (*R.L.L. Limited*)

consin. I was lucky. I found a nail and a rock in the road and with some time, some patience, a lot of cussing and even more luck, was able to pound out the damaged link and pull the chain up another link and pound the rivet back into place. I do not recommend this procedure, believe me. You'll save yourself a lot of trouble if you remember to take your rivet tool with you on any long bike trip.

Okay. To use the rivet remover, make sure the rivet pushing end of the tool is lined up exactly on the rivet, so you don't damage the side plate. Screw down the handle until the rivet end just touches the rivet and note where the end of the handle lies—which o'clock position it has assumed. Then, with that position as a reference point, turn the handle exactly five times up to that reference point. Now you should be able to back off the tool, put it down, take the chain between the fingers of both hands, one hand on each side of the rivet you have pushed out, and twist the chain sideways, until the chain comes apart. If you will look at what's left of the rivet inside the plate you will see perhaps ¹⁄₃₂-inch of the rivet still visible. This is just right, because when you reassemble the chain (I am assuming here that you are not replacing the chain, just removing it for cleaning) you will have that little bit to hold the chain together. All you do is snap the chain back together—the little bit of rivet showing will hold it until you can get the rivet tool back on it to push it in again. Make sure that the rivet is in as far as the other rivets, but no farther.

One additional point about chain removal and reinstallation: When you push the rivet through, the rivet is now protruding from the left side of the chain, where it is hard to get at to replace. The temptation is to reinstall the chain with this rivet facing outward, toward you, where you can reach it. And for most of us it's a matter of sheer chance which side of the chain goes back on. If you reverse chain direction at the top and bottom, both, you could have some chain chatter, because it will have

Fig. 6-3: This is how the chain goes on. Starting at top, the chain goes around the freewheel (it's easier if you shift to high gear, small cog), in front of the top derailleur pulley and down and around the rear of the bottom pulley, then forward and around the small front chainwheel, going up from underneath. It doesn't really matter which way you start, just so long as you wind up with the chain in the above position. People who have difficulty visualizing things three-dimensionally should find this photo a big help. If you are wondering what became of the wheel, well, I used a sample hub without rim or spokes so you can see what gives.

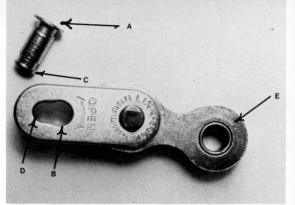

Fig. 6-4: Shimano quick-link eliminates need for chain rivet tool. Parts are: (A) Bushing, showing wide end and (C) showing smaller end that fits into hole (B) in side plate and when chain is in use slides into (D) area of side plate. (E) is conventional chain bushing that fits into your chain (rivet goes through).

worn in the opposite direction. To avoid this, I suggest you push out the rivet on the left side (rear of bike) of the handiest side plate. Now the end of the chain on your right (toward front of bike) will be free and will be the end without the protruding rivet. Remove the chain, sliding it out of the derailleur wheels, over the rear cogs and the front derailleur cage. To reinstall the same way, start with the protruding rivet facing away from you, with that end of the chain toward the rear end of the bike. Take the other end and pull it over the chainring, down through the front-derailleur cage, over the smallest (high-gear) rear cog and through the derailleur pulleys (see Fig. 6-3). If you have done all this right, when you snap the chain together (it's easier if the chain is off the chainwheels and lying on the bottom-bracket shell) you should have put the chain back just the way it was before you removed it. The rivet will be facing toward the left side of the bike, which will make it a bit more difficult to use the rivet tool, but you can do it. I hang the bike from the ceiling and work on the chain with the tool from the left side.

There are two brands of instant come-apart links, one made by Shimano (Fig. 6-4) and one by RLL Limited, Box 296, River Forest, Illinois 60305 (Fig. 6-5). The Shimano version does not require any tools, once you have installed it with your rivet tool on one link. It simply pushes together. You twist the chain up and together so as to force the special little rivet (A) (Fig. 6-4) back into the enlarged section of the hole (B). Then you push the small end of the rivet (C) out and, presto, the chain is apart. If you're lucky, you did not drop the tiny rivet on the floor where it will be promptly lost to view forever. Just be careful to cup

Fig. 6-5: R.L.L. Limited Super Link, which uses either a tiny Allen wrench bolt and nut or screwdriver end bolt and nut instead of a rivet. Also eliminates need for rivet remover.

your hand under the chain to catch it. To reassemble, reverse the process and check to make sure the rivet (A) now rests securely in the small end of the plate hole (D). The quick-release end (E) is where it fits into your chain. This system is a very good idea, unless you lose the special rivet, because now you can take your chain apart on the road without having to carry a heavy rivet remover. I hope Shimano makes it possible to buy extras of these special rivets, because I'd be much happier away on the road with a couple of extra ones stowed in my handlebar bag, wrapped in a small plastic bag.

The other RLL quick-release uses either a tiny screw, which takes a tiny screwdriver, or a 1-millimeter Allen wrench. I'd opt for the screwdriver, because the 1-millimeter Allen wrench is so tiny it's easy to lose; you can at least use the point of a pocket knife if you lose the screwdriver. One or the other is furnished with the RLL master link. Like the Shimano master link, you also run the risk of dropping both the link and its attaching screw, which, if dropped, will disappear. Well, you can always take the chain up one more link to get home, if you have also brought along a rivet tool. At this point I feel that I am leaving the impression with you that I drop things a lot. That's a slanderous, libelous and fairly accurate conclusion. I drop teensy, itsy, bitsy things easily and permanently lose them—which is why I surround myself with so many itsy, bitsy parts such as ball bearings and microscopic sizes of bolts and nuts. Saves a lot of running around looking for spares.

Now, about chain lubrication. I know I recommended that you throw away old chains so you don't use them for spare links. I keep mine because I have been testing a lot of different lubricants on my chains over the years. I have an odometer on my bike, so I know how many miles I travel, and because I test bike components, I keep track of mileage and other things such as how long the chain lasts before it stretches to the replacement point. I've used just one lubricant on each chain until the chain stretched too far. After trying a zillion lubricants, and without boring you with the hundreds of chicken scratchings on my record pads, I can tell you that the lubricant that made my chains last longest, with least stretch, is a heavy-gear oil with a viscosity of around 140 SAE, which is something like cold molasses. You can buy such an oil in any auto-supply store; just ask for gear lube. This oil is so heavy you have to heat it to get it thin enough to penetrate the chain parts. I use a hot plate, an old pot (stolen from the kitchen) and soak the chain in the warm oil overnight. The hot plate has a thermostat which I set to low. Don't try this method unless you are in a room with lots of ventilation or outdoors, and keep the heat low and on long. Spray-type lubricants such as those sold in motorcycle stores will work, but they are not good enough to prevent chain wear from occurring fairly quickly. In

Fig. 6-6: Shimano UltraGlide (UG) chain has bowed-out side plates.

fact, I found that my chains, lubed with the heavy-gear oil (well, you can use 85 or even 80 SAE viscosity thickness and still get good results) lasted up to five or six times as long as the chains lubricated with the spray lubricants. The one drawback to the heavier oil is that it does attract more dust. I simply relube after every trip, or once a month, as necessary, and wipe off all extra oil before remounting the chain. I didn't dream up this method of chain lubrication, by the way; it's been practiced by experienced cyclists for at least fifty years.

Now let's look at some of the newer chains that have been introduced recently. Probably the most controversial is the new Shimano Ultra-Glide chain (UG) (Fig. 6-6). As you can see in this picture, the UG chain has widened or bowed-out outer chainplates. The theory is that with conventional chains, the chain roller (see "A" in Fig. 6-7) hits the teeth of the larger gear when shifting to a lower gear, before outer chainplates

Fig. 6-7: Dissected chain showing parts: (A) roller; (B) outer side plate; (C) inner side plate; (D) rivet; (E) bushing. This is a SunTour New Winner chain. Note chamfered inside of outer plate which reduces overall chain weight.

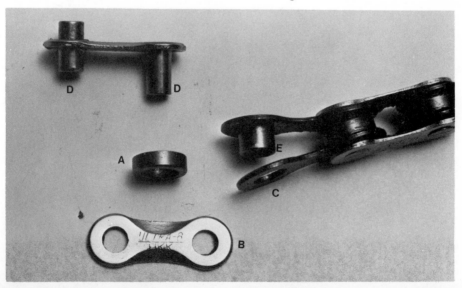

can engage that gear. According to Shimano, this creates friction, and can cause overshifting. Shimano claims that the increased width between the outer plates makes shifting easier and more accurate. I measured the widest point between the two Shimano UG outer plates as 5.5 millimeters. The widest point between the new Ultra Six SunTour outer plates is 4.5 millimeters and between these plates of a Regina chain the measurement is 5 millimeters. I used the Shimano UG chain and found little difference between it and conventional chains when used with a conventional freewheel. But when used with Shimano's new freewheels which have cogs twisted at an angle, I found shifting to be snappier and more precise. Therefore I suggest the UG chain be used with Shimano freewheels. With this combination I also discovered that shifting under high pedal torque while hill climbing was much easier, although I still recommend that you shift down before the hill grade forces you to do so. I feel that the Shimano UG chain and twisted-tooth freewheel cogs (Uniglide freewheel) should be used together on a tandem, where torque is at a maximum. At this writing these cogs go up only to 28 teeth, but I hear that Shimano will eventually go to 32 or 34 teeth for the wider range that you need on a touring tandem. As noted earlier, you should use a special chain-rivet tool to avoid bending the bowed-out plates, although with care you can use your old tool. Because the plates are bowed out, my survey of bicycle mechanics in the Chicago area as to their experience with these chains reveals that they are concerned about undue chain stretch. This is contrary to Shimano's claim that the UG chain will stretch half as much and last twice as long as the conventional chain. We will just have to wait and see. At the moment I am neutral.

SunTour has come up with a nice chain which works well with their freewheels. It's the Ultra-Six model which has thinner side plates and smaller roller pins. Say, let's stop here for just a moment and look at the parts of a chain link. It's a legitimate detour because my illustration is a SunTour link. Going from the outside in, we have, in Figure 6-7: (A) the outer side plates; (B) the inner side plates; (C) the bearing surface on which (D) the roller rotates; and (E) the rivet that goes through the bearing surface, the inner side plate and the facing side plate to hold the whole shebang together. Wear points of a chain are inside surfaces of plates, the roller and the roller journal. Stretch is due to internal rearrangement of molecules in chain plates and wear on rollers, bearing surface and rivets. You will note, I hope, that the Ultra-Six outer plate has a slight bevel to the inside. This has the effect mainly of lightening the chain, an effect enhanced by the narrower, smaller rollers. The Ultra-Six works on a variety of brands of freewheel cogs as well as on SunTour's new line of freewheels, with a slightly narrower space between rear cogs. I would not recommend using the Shimano UG chain

Fig. 6-8: Regina chain is one of the most reliable I have used, and after five years on one chain, I have yet to have it break. Of course I cleaned and relubricated it regularly.

on the SunTour New Winner freewheels, because spacing is narrower on this freewheel and the Shimano UG plates are ½ millimeter wider than the Regina and 1 millimeter wider than the SunTour Ultra-Six side plates. Eyeballing the clearance, I would say there is darned little between the wider side plates of the Shimano UG chain and the adjoining cogs of the SunTour New Winner freewheel.

When all is said and done, however, my favorite is still the old faithful, the Regina line of chains (Fig. 6-8). These have the hardest plates and the best metallurgy of any chain I have tested. They have given me many thousands of miles of good and faithful service, and they work well on the more conventional components.

BOTTOM BRACKETS

I think we need to clarify some nomenclature at this point. A bottom-bracket shell is the part of your bicycle frame at the bottom, where almost all the tubes are brazed on. The downtube, the seat tube and the chainstays are all brazed onto the bottom-bracket shell, as shown in Figure 6-9.

Inside the bottom bracket you will find the bottom-bracket set, consisting of the spindle (you might call it an axle, but we bikies call it a spindle), the bearings, the adjustable cup on the left side and the fixed

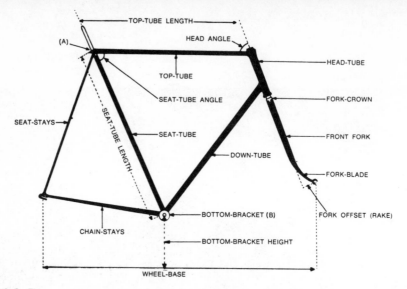

Fig. 6-9: The parts we are concerned with here are the seat tube, downtube and stays, all brazed to the bottom-bracket shell.

cup on the right side, all as shown in Figure 6-10. There's also a lock-ring, (Fig. 6-11) which locks the adjustable cup in place after you have adjusted it to eliminate endplay or sideplay and, if it's a cotterless crank, the washers and crank lock bolts. Figure 6-10 shows a typical cotterless crankset, in this instance a Shimano set. I have identified the parts for you, as you will see in the caption.

Attached to the bottom-bracket spindle are the left and right cranks and to the right crank are attached the chainwheels, as shown in Figure 6-12. Again, this is a cotterless aluminum alloy crankset. To the cranks are attached the pedals—which is as good a place as any to stop and review the three basic types of bottom brackets and their cranksets.

Fig. 6-10: Typical bottom-bracket set assembly. (A) spindle, showing left side; (AA) right (chainwheel) side, note that it is longer to provide space for the chainwheel; (B) fixed cup, goes on right side of bottom-bracket shell; (C) adjustable cup; (D) crank fixing bolts; (E) lockring, goes on adjustable cup (C); (F) bearings in races; and (G) crank fixing bolt washers, go under bolt heads.

Fig. 6-11: Adjustable cup lockring, shown removed from adjustable cup.

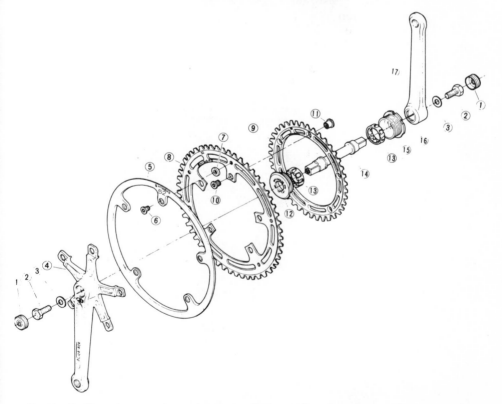

Fig. 6-12: Complete crankset, this one a Shimano DuraAce design. Going over the parts, they are: (1) dust cap; (2) crank-fixing bolt; (3) washer; (4) right crank; (5) chain guard (you don't need it and I would remove it); (6) chain-guard bolt; (7) chainwheel mounting bushing; (8) chainwheel; (9) chainwheel; (10) chainwheel mounting bolt; (11) chainwheel mounting nut; (12) fixed cup; (13) bearings; (14) spindle; (15) adjustable cup; (16) lockring; (17) left crank.

TYPES OF CRANKSETS

For convenience I am going to forget about bottom brackets and just talk about cranksets, and include in cranksets their associated bottom brackets.

When the safety bicycle, with its chain drive and two small wheels of more or less equal diameter drove the dangerous antique high wheel (also called a "Penny Farthing" or "Ordinary") off the market, the method of attaching the cranks to the bottom-bracket spindle was retained. Figure 6-13 shows a cottered crank of an antique high wheeler, where the cranks are fastened to the spindle by a sort of wedge, or as we call it today, a cotter or key. Fig. 6-14 shows a cross section of a cottered crankset and Fig. 6-15 shows an actual crankset.

The final type of crankset I will mention here is the so-called Ashtabula or one-piece crank, shown in Figure 6-16, on an old balloon-tire Schwinn, circa 1930, and a modern version on a Monarch-Crescent (Swedish) bicycle (Fig. 6-17). These cranks are solid, one-piece steel. The cranks and the chainwheel are all one piece of steel, and the left

Fig. 6-13: Early form of cottered crank design on a high wheeler of the 1880s.

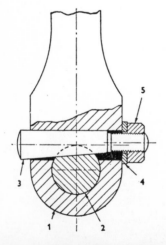

Fig. 6-14: Cross section of cottered crank: (1) crank; (2) spindle; (3) cotter pin; (4) washer; (5) nut. *(Temple Press)*

Fig. 6-15: Cottered crank. Chainwheel is steel. Note that to remove this crank you lay the crank base over a notched 2-by-4, supported at points "B" and "C." The cotter pin nut (A) is loosened a few turns and hit squarely with a mallet to drive pin down into notch. This way you avoid damage to bearings because hammer shock is absorbed at base of crank and by the 2-by-4. Remember, the nut on a cottered crank is **not** intended to pull the pin up tight; the pin must be hammered back in. You just turn the crank around until the top of the pin is over the notch, the reverse of the position in this photo. A special (expensive) shop tool is available for pin withdrawal and installation.

Fig. 6-16: One-piece crankset (arrow) on old balloon-tire Schwinn bike of the 1930s.

Fig. 6-17: Modern version of one-piece crank.

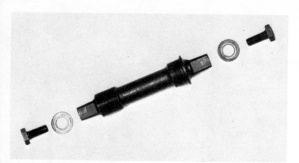

Fig. 6-18: Conversion unit, to convert one-piece crankset to cotterless alloy crankset. Spindle threads fit one-piece cups, old bearings are used.

crank is pulled out through the bottom bracket to disassemble it, as detailed later on in this chapter. Schwinn sells a replacement spindle (Fig. 6-18) that turns a one-piece crankset into a cotterless crank. You buy the spindle and the cranks and chainwheels separately. You use the old bearings. The replacement spindle costs around $35. But I'm hanged if I can figure out why you would want to spend any money on the type of bicycle that comes with an ungainly, heavy, ugly one-piece crankset and have to replace that crankset with a lightweight aluminum alloy crankset. Well, there is one bike I know of that *is* worth the changeover and that's the old Schwinn SuperSport, which has a fine, lugless, high chrome moly steel frame. If you have a SuperSport, by all means make the conversion. Then you will have a bike the equal of some of the $400 or even $600 models being sold these days. I'd add aluminum alloy 700-centimeter rims and Shimano DuraAce side-pull brakes and hubs to totally upgrade the SuperSport, though. If you have an otherwise good BMX bicycle, you might also want to go to a cotterless crankset. A supplier of sealed-bearing replacements is Durham Bicycles, who make a unit that clamps into the bottom-bracket shell (Fig. 6-19). Now let's get into bottom-bracket maintenance, because I imagine most people will want to know how to go about this important procedure, after which we will cover the selection of bottom brackets or cranksets and the features of major brands.

Fig. 6-19: Sealed-bearing bottom-bracket set to convert one-piece cranks to cotterless cranks: (A) long bolt and nut holds this unit in place (three supplied); (B) end pieces fit bottom-bracket shell. (C) thrust collars have Allen bolts that permit movement of spindle to adjust it for correct chainline (lateral movement). *(Durham Bicycles)*

MAINTENANCE OF BOTTOM BRACKETS AND CRANKSETS

Let's break this section down into four parts: (1) new bicycle checks; (2) cotterless crankset maintenance; (3) cottered crankset maintenance; and (4) one-piece crankset maintenance. Starting with a new bicycle . . .

Before you wheel the bike out of the shop, I strongly recommend that you check, among other things, adjustment of the left-hand adjustable cup of the bottom-bracket spindle. Do this by having the shop put the bike on a bike stand so the wheels are free to rotate. Grasp each pedal with your hands and rock the cranks from side to side. There should be no side play. Hold the cranks by the top, just above the pedals. Then slip the chain off the chainwheels and spin the cranks. The cranks should rotate freely, without evidence of binding. If you spin the cranks and they come to rest with a sort of sudden stop as they slow down, that's binding. If the stop or slowdown is very gradual, that's okay. Have the shop adjust the left-hand cup as needed.

On a new bike, remove the dust cap (Fig. 6-20) (Campy dust caps take a 5-mm Allen wrench) and tighten down the spindle locking bolt every 50 miles or so for the first 200 miles (Fig. 6-21) with 215- to 240-inch pounds of torque (18–20 ft. lbs.) using an automotive type of torque wrench (or enough muscle to move the bolt slightly). Depending on the brand, bottom-bracket bolts take a 14-, 15- or 16-millimeter wrench. Most common metric sockets will be too thick to fit into the crank open-

Fig. 6-20: Dust cap on cotterless crank-set.

Fig. 6-21: Fixing bolt forces tapered crank up onto taper of spindle.

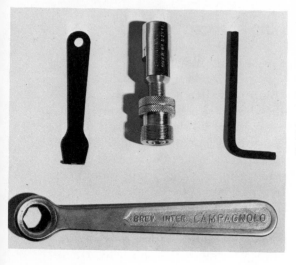

Fig. 6-22: Some of the tools you will need to remove and reinstall cotterless cranksets. Top row, left to right: chainwheel fixing nut tool; crank puller; Allen wrench to fit chainwheel fixing bolt. Bottom, crank fixing bolt tool (also shown in Fig. 6-21).

ing to get at the pedal, so you will need a special wrench, such as the Campagnolo spanner shown at the bottom of Figure 6-22, or the four-in-one wrench made by Park Tool Company (Fig. 6-23), which has 14-, 15- and 16-millimeter ends plus a 5-millimeter Allen pip for dust caps (available in Schwinn bike stores, among others). Remember, the spindle-tapered shank is hardened steel . . . the crank is relatively soft aluminum. If the crank is not firmly pushed up on the tapered shank it will be loose, and just a few miles of pedaling with the crank hanging loose will destroy the tight tapered fit, and you will never be able to get the crank to fit properly again on the spindle. You will then need a new crank for from $10 to $28.

Also on a new bike, check the mounting bolts holding the double or

Fig. 6-23: Shimano lockring remover is a better tool because it has a shield that helps keep it from slipping off the narrow lockring.

Fig. 6-24: Here's how the chainwheel fixing bolt tools shown in Figure 6-22 look in use. Use them to tighten this bolt every few months, and to remove chainwheel if necessary.

triple chainwheel set together (Fig. 6-24) with the special pronged tool shown at top left of Figure 6-22 and an Allen wrench, usually 5 millimeters. Hold the inside (left) bolt with the pronged tool (bushed nut wrench) while you tighten with the Allen wrench. These and other tools are available at your bicycle store.

I have a very good reason for asking you to check the tightness of the chainwheel bushed bolts occasionally, especially on a new bike. I was test riding some new bikes for one of the consumer testing magazines some years ago and, on a hard uphill climb, the chain suddenly slipped off the inner chainwheel and in between the two chainwheels. Looking down I discovered that the inner ring was distorted, wavy, which had thrown the chain off. The reason for the distortion was that one of the bushed bolts had come loose and had fallen out somewhere along the road, and the other bolts were about to do the same. From now on I check these bolts on every new bike I test ride. And I can tell you that, with the exception of Campy equipment, I have found many chainwheels with bushed bolts which, although not exactly loose, could be taken up from a half to a quarter turn—and that's incipient trouble up the road. I do check all chainwheels, regardless of brand, and although Campy equipment has been tight so far, I still check them just to make sure. I would check *all* chainwheel sets at least twice annually, because vibration from road shock can loosen these bolts eventually. The few minutes you spend going over them can save downtime on the road or the cost of a new chainwheel. Here are steps in complete cotterless crank maintenance:

STEP ONE: Remove the dust cap (Fig. 6-20).

STEP TWO: Remove the crank mounting bolt with the crank bolt wrench (Fig. 6-21). Remove the washer behind the bolt head (don't lose it).

STEP THREE: Now you will need a crank puller. This is the type of tool shown in the top center of Figure 6-22. This particular tool is made to fit Shimano cranks but it will also fit Campagnolo cranks, although a bit loosely. Far better than this type of crank puller is the multiple crank puller that fits French, Italian and Japanese cranks, Fig. 6-25. The smaller threaded section fits Campagnolo, Sugino, Shimano and Sun-Tour cranks, the larger section fits Stronglight, T.A. Cyclotouriste and other French chainwheels. To use any of these crank pullers, you will note first that there are actually two threaded sections, the larger one threading over a central threaded shaft. Turn the larger section counter-clockwise until the end of the inner section is flush with it, as shown in Figure 6-22. Here the larger section of the crank puller (top, center) has been screwed forward until it is flush with the end of the inner section. Now insert the larger, outer section into the threaded part of the crank, the part where you have removed the dust cap. Be sure to get the crank tool *all the way inside the crank,* because, to pull the crank off the tapered spindle, the tool depends on the threads of the aluminum crank to hold it while the center section is turned to exert backing force on the end of the spindle. With the puller in the crank, turn the center section with a wrench clockwise (the Park puller, Fig. 6-25, has its own wrench handle). If you can't get the crank to budge, tap the end of the puller smartly with a ball peen hammer (not too hard) two or three times to help loosen it. Then turn some more, tap some more and finally you should be able to pull the crank off the spindle (Fig. 6-26). Remove the right-hand crank complete with chainwheel.

STEP FOUR: Now remove the left-hand adjustable cup lockring. Figure 6-27 shows a Campagnolo lockring wrench; but I prefer the new Shi-

Fig. 6-25: A more convenient, easy-to-use crank puller than the one in the top center of Figure 6-22, this Park tool has its own handle. The tool threads into crank dust cap threads. This part is reversible to fit Stronglight and T.A. cranks as well as Campagnolo, Shimano, SunTour and other makes.

Fig. 6-26: When puller has loosened crank, it comes off tool and all.

Fig. 6-27: Lockring remover

mano lockring wrench (Fig. 6-23) because it has a crescent plate or guide over the jaws of the wrench. This guide helps keep it from slipping off the narrow lockring, which is only around 3.5 millimeters thick (or thin). If the wrench were to slip, you could mangle the lockring indents and it would be more difficult to remove; and/or you could ruin the paint finish on the tubes just behind it, and your knuckles. The lockring threads off counterclockwise. *Unless you are going to replace the entire bottom-bracket set, there is no need to remove the right-hand, or fixed, cup, which I will discuss later.*

STEP FIVE: With a pin wrench (Fig. 6-28) remove the adjustable cup (Fig. 6-29). It threads off counterclockwise. Shimano makes a fixed-pin

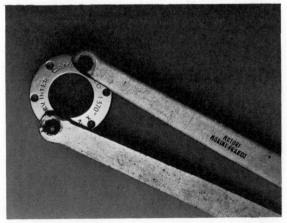

Fig. 6-28: Adjustable pin wrench fits holes in adjustable cup.

Fig. 6-29: Adjustable cup removed. Spindle lies on bottom-bracket shell. Bike is upside down.

wrench (Fig. 6-31) which fits their own and Campagnolo adjustable cups, and which has a 32-millimeter wrench on the other end. If you have an older bike, the ball bearings may be loose, not in a race, so be prepared to catch them. You might have the bike, with wheels removed for convenience, lying on its side on the workbench, with a rag underneath the bottom-bracket shell to catch loose balls. Pull the spindle out. Remove all balls. If balls are in races (Fig. 6-31) remove the left-hand set, reach in and remove the right-hand set, after you pull out any dust shields. Some dust shields, such as the Campy, are in two sections.

I *do* recommend a dust shield (Fig. 6-32) over the spindle inside the bottom-bracket shell, because dust and dirt and water can drift down onto the precisely machined surfaces of cups and bearings from the tubes. You can make your own dust shield from an old beer can. But whatever you do, do not succumb to temptation and make a dust shield out of paper or cardboard! Cardboard dust shields crumple at the first

Fig. 6-30: Shimano makes a very nice pin wrench that fits their adjustable cups. This is not an adjustable pin wrench; pins are fixed.

Fig. 6-31: Adjustable cup removed, showing bearings set in race. Some bikes have loose bearings, so be ready to catch them as you remove cup. Pull spindle out carefully, with bike lying on right side, if you have loose bearings, so you don't lose them up the tubes or on the floor.

sign of moisture or water, and the resulting gunky mess will clog bearings, absorb and so rob bearings of grease.

STEP SIX: Clean bearings and cups of all old grease, with a solvent such as Carbo-Chlor, available from your local hardware store. *Do not use gasoline or any other flammable, explosive liquid!* When using any other solvent, even kerosene, try to have plenty of ventilation around you, such as an open window or, better still, the great outdoors. Wipe out the inside of the bottom-bracket shell thoroughly and take this opportunity to inspect the inside of the tubes for signs of rust. If you spot rust inside the tubes, remove it with fine sandpaper and, with a small brush, coat with two or three layers of aluminum paint. With a rag on the end of a coat hanger wire, coat the tubes with grease as far up as you can reach. You may have to remove the saddle to get at the seat tube

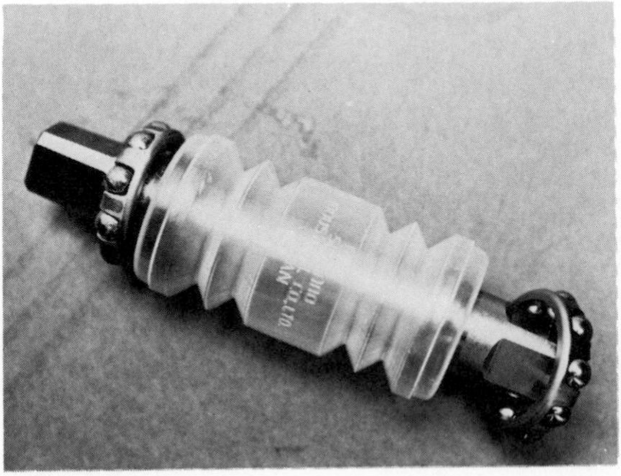

Fig. 6-32: Plastic dust shield keeps dust from bearings.

from the top. Squirt oil into any small "breather" holes in the seat or chainstays.

STEP SEVEN: If you have loose bearings, loose balls, replace them by first dabbing a layer of grease on the right-hand fixed cup. With the bike on its side, lay in all the balls, replace the spindle, making sure the long end goes in first, because this is the end the crank/chainwheel fits onto. If you will go back and look carefully at the spindle in Figure 6-10, you will see that the right side, "AA," is longer than the left side, "A." Side "A" goes in first. Of course, if you have bearings in a cage, the cage should go in first. Remember, there is a convex side (outward curving) and a concave side (inward curving, like the inside half of a tennis ball) to the caged bearing set. The convex side faces toward the cups, the concave side toward the concave side of the spindle. Figure 6-33 shows the correct position of the caged bearing and spindle; for example, you will note that the outwardly curving portion (convex) of the spindle faces the inwardly curving portion (concave) of the caged bearing set. I am not going to take any chances that the instinctive mechanical ability of most of us will automatically ensure that we get these bearings in straight. It's just too easy not to, and too expensive if you do it wrong.

Okay, now you have either coated fixed and adjustable cups with grease for loose balls; or filled the now clean and empty cavities of the caged bearing sets with some good waterproof grease such as Lubriplate or Phil Wood grease lubricant; added a dab more on both sides and moved the right set of bearings into position; and slid the spindle, long end in first, into the bottom bracket and out the right-hand side, through the bearings. Now insert the dust cover.

The left set of bearings should be in the adjustable cup. If loose, it

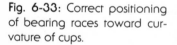
Fig. 6-33: Correct positioning of bearing races toward curvature of cups.

should be held there by grease; if a caged set, you should slide it onto the spindle. Now you can thread on the adjustable cup.

STEP EIGHT: Thread the adjustable cup all the way, by hand, and then with the pin wrench, tighten up very slowly and carefully until just snug, no more, and back off half a turn.

STEP NINE: Thread on the lockring by hand till snug. Holding the adjustable cup in place with the pin wrench, tighten the lockring. Use some muscle on it. Now grasp the spindle at both ends and move up and down to check or feel for too much "play" or looseness. If the spindle moves vertically, it's too loose. If the spindle feels tight when spun between thumb and forefinger, it's too tight, especially if you feel a metallic sort of grittiness as you spin it. Loosen the lockring, holding the cup with the pin wrench, and either tighten the cup slightly or loosen it, as needed; then, holding it with the pin wrench, tighten the lockring down. Remember, you will probably have to make one or two more minute adjustments, unless you work in a bike shop and do this all day.

STEP TEN: Install the cranks. *Do not grease the taper on the spindle or the inside of the crank!* If you add grease here, you can force the soft aluminum alloy crank too far up on the spindle and ruin the crank. The spindle taper ends should be clean and dry and free of grease, as should the matching taper of the inside of the crank. After you slide the crank on by hand, install the washer, then the locking bolt, and tighten the locking bolt 215- to 240-inch pounds (18–20-ft. lbs.) or with moderate to strong muscle until snug. Then, with a piece of wood such as a one-foot length of 2-by-4, using a ball peen hammer over the wood, tap the crank smartly; then tighten the locking bolt once again. Remember, from now on tighten up the locking bolt every 50 miles for the next 200 miles.

STEP ELEVEN: With both cranks installed (I hope in the right direction, perpendicular to each other) grasp the end of each crank and move laterally—sideways—to feel for looseness. Spin, and listen for tightness and feel for tightness. Readjust adjustable cup as necessary. There should be no sideplay or tightness or binding. If in the future you have trouble getting the spindle just right, you might try installing the right-side crank all the way, as in Step Ten; then install the left-side crank just tight enough, with the locking bolt in place, so as to remove looseness from the crank arm; then check for proper cup adjustment. That way the left crank won't be on so tightly that you have trouble backing it off to make cup adjustments.

Cottered Crank Maintenance

Note in Figure 6-15 that in order to remove the cotter pin or wedge, you should support the crank over a notched-out piece of 2-by-4 lumber, loosen the cotter bolt about three turns, and tap smartly straight down on the bolt with a ball peen hammer. The wood brace absorbs the shock of the hammer and keeps it from harming the spindle bearings. Installing the cotter is just the reverse process. You turn the cotter so its top is where the nut is in Figure 6-15 and smack it firmly down into the wedge. As Figure 6-14 shows, the wedge or cotter fits into a slot in the spindle. The slot is at an angle that matches the cotter, and the crank is held onto the spindle shaft by the drive fit between the spindle, the cotter and the crank. Most cottered cranksets (and their chainwheels) are made of steel, as is the one shown in Figure 6-13. Up until 1973 or 1974, most of the inexpensive bicycles had such cranksets. They are heavy, difficult to remove and reattach and, as far as I am concerned, are totally without merit when compared with even the cheapest cotterless crankset. If you have a bicycle with which you are inordinately in love, and it has a steel cotterless crankset, I urge you to substitute one of the less expensive lightweight aluminum alloy cotterless cranksets, such as the Shimano 600 EX—about which, more later.

Maintenance of One-Piece Cranksets

Unlike the other two types of cranks, on one-piece cranks you will have to remove both pedals for complete disassembly. All you need remember for pedal removal is that the right-side pedal threads on clockwise and the left-side pedal, counterclockwise; and that for removal, the reverse applies. The rule here is that pedals *always* thread on in the direction of crank rotation, but because the crank rotates clockwise when you look at it from the right and counterclockwise when you look at it from the left, the same applies to pedals.

With pedals removed, just remove the lockring and adjustable cup, and pull the entire one-piece crank assembly through from the right side. Clean bearings and chainwheel(s), and reassemble.

A Final Word about Adjustment

Inexpensive bikes may have the bottom bracket out of alignment with the stays and dropouts. Or the face of the bracket shell may not be accurately machined. Or the less expensive bike may have been dropped on its side so the bottom-bracket shell or its spindle became misaligned upon impact. Also the bottom-bracket threads on these less expensive bikes are not as precisely machined as the threads on the better bicycles. There is going to be a lot more slop in these threaded part fits. So what may seem to be proper alignment when the adjustable cup is threaded down and backed off a half turn may well turn out to be so tight as to greatly shorten the life of bearing surfaces. *Any* bearing surfaces, no matter how expensive the bike, will have a far shorter life if too tight, not to mention the fact that pedaling will be a lot harder when bearings are too tight. So remember that when you tighten up on the lockring you will, unless you hold the cup in place, also move the cup so bearings will be too tight. If you do hold the cup in place, tightening the lockring can move the cup slightly out, so what was just right before is now too loose. Sideplay in a bottom bracket can flatten bearings and score the cups because it tends to concentrate instead of spread the load among all the bearings.

HOW TO SELECT A BOTTOM-BRACKET SET OR CRANKSET

If you have a good frame you may want to upgrade the bottom-bracket set or the entire crankset. Or you may want to change from a double to a triple crankset, which will require a long bottom-bracket spindle to accommodate the third chainwheel. I think the best reason of all to change bottom-bracket sets, though, is to go to a sealed, precision-bearing bottom-bracket setup, such as the Phil Wood, Durham or Avocet designs. These sealed-bearing sets end for years the hassle of bottom-bracket maintenance and adjustment. If your chainwheel is worn to the point where the chain jumps off, you will, of course, need a replacement. Check chainwheel teeth, look for wear that causes them to come to a point, to have a hook at the trailing edge or to be thinner at the top than at the base of the teeth, particularly when compared with a new chainwheel of the same make. If you change chainwheels, you should also change the chain, unless it's new.

To select a new bottom-bracket assembly of the right size, first measure the end-to-end distance of your bottom bracket, as shown in Figure 6-34. If you are going to another double chainwheel and your bottom-bracket shell is anywhere between 67 and 69 millimeters, it takes a 68-millimeter spindle. The problem is that you can't really *measure* the 68 millimeters on the spindle; there is no reference point where, with a metric caliper ruler, you can measure off 68 millimeters and have it make any sense with reference to end of bearing lands (the convex part where the bearings ride), or any other point. All the 68 millimeters

Fig. 6-34: To determine correct size of bottom-bracket spindle, measure length of bottom-bracket shell. This one measures 68 mm. (2.68 in.)

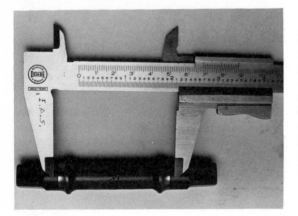

Fig. 6-35: The "invisible" measurement of a 68-mm. spindle is simply to specify that a 68-mm. bottom-bracket shell will not "swallow" the adjustable cup so all the threads go inside the bottom-bracket shell with no room for the lockring; you **must** use the lockring.

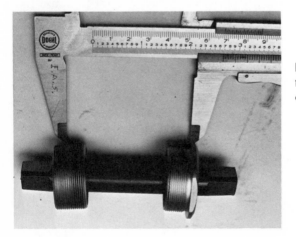

Fig. 6-36: At 68 mm. wide, the adjustable cup leaves four or five threads for the lockring.

means is that the bearing lands will be such that when you screw home the adjustable cup there will be room for the lockring, as shown in Figure 6-35. Here I have set the metric caliper ruler at 68 millimeters with the cups removed. You can see it applies to nothing visible on the spindle. With cups in place (Fig. 6-36) you can see there is room (I count five threads) for the lockring. So that's what the 68 millimeters means— you get a spindle long enough between bearing lands to allow room for the lockring on the adjustable cone side. By the way, here is one good reason never to interchange different makes of cups. Cups have different widths, and if you switch to a narrower (thinner) set of cups, the adjustable cup is going to screw all the way flush with the left side of the bottom-bracket shell, leaving you no room for the lockring. Without the lockring, the adjustable cup can move as you pedal, and change adjustment, because it will be quite loose. Need I say, after all the preceding, that such movement will be an unmitigated, expensive disaster? Figures 6-37 and 6-38 show the difference in width, for example, between Shimano and Campagnolo adjustable and fixed cups. I also would not advise changing or interchanging brands of bearing sets in cages. It's okay to change individual ball bearings, as long as they are the same size. By the way, apropos of nothing at all except measurement, you can buy an inexpensive metric caliper ruler from a local hardware store or from a metric specialty supply house such as Ametric. To read this ruler, which measures inside diameter (A); outside (B) and depth (C) in both inches and millimeters, put the jaws or the depth gauge on whatever you want to measure. For example, let's say that what you measure reads 69 plus, someplace between 69 and 70. Each large number at the top of the scale is 10 millimeters, each of the smaller divisions represents one millime-

Fig. 6-37: Left, Shimano adjustable cup. Right, Campagnolo adjustable cup.

Fig. 6-38: Left, Campagnolo fixed cup. Right, Shimano fixed cup.

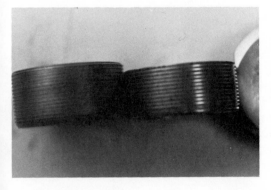

ter. So if the end of the vernier (Fig. 6-39) is at plus 9 and a fraction, which totals 69 millimeters plus a fraction of a millimeter, now we have to find out what that fraction represents. This is where we turn to the vernier scale on this ruler (Fig. 6-40). The vernier ("A") is not numbered, but is divided into ten major divisions and two smaller divisions between each of the major divisions. Each of the major divisions represents one additional decimal point to the right and each of the smaller divisions an additional decimal point. For example, in Figure 6-40, the left side of the vernier is just above 69. To read the additional fraction, go to the vernier division closest to being aligned with the division in the main metric scale underneath it. In Figure 6-40, the division in the vernier main scale is 3½ vernier divisions . . . that is three major divisions plus half a division. So the closest we can come to an accurate reading with this vernier metric caliper ruler is 69.35 millimeters. Got it? No? Ah, well, I tried. Buy yourself a vernier metric ruler anyhow—it comes with instructions and you'll get a real feeling of accomplishment by using it. Unless, of course, you are a machinist or an engineer, in which case this description is strictly ho-humsville, and I don't blame you for thinking so.

Now back to bottom-bracket selection. Important dimensions of the spindle are shown in Figure 6-41. Note that dimension (A) is longer than dimension (B); this is because (A) is the chainwheel side of the spindle. On the spindle body in the dimension (B) section is stamped 68 and 112, which means that the spindle is for a 68-millimeter bottom-bracket shell and that the total spindle length is 112 millimeters. All of which is fine, but you still have to have room for the chainwheel to clear the stays. You need a good healthy 10-millimeter clearance between the inner chainring and the chainstay to avoid chain rub in low gear. With the conventional bottom-bracket set consisting of balls loose or in a race, a fixed cup and an adjustable cup with lockring, you have absolutely no way to change the clearance between the chainwheel and the chainstay. This is a fixed dimension depending directly on spindle length. If you are going from a double to a triple chainwheel, keep the cups and bearings, and change to a longer spindle to accommodate the triple chainwheel set. For example, Campagnolo's double-plateau chainwheel uses a spindle with an (A) dimension (Fig. 6-41) of 31 millimeters, but this dimension goes to 35 millimeters for their triple chainwheel. Of course the triple chainwheel is now longer by the 4-millimeter difference between the two (A) dimensions; the double-chainwheel spindle is a total of 112 millimeters long and the triple is 116 millimeters long. But both will fit a 68-millimeter bottom bracket; the only difference is the (A) dimension, which is longer for the triple chainwheel.

It's risky to interchange cranks. For example, you can count on Cam-

Fig. 6-39: Vernier caliper ruler is a very handy tool for quite precise measurements in both millimeters and inches. (A) measures inside diameters; (B) measures outside; (C) measures depth.

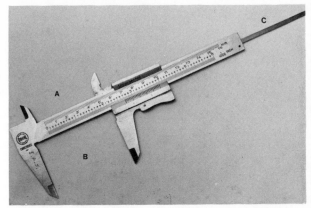

Fig. 6-40: Close-up of vernier scale section. Read measurement where vernier line comes closest to mm. line below it. Vernier scale is in 100th of a mm. Each major vernier scale is 1/10 of a mm. So if the major scale below is, say, 69 mm., and vernier lines up with the third major vernier line plus one, over the major scale, the reading would be 69.35 mm.

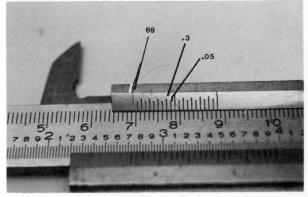

Fig. 6-41: Important measurements of a bottom-bracket spindle. Although you can read the manufacturer's marking on the spindle as 68 W 112, which means that the spindle will fit a 68-mm. bottom-bracket shell and the 112 is the spindle length, there really is no measurable place on the spindle that you can say is 68 mm. Dimension (A) shows the length of the right side, for the chainwheel side; (B) is bearing surface to bearing surface; (C) is left side of spindle; (D) is spindle diameter; (E) is overall spindle length and taper° is just that (most spindles have a 2° taper, the way we measure it).

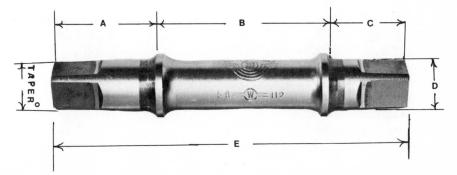

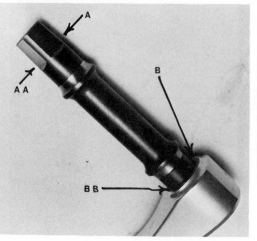

Fig. 6-42: If the crank can be pressed by the crank fixing bolt so far up the spindle taper that it butts against the spindle shoulder, the crank is a poor fit and will not be tight enough. This is a sure way to destroy the crank. Crank is too far up at points (B) and (BB). (A) and (AA) show that some of the taper should show.

pagnolo cranks and spindles to be up to specs, the taper cut to 3½ degrees exactly. But other cranks may have a specified 3½-degree taper but be slightly off that mark, or even be cut to 3 degrees. Also, you will find the tapered end of the spindle to be longer on some makes than on others, as shown in Figure 6-41. This means that it may be possible to force the crank too far up onto the spindle so that the shoulder of the crank abuts the inner rise of the spindle taper, as shown in Fig. 6-42. Here I have placed a Shimano 600 crank on a Campagnolo spindle. The tapered opening in the Shimano crank is enough larger than the Campy shank so that the Shimano crank is actually loose. The fit between the crank and the spindle should be a press fit, so tightening the spindle bolt will force the crank tightly up on the spindle's tapered end. You will note in Figure 6-42 that the crank is so far up into the spindle that you can't even see the shoulder of the tapered end. You can tighten down on the spindle locking bolt, sure, and the crank will now *feel* tight. But believe me, that tightness is not good—there's an awful lot of air between most of the inside of the crank and the spindle, so that the crank is hanging onto the spindle by just a fraction of its body. It won't take very many miles of pedaling before this type of crank-to-spindle fit will shear off the insides of the crank and leave you with a nice, free-wheeling crank that can only be repaired by buying and installing a new, properly fitted and mated crank. If in doubt about the crank-to-spindle fit when buying a new crank, bring along your old spindle to the bike shop, put the new crank on it, and tighten it down to check the fit before you leave the store. You'll know, right away, if the fit works or not. In some fits, the end of the spindle is flush, or close to being flush, with the bottom of the crank-puller hole. After tightening the bolt, re-

Fig. 6-43: Crank end is about right distance from end of spindle. If spindle protrudes beyond inside flat of crank, fixing bolt can't tighten so crank will be too loose and will be ruined.

move it and check to make sure that you have a clearance of at least ¹⁄₁₆th to ¹⁄₈th inch between the end of the spindle and the inside surface of the squared end of the crank, as shown in Figure 6-43. If the crank is closer than that, or flush with the spindle end, the bolt is tightening against itself and not against the crank. If the bolt tightens on itself, further tightening will only shear off the bolt and not bring the crank tight enough up on the spindle. If you don't shear the bolt off, you will also have a loosened crank eventually, and because the spindle is steel and the crank softer aluminum, the result can be a ruined crank.

As another example of spindle length for double versus triple cranks, Stronglight's double has an (A) dimension (see Fig. 6-41) of 32.5 millimeters and the triple has an (A) dimension of 39.5 millimeters—a difference of 7 millimeters. Overall length (Fig. 6-41) (E) dimension for the double is 118.5 millimeters, for the triple, 125.5 millimeters, a difference of 7 millimeters. So the difference is in the longer crank end, dimensions (B), (C) and (D) remain the same, and if one fits a 68-millimeter bottom-bracket shell, the other will also fit it.

National Differences

The threads that are cut into the bottom-bracket shell, into which are threaded the adjustable and fixed cups, are not the same for all bottom brackets. Would, indeed, that they were. As it is, the national differences make bottom-bracket set selection a real mess. As a guide, *if your bicycle was made in the U.S.A., England or Japan,* it is most likely to have the bottom-bracket threads of 1.370 × 24 threads per inch, which is British Standard Coarse. *The adjustable cup will have right-hand threads* and so will thread on clockwise, as will its lockring. *The fixed cup will have left-hand threads* and so will thread on counterclockwise. The crank will be threaded $9/16 \times 20F$ for pedal threads with those dimensions. *The bottom bracket will most likely be 68 millimeters wide.*

If your bicycle was made in France or Belgium, the bottom-bracket threads will be 35 millimeters $\times$ 1.00 millimeters and the pedals will be threaded 14×1.25 millimeters. Because it is difficult to find pedals with this thread cutting, any good bike shop can chase these threads out to the more standard $9/16 \times 20F$ in a few minutes—and don't hesitate to do it if it's necessary. The bottom bracket will most likely be 68 millimeters wide from edge to edge (Fig. 6-34). The fixed and adjustable cups will be right-hand threaded (threads on clockwise).

If your bicycle was made in Italy the bottom-bracket threads will be 36 millimeters $\times$ 24 threads per inch, and pedal threads will most likely be $9/16$ by 24 threads per inch. The bottom bracket will probably be 70 millimeters, which means you will need a 70-millimeter spindle (that's the nondimension I noted above and illustrated in Figure 6-35. Both fixed and adjustable cups will be right-hand threaded (thread on clockwise). Figure 6-44 shows the difference between right- and left-hand threads, in case there is any doubt. Note that the right-hand thread (which is normal thread direction found on most bolts and nuts) slopes to the left, and left-hand threads slope to the right. On finely cut threads you will need a magnifying glass to tell the difference.

If, God help you, *your bicycle was made in Switzerland,* your bottom-bracket threads will be a cross between English and Italian, and will be 35 millimeters $\times$ 1 millimeter pitch and the fixed cup may be left-hand threaded. Or, it *may* be right-hand threaded. You never know, and you will need to make a visual check (Fig. 6-44). If the fixed cup is right-hand threaded, the bottom bracket will accept the French bottom-bracket sets. But if the fixed cup is left-hand threaded, then your replacement is going to be a problem, and may have to come from a Swiss source. Good luck!

Table 6-1 shows basic spindle dimensions of common makes of bottom-bracket spindles. Table 6-2 shows chainring interchangeabilities. Table 6-3 shows chainring-teeth availabilities. For example, from Table

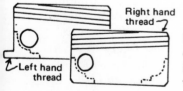

Right hand thread

Left hand thread

Fig. 6-44: Difference between left- and right-hand threads can usually be determined by inspection. Here's what to look for. Left-hand threads are "normal," and spin on clockwise. Right-hand threads are on British, American and Jap-

Table 6-1   Bottom-Bracket Spindle Dimensions (See Fig. 6-38)

Make	Type	Dimensions (millimeters)					Taper*	Axle Marking
		"A"	"B"	"C"	"D"	"E"		
Campagnolo	Double	31	54	27	13.5	112	3.5°	68 SS 120 †
Campagnolo	Triple	35	54	27	13.5	116	3.5°	68 SS 120 X 3
Campagnolo	CycloCross	31	54	30	13.5	115	3.5°	68 SS
Campagnolo	Double SR (Titanium)	34	54	30	13.5	118	3.5°	68 SL 120
Campagnolo	Track	28	54	27	13.5	109	3.5°	68 P 120
Stronglight	Double	32.5	56	30	13.5	118.5	3.5°	113
Stronglight	Triple	39.5	56	30	13.5	125.5	3.5°	125
Stronglight	Double Long	34.5	56	30	13.5	120.5	3.5°	120
Stronglight	Double X Long	38	56	30	13.5	124.0	3.5°	124
Sugino	Double	34	50	29	13.5	113	3.5°	MW 68
Sugino	Track	29.5	50	28.5	13.5	108	3.5°	MS 68
TA	Double	32	56	26	14.0	114	3.5°	344
TA	Triple	36	56	26	14.0	118	3.5°	374

* This chart was taken in part from manufacturers, and I wish to note that the taper measurement is controversial in that Sutherland and Phil Wood measure of these spindle tapers is 2 degrees and not 3.5 degrees. The variance may be due to how the taper is measured, that is, whether from the centerline of the spindle to either end of the taper, or from the difference between the tapers. I fail to see how this major a difference can exist, however. I am inclined to stick with Sutherland and Phil Wood, because my own measurements indicate closer to 2 degrees than to 3.5 degrees.

† For Campy only, the code means 68 (for 68-millimeter bottom bracket); 120 means recommended rear-hub axle length for accurate chainline.

6-3 you will note that TA makes a low-gear inner ring for a triple chainset of only 26 teeth, which can be fitted to a Stronglight triple chainwheel set to replace their low of only 38 teeth.

Most of the bottom-bracket chainsets on the market come in English, French and Italian thread specifications. If in doubt, check with your bicycle shop, because availabilities change fairly frequently.

Table 6-2   Chainring Interchangeability

Make	Number of Chainwheels	Model	Crank Arm Type	Interchangeable With
Stronglight	Double	49 D	5 pin	TA
Stronglight	Double	93	5 arm	—
Stronglight	Double	Criterium	5 pin	—
Sugino	Double	Mighty Compe MCD	5 arm	Campy Rec. S
Sugino	Double	Mighty Custom MCC	5 arm	Campy Rec. S
Campagnolo	Double	Super Record S	5 arm	Super Record P Avocet
Campagnolo	Double	Super Record P	5 arm	Super Record S Avocet
Campagnolo	Double	Record S	5 arm	Sugino
Avocet	Double	Racing/Touring	5 arm	Campy Rec. S & P

Table 6-3   Chainring and Crank Length Availability

Make	Model	Inner Center Outer (Number of Teeth, Minimum/Maximum)			Type	Crank Lengths (In millimeters)
Campagnolo	Nuovo Record	42–52*		53–57	Double	165,170,177.5
Campagnolo	Nuovo Record	(any combination of above)			Triple	Same
Shimano	DuraAce	Inner and Outer rings are interchangeable with teeth from 39 to 55			Double	165,170,172.5,175
Avocet	Racing/Touring	24–40	41–54	41–54	Triple	170,172.5,175
Sugino	Maxi 2	Comb. of 32–57			Double	165,171
Sugino	Mighty Comp.	Comb. of 42–54			Double or Triple	165,168,171,175
Sugino	Maxy 5	Comb. of 32–57			Double	165,171
Sugino	Mighty Tour	34–45	40–52		Double	
Sugino	Mighty Tour	34–45	34–45	40–52	as Triple	165,171
SunTour	Superbe CW-1000	42–47		47–54	Double	167.5,170,172.5, 175
SunTour	Road VX	34–48		48–53	Double	165,170
TA Cyclo-touriste	W1690 Pro	26 to 68 as one to triple			Single, Double, Triple	160,162.5 165,167.5 170,172.5 175,177.5 180

* Interchangeable as inner or outer chainrings

About that Fixed Cup

You may be under the impression that I am avoiding the subject of how to remove the fixed cup. I really am not, honest. For one thing, there's no reason why you should *ever* remove a fixed cup unless it is worn out or unless you are changing over to another brand of bottom-bracket set or to a sealed-bearing bottom-bracket set (yes, I recognize the redundancy). To remove the fixed cup, which you might think is *welded* on the bottom bracket because it's so tight, first think through which direction you should turn it. If your bike was made in England, France, the U.S.A. or Japan, it's 99.9999 percent likely you have a left-hand-threaded fixed cup, *which means it unthreads clockwise.* If your bike was made in France or Italy, the bottom bracket is most likely to be right-hand threaded and will thread off counterclockwise. If your bike was made in Switzerland, the fixed cup could be right- or left-hand threaded. Try it counterclockwise first.

If the flats on your fixed cup measure 36 millimeters, you are lucky,

Fig. 6-45: Shimano fixed-cup wrench is a terrific tool. If you change bottom-bracket sets and wish to remove the fixed cup, I would advise you to buy one. Fits 36-mm. fixed cups.

because you can use a Shimano 36-millimeter fixed-cup wrench (Fig. 6-45). If your fixed cup is some other size, you can have a problem without a special wrench, because the *shoulder* of the fixed cup is only 3.5 millimeters wide, tapering to 3 millimeters at the ends, and the bottom-bracket shell is right next to the flats, so it's virtually impossible to get a good enough grip to turn the fixed cup with, say, a monkey wrench or adjustable crescent wrench. One way I have removed fixed cups is by removing both wheels and holding the bike up over a large machinist's vise and tightening down the vise on the fixed-cup flats; then I twist the whole bike. Remember that if the cup is right-hand threaded the bike must twist clockwise, vice versa if left-hand threaded. If the vise jaws are not mangled and you have tightened them down fair and hard, you can usually unscrew the fixed cup at the first try. But resign yourself to scraping paint off the edge of the bottom-bracket shell. It's hard to avoid when you use the bench vise method.

SEALED-BEARING BOTTOM BRACKETS

At this writing there are three brands of sealed-bearing bottom-bracket sets on the market, available either in bicycle stores or directly from the manufacturer. The manufacturers use commercially available sealed precision bearing sets which are replaceable but which should give you at least 5,000 miles before requiring relubrication. You can, on all of them, pry the outer dust seal off if you are careful. Do it with the point of a sharp knife inserted *underneath* (not into!) the seal, between it and the bearing, and pry up and out. With the seal removed you can visually inspect the bearing for lubrication, clean it if necessary with a small brush and solvent such as Carbo-Chlor and force a mild grease such as Phil Wood or Lubriplate into the cage. Be careful not to overforce the grease or you might push out the seal on the other side. Some bottom-sealed sets cannot be taken apart except at the factory, so if you push in the inner seal, you won't be able to replace it. I would like to review the three brands in some detail at this point.

Phil Wood Bottom Brackets

I mention Phil's bottom brackets first because he's the granddad of sealed bicycle components with precision bearings in the U.S.A. Two other firms make them now, but Phil Wood was the first, outside of a few machinists/cum/bicyclists or bicyclists/cum/machinists in Detroit and California whose production is extremely limited. You can buy one of these elegant bottom-bracket sets for around $45 in your local bike store, or should be able to. If not, write Phil Wood directly at 153 W. Julian St., San Jose, California 95110 or phone 408/298-1540. Phil makes his bottom-bracket spindles with a 2-degree taper (see first note, Table 6-1) so you should have no problems with fitting your old cranks on the spindle. Just make sure they don't bottom out. Here are the sizes available:

Phil's bottom brackets are available in British, Italian, French, Swiss, Raleigh Super Course, 1.370 × 26 right adjustable cup, left-hand fixed cup; and Chater Lee, 1.450 × 26 right adjustable cup and left-hand threaded fixed cup. You will need to order the cups that fit your bicycle. Specify which one.

You will need special tools to install Phil Wood bottom brackets. Figure 6-46 shows a shop version of this tool, which costs around $10; however, there's a much less expensive version, suitable for home use, for around $3.50 (Fig. 6-47). Figure 6-48 shows one end of an installed Phil Wood bottom bracket, Figure 6-49 shows a close-up of one of the "cups."

As you might guess, there is considerable leeway in moving the spindle laterally by adjusting both cups. You can move the spindle to one side or the other at least 5 millimeters (0.197 in.) for correct chainline (which we discussed earlier). You can tighten up both cups without causing binding pressure on bearings, so lateral adjustment is no prob-

Table 6-4 Phil Wood Bottom-Bracket Sizes

Campagnolo and copies	TA or Stronglight	Phil Wood Part Number	Spindle Length (millimeters)
Single	—	1	108 (4.25″)
Double	Single	2	113 (4⁷⁄₁₆″)
Triple	Double	3	119 (4¹¹⁄₁₆″)
—	Triple	4	125 (4¹⁵⁄₁₆″)

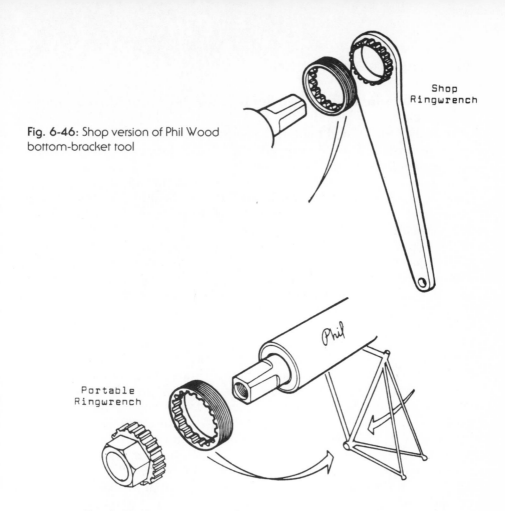

Fig. 6-46: Shop version of Phil Wood bottom-bracket tool

Shop Ringwrench

Phil

Portable Ringwrench

Fig. 6-47: Home version of Phil Wood bottom-bracket tool

Fig. 6-48: One end of Phil Wood bottom-bracket adjustable bearing retainer

Fig. 6-49: Phil Wood bearing retainer. Nonserrated end goes in first.

lem. Just be sure to leave two-thirds of the threads inside the bottom-bracket shell.

To install Phil Wood bottom brackets, disassemble the old set as per previous instructions, thoroughly clean bottom-bracket shell threads with a nonoily solvent and dry off. Insert the bearing cartridge in the shell, long side of the spindle first, toward the right side of the bike (No. 1 model will have both spindle sides the same length). Apply mounting compound to ring threads (supplied) and screw both rings in by hand. Rings must have the plain or nonserrated end facing toward the center of the bottom-bracket shell (arrow in Fig. 6-49). Adjusting them so that both rings are about centered or screwed in the same amount, hold one ring with one of the tools (you should have two) and tighten up the other to about 25 foot pounds. Tighten the remaining one the same way. If you are using the British thread on the right-hand cup, the cup or ring will be marked by a red-painted face on the inside of the ring. Remember to thread this one in counterclockwise since it will be left-hand threaded. Make chainline lateral adjustments before tightening shells.

Phil also makes a youth adapter bottom bracket for your small child, say from five to ten years of age, whose legs would otherwise be too short to reach the pedals on your tandem. The adapter (Fig. 6-50) bolt/clamps onto the seat tube. You're looking at around $30 for this unit. It fits either a 1⅛-inch seat tube or a 28-millimeter (slightly smaller) seat tube. A neoprene liner is provided to protect the paint. This is *not* the complete unit. You still have to install a bottom-bracket set, and the adapter will (of course) accept one of Phil's bottom-bracket cartridges. Or you can use an old bottom-bracket set, if you have one, and the cranks and chainwheel from another bike.

Fig. 6-50: Phil Wood bottom-bracket shell child adapter for tandems. Shell clamps on seat tube. Requires Phil Wood bottom-bracket set, an extra purchase.

Fig. 6-51: Phil Wood crank shortener, for people with orthopedic requirements

Crank Shorteners

If you have one leg shorter than the other, it's a lot easier to pedal if one of the cranks is shorter than the other one. They bolt to crank arms. If the right leg is the problem, you will have to dispense with the right or outer chainwheel, to make room for the adapter (Fig. 6-51). They run around $30 each.

Durham Bottom Brackets

Roger Durham, engineer and cyclist, has come up with a dandy bottom-bracket set (Fig. 6-52) that mates well with your old cotterless crank spindle length. Roger's spindle lengths are: 114 millimeters (4.5 in.), 127 millimeters (5 in.) and 140 millimeters (5.5 in.). English, Italian or

Fig. 6-52: Durham bottom-bracket sealed-bearing set. Parts are: (1) spindle; (2) bearing retainer or holder; (3) needle bearings in sealed races; (4) thrust collar can be adjusted by loosening Allen screws (5) to allow lateral movement of spindle for chainline alignment (lateral movement can be as much as needed up till chainwheel rubs on tubes.); (6) thrust ball bearings in race; (7) machined, hardened flat washers; (8) an aluminum shell that is precisely machined so you can't overtighten bearing holders (2) with pin wrench. Shell is a spacer.

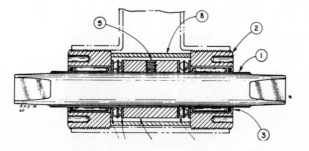

Fig. 6-53: Durham bearing retainer, showing needle bearings.

French threadings for bearing carriers replace adjustable and fixed cups. The spindle is 15.9 millimeters versus 15.06 millimeters for the Phil Wood bottom-bracket diameter, so there is a mite of added strength here. I have never had a bottom-bracket spindle break, or even bend, but then my cycling torque is far below that of a road-racing athlete. Roger uses four sets of bearings. In the description that follows, please refer to the keyed numbers in Figure 6-52. Number 1 is of course the spindle. Number 2 are the aluminum bearing carriers, one on each side of the spindle. Number 3 are the caged roller bearings carried inside the bearing carriers (Fig. 6-53). These bearings sets are rated at 2,000 pounds capacity *each* so the total capacity of the two of them is two tons. In the center of the set is an aluminum thrust collar (4) (see also Fig. 6-54), which is held on the shaft by two socket set screws (Allen wrench

Fig. 6-54: Bottom, Durham spindle with machined flat washer (A); thrust bearings (B); and thrust collar (C) above is conventional spindle.

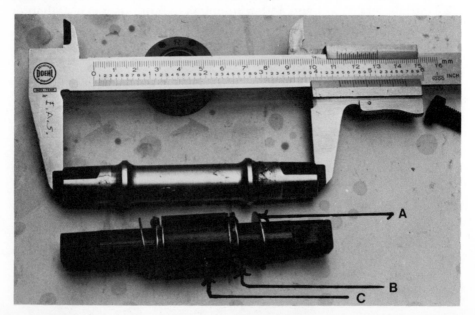

provided with the set). This thrust collar can be loosened and moved laterally on the spindle for chainline adjustment. I found I could get 7 millimeters (a bit over ¼-inch) lateral adjustment by moving the thrust collar on the spindle and still have the bearing carriers threaded far enough inside the bottom bracket for comfort. Between the bearing carriers are hardened steel thrust washers (7) which are on either side of a pair of retainer-type thrust bearings (6). The thrust bearings take up lateral thrust (Fig. 6-54). Finally, there is an internal sealing sleeve (8), consisting of a hollow tube of aluminum which protects thrust bearings from being end-loaded by the bearing carriers and which also provides precise bearing clearance. The sleeve prevents you from tightening the threaded bearing carriers in the bottom-bracket shell so tightly that you cause the spindle to bind. The sleeve also seals bearings from contaminants such as water or rust in the frame and keeps bearings from loosening.

To install: Remove old bottom-bracket set as previously instructed. Clean threads in bottom bracket. Screw in right-side bearing carrier by hand. Make sure there is a washer next to the thrust collar, followed by thrust bearings, followed by another washer (Fig. 6-53). Reverse this sequence on the left side. The thrust collar Allen screws should be tight and the collar in about the center of the spindle. Now thread in the left-hand bearing carrier by hand. If you have a bracket set of the right size, you should have the carriers pretty nearly flush with the ends of the bottom-bracket shell. Tighten both carriers with an *adjustable pin wrench* (the Shimano fixed-pin wrench won't fit). Now check for end play by trying to move the spindle up and down. If you find play, remove the left-hand carrier, make a paper washer out of a business card, and locate it between the carrier and the flat washer. If one of these paper shims does not take out play, use two. I used three in my installation. This is a bit of extra trouble, but not much, and it is certainly worthwhile, considering how well the bracket set works. The sealed bearings add very little friction; in fact, my set showed none worth mentioning, compared with the old conventional set. As you have guessed by now, I am sure, the bearings are easily get-attable, and simple to remove and replace if necessary. All bearings are the standard commercial precision type available either from Durham or from a bearing supply house.

Now check chainline. Please review chainline specifications for your gear setup. One easy way to arrive at a reasonable approximation of correct chainline (eyeballing won't do, and it's difficult to get a straight-edge on the chainset and freewheel cogs due to their location and size) is to measure the distance between the freewheel cog that you are using as the chainline reference point and the wheel rim. I hope you have the wheel in the dropouts straight and that the rim is accurately trued. If

you have a five-speed freewheel and a double chainwheel, correct alignment is when the centerline *between* the chainwheels lines up with the
number-three rear cog (Fig. 4-21). If you knot a piece of string around
the chainwheel bushing, between the two chainwheels, and bring it
back and tie it to the seat stay, you will have a reference point to check
chainline. You should have the same distance between the rim flat closest to the chainwheel and the string as between the rim flat farthest to
the rear of the bike and the chainwheel; and the rear part of the string
should be lined up with the number-three cog of the freewheel. Measuring in both locations gave me 29 millimeters; and, because I had the
chainring end of the string close to the centerline between the chainwheels, and right over number 3 rear cog, it indicated that the chainline
was pretty surely on the mark. This is a rough gauge of chainline, but
unless you are a racing cyclist, it is good enough. If the chainline is off,
you can unscrew the Durham left-side bearing carrier, pull out the spindle (watch that you don't lose the washers) and move the thrust collar as
needed.

You will note that the spindle is threaded for a bolt and that the bolt
and a washer are supplied to replace your old crank bolt. Your old crank
bolt will *not* fit the Durham spindle because it's not metric thread, but
⁵⁄₁₆ by 24 TPI. The bolt also takes a ½-inch socket, so it's small enough
to permit entry of the socket into the crank, which is a real convenience,
because the tight fit of the larger bolts that come with the crankset makes
it easy for the wrench to slip off; and I clearly remember skinned
knuckles, once on the chainwheel teeth. The Durham set sells for
around $40.

Avocet Sealed Bottom-Bracket Set

The Avocet version of a sealed bottom bracket (Fig. 6-55) is a new
introduction to American bicyclists, and should be available in volume
in early 1981. The design is substantially different from the Phil Wood,
but similar to the Durham in that the bearings are inside threaded hold-

Fig. 6-55: Avocet sealed-
bearing bottom-bracket set

Fig. 6-56: Cross section, Avocet sealed-bearing bottom-bracket set

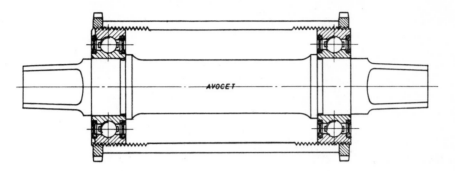

ers. There is a lockring for both the left and right side of the spindle, and some lateral adjustment for the chainline is available. The set can replace most high-quality conventional bottom-bracket sets such as Campy, Sugino, T.A. and Stronglight, and is available in English, French, Italian and Swiss threadings. Complete weight is 260 grams (9.17 oz.). Cost, around $33. Installation is straightforward; the only tool you need is an adjustable pin wrench.

CHAINWHEELS

We have already covered chainwheel interchangeability. I would only like to add a word about some of the new developments in chainwheel design. For example, Shimano has a new line of what they refer to as "W" cut gear teeth on their chainwheels. Figure 6-57 compares their chainwheel with Campagnolo, to give you an idea of the differences. In addition to the wider "W" cut, Shimano has shortened the two teeth just behind the crank and the two on the opposite side of the chainwheel

Fig. 6-57: Shimano "W" cut chainwheel teeth, left, versus Campagnolo chainwheel teeth, right.

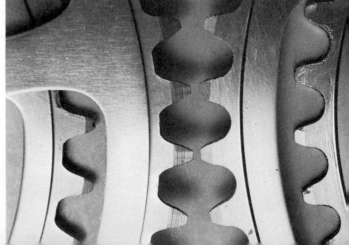

from the crank. The theory is that it is at these two points where chain stress is greatest; so the shorter teeth means that the chain does not have to lift as far to be nudged by the derailleur cage from one chainwheel to the other. However, the difference in teeth height is only one millimeter (about $\frac{4}{10}$ inch). I found no noticeable difference in shiftability between the Shimano chainwheel with these four shorter teeth. The wider spacing at the base of the teeth has nothing to do with ease of shifting, but is better designed to accommodate the Shimano Uniglide chain, about which, more later.

Shimano has one new development which I applaud, and that is their one key-release mechanism on cranks (Fig. 6-58) that takes only a 5-inch-long, 6-millimeter Allen wrench (supplied), both to tighten the crank onto the spindle-tapered shaft, and the same Allen wrench, turned counterclockwise, to pull it off. Turn the wrench clockwise to fasten the crank on the spindle; counterclockwise, the crank comes off the spindle. When the crank comes loose you have to give four or five more turns to unscrew the fixing bolt. This mechanism is on the top line of DuraAce cranks, as well as the special DuraAce pedal. I'll discuss these pedals in detail in Chapter 8, coming right up. Figure 6-59 shows a conventional crank-pedal threading and the new DuraAce pedal crank. Obviously you have to buy the whole shebang if you want these excellent pedals. Clearly this product is for the original-equipment market, because you

Fig. 6-59: Conventional crank, left, and new Shimano crank, right, for their new pedals. Note that pedal end has opening of a much larger diameter.

are not buying just a pedal, you're buying a system of mated, designed-together components that will, for the most part, only work with each other. The new Shimano UG chain will not work well except with Shimano matching freewheel cogs and derailleurs. If you install the DuraAce freehub you must use Shimano's rear derailleur with a hatch plate (half inner plate so you can slide the chain out and remove the freewheel without removing the chain, and without "breaking" the chain with a rivet remover). To "break" the Shimano chain with its fatter bowed plates you should use a special Shimano rivet remover in order to avoid bending the plates flat again, or else be darned careful when you use a conventional rivet remover, which I have used on these chains successfully. And so on . . . You need to select Shimano components, at least the newer ones, with great care to be sure that what you buy will fit what you have unless you buy the entire system, freehub or hub and freewheel, chainset, bottom-bracket set, chain and rear derailleur.

To digress a moment, I will say that the Shimano Crane GS derailleur is the best wide-range derailleur on the market that I have tested, and that it can be used on any system or combination of components. The DuraAce derailleur line is usable anywhere as is the excellent DuraAce front derailleur. I merely wish to note that when it comes to Shimano, be aware that in the third-line component series especially (Altus, for example) you need matched components. True, most of Shimano's DuraAce conventional line, such as the chainwheels, derailleurs, and hubs, are standard and can be used with equipment made by other companies, except that Shimano chainwheels are not interchangeable with any other make, at least as of this writing.

THE GREAT CRANK-LENGTH CONTROVERSY

A few years ago a fellow who owned a foundry made some extra-long cranks and a frame with higher ground clearance so the cranks would not hit the ground and a longer frame so pedals would not hit the front wheel on a turn, and he set off up a mountain. He claimed a new world record for that particular peak, which, he said, could only have been made with those extra-long cranks. I don't recall the exact length of the cranks, but they were substantially longer than any commercially available size, probably over 200 millimeters. But when other cyclists in good condition attacked that same mountain with conventional-length cranks they found this "record" easy to beat: The original speed was made some forty or fifty years before when bikes were not as efficient as they are today.

Still, there seems to be rather a lot of controversy over crank length.

Theoretically, from the simple standpoint of the lever (Archimedes said something like "Give me a lever long enough and I will move the world," but he never said where he would stand, and he knew nothing about roughage) the longer lever would appear to give you more torque, but at the expense of crank rpm capability. There's always a trade-off, always a penalty. Nevertheless, the theory is that the longer the crank (lever), the higher the gear that can be used without undue fatigue. Somewhere there is a point where the longer gear impedes smooth pedaling action (the French have a nice, silky-sounding smooth word for this action which is *soplesse*) and crank rpm and therefore speed. The problem, then, is really not whether the crank is too long or too short, but what the correct crank length (Fig. 6-60 shows a variety of crank lengths) is for your particular leg length and physical stamina and gear ratios available on your bike. Another limiting point is how far your bottom bracket is above ground and the pedal clearance from the front wheel. Also on short-wheelbase road-racing type of bikes there is going

Fig. 6-60: Selection of various crank lengths. Left to right: (A) Shimano DuraAce with new pedal threading and integral crank puller, 170 mm.; (B) Shimano DuraAce conventional crank but with integral puller, 175 mm.; (C) SunTour Road VX 170 mm. crank; (D) Campagnolo Strada 170 mm. (note beautiful machined finish); (E) Shimano Selects with octagonal female joint to fit their octagonal spindle on this less expensive crankset, 165 mm., and (F) Shimano 600EX crank, 170 mm.

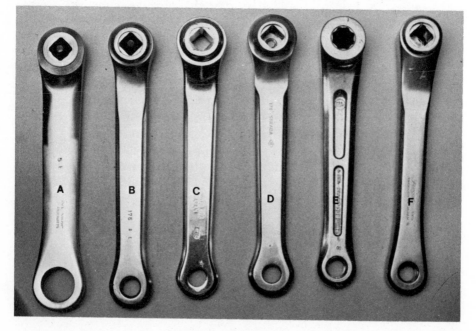

to be a minimum front-wheel clearance at best, so before you change to longer cranks turn the front wheel until it is at its closest point to the toe clips or pedal, measure that distance and decide whether you can go, say, from 6½-inch cranks (165 mm.) to 7-inch cranks (178 mm.). Of course, there are smaller gradations between available crank lengths, as shown in Table 6-3. The widest range of cranks is made by T.A., and goes from 160 millimeters (6.3 in.) in 2½-millimeter increments all the way to 180 millimeters (7.1 in.).

Let's see if we can come to some rational method of deciding upon the correct crank length for you. We have already mentioned two limiting factors, bottom-bracket-to-ground clearance and wheelbase. Apropos of ground clearance, I'm not worried so much about bottom-bracket-to-ground clearance while the bike is upright. The problem is when you bank for a turn, because then the pedal comes much closer to the ground. You also need to consider leg action as well as leg length as measured on the inside (inseam). What you want is a pedal action that simulates, as closely as possible, the natural action of the knee. A pedal that's too long or too short exaggerates this natural action, which can lead to knee problems as well as decrease pedaling efficiency. If you are doing a lot of hill climbing, as long a crank as will fit you is going to give you more leverage. I might note here that the difference between 160 millimeters, the shortest crank available commercially at this writing, and 180 millimeters, the longest crank available, is 20 millimeters, which is .7874 inches (call it ¾ of an inch). I might also note that the 160-millimeter crank available from T.A. is on their single chainwheel. I mention this only to let you know its availability.

Another formula, which makes a lot of sense to me, has been derived after extensive study of the physiology of pedaling by three doctors in France, as reported in a cycling journal from that country. The formula is that the crank length should be around 20 to 21 percent of the inseam measurement. You measure your inseam in stocking feet from the floor to the crotch. Thus if your inseam measurement is 32 inches, 32 × .2 = 6.4", you would use a 6.4-inch crank, which converted to millimeters (6.4 × 25.4) = 162.56 mm. Call it 162.5 millimeters, because T.A. makes a single chainwheel crank this short. I would go to the 21-percent end of the scale, which gives us .21 × 32 inches (my inseam measurement) = 6.72 inches × 25.4 = 170.688 mm. For the same inseam measurement, that's a difference of around 8 mm., which is only around 5 percent, or .31496 inches (8 × .03937), or a tad over ¼ inch. I'm not trying to minimize the importance of the ¼-inch+ difference, because this can be fairly major if it means going beyond your natural pedaling action of the knee and associated bones and tendons and joints and musculature. But the longer crank gives more leverage on uphill climbs.

Another way to look at selection of crank lengths is more experiential, but based on the following factors: How fast do you routinely "spin" the cranks? If your normal pedal cadence is 80 rpm, I suggest you use as long a crank as is comfortable for you. The reason for this is that the longer cranks give you more leverage. If, however, you twirl along at, say, 90 or 100 or greater crank rpm, then you can use shorter cranks which facilitate faster rotation. This would be true particularly if you are a strong rider. If you are heavy plus strong, but pedal slowly, I would use the maximum crank length with which you are comfortable. I changed from 165-millimeter to 170-millimeter cranks and found that my own pedaling was smoother and that I had more power to climb hills. I also found my normal cadence to be unaffected by the longer cranks; I still crawl along at 72 to 80 rpm. I have what pants manufacturers call a statistically normal relationship of inseam to overall height. The waist relationship I would rather not discuss. That is, I am just average in terms of inseam to height. Among other things. I won't bore you with a recitation of what all the experts in racing, physiology and cycling in general have had to say about crank length. Needless to say, there is no magic formula for determining crank length that is hard and fast and works for everybody. My own conclusion is that the 20-to-21-percent formula of crank length to inseam measurement is a good starting point. At least you won't subject your knees to damaging abnormal stresses from too short or too long a set of cranks. On the other hand, it's expensive to buy a lot of cranks just to experiment to see which length is best for you, under widely varying conditions of cycling such as cadence rpm's, cycling on the flats and on different percentages of road grade and your own physical condition which can change from day to day. Figure 6-51 shows Phil Wood crank shorteners, which sell for around $30; but that, too, is a fairly costly investment unless you have an orthopedic reason to use them. On the other hand, if you have invested $600 or more in a really fine bicycle, you might want to go the one step further and experiment with different crank lengths. You don't have to buy new chainwheels, because you will only need the cranks and can transfer the chainwheels from one to the other if you can find a bike store that will sell you the naked right-side crank. Or, you might borrow cranks of a different length from a friend (does anyone have that good a friend?). Figure 6-61 shows a shop tool chainwheel straightener. But re-read the section earlier in this chapter on fitting cranks to spindles, before you start changing cranks.

Fig. 6-61: Shop chainwheel straightener

ELLIPTICAL CHAINWHEELS

Before leaving cranks and chainwheels, I would like to discuss, briefly, the elliptical chainwheel, a Roger Durham design shown in Figure 6-62. I hasten to add that although Roger makes a modern version, the elliptical chainwheel has been around since the late 1890s and has varied from a plus or minus ovality of 8 percent to the Durham version of plus or minus 25 percent. I have used the Durham model and can report that it does smooth out my power stroke on hill climbing, if the hills are moderate. But if you will look at the chainwheel in Figure 6-62 you will quickly see that you can't use a front derailleur with it because the top of the ellipse would hit the derailleur cage. To shift into the lower-gear chainwheel you have to stop and move it over by hand, ideally lifting up the rear wheel, twirling the pedals and shoving the chain over. But since I do not have three hands, my preferred way is to use the heel of my foot as the derailleur (I have grease marks on my right shoe) to move it over, while pedaling with my left foot. This is not the safest procedure in the world and *must* be done before approaching the hill, unless you are strong enough to hill climb with one leg. I did not find the elliptical chainwheel to be any substitute for the lower gear possible with the inner, smaller chainwheel. But I did find that the ellipse design made cycling on the flats smoother. I don't think I would want to tour any great distance with the Durham design, though, because I need the instant availability of all my gears, particularly my low, low "Granny" gear on steep hills. But for around town and on the flats, the elliptical chainwheel is a real eye-catching conversation starter, and it is somewhat helpful in eliminating the dead spots in crank rotation. To see what I mean at this point, I suggest you go to your bike (or do it mentally if you are good at three-dimensional visualization) and put a crank at the 12-o'clock position. The other crank will of course be at the 6-o'clock position. Here you now have zero torque on the pedals. Torque increases with the angle of pedal and falls off rapidly as you approach the noon position with one crank. If you look at Figure 6-62 you can see that as the pedal approaches the noon position the chain-

Fig. 6-62: Durham elliptical chainwheel

wheel becomes smaller, which in effect gives you a lower gear automatically. Conversely, as your pedal swings past noon the ellipse begins to pick up more teeth, creating a bigger chainwheel effect, and you swing automatically into a higher gear.

You might think that the switch from the big to the small portion of the chainwheel will be beyond the capacity of the rear derailleur, but not so, any more than the difference between a 42 and 52 dual chainwheel and a 14-to-28-tooth freewheel would be. Of course if you have a 14-to-34-tooth freewheel, you will be using a longer cage wide-ratio derailleur, so again I see no problem. Except that as the chain swings over the oval chainwheel, the derailleur will move back and forth, so derailleur bushings wear a lot faster.

GEAR RATIOS

I have suggested, elsewhere in this chapter, that you may not be satisfied with the gear ratios on your bicycle—that you may wish to change to wide-ratio gears for touring and hill climbing on tours, or to close-ratio gears for riding on the flats or for road racing. We have already discussed *how* to change gears; now let's discuss *which* gears to select to meet your needs. If you pedal on flat terrain only, and at most five or six miles at a trip, you don't need gears at all. Any single-speed gear within a moderate gear ratio (see below) will get you there and back.

But if you plan to ride longer distances over hill and dale, through flat country, into varying wind conditions, you will need a wide range of gears. The broad selection of gears, say from ten to eighteen gear selections, will let you compensate for the incredible variations in cycling conditions you will encounter on any cross-country trip. Gears are particularly important when you cycle tour and carry thirty or more pounds of camping gear on your bike.

When you buy a bicycle from a dealer, you are stuck with the gears that come with it. You don't have to keep them, however, if you want a wider gear range. For example, a ten-speed bicycle often comes with gears something like this: front double plateau chainwheel with 40 and 50 teeth, rear five-cog freewheel with 14, 17, 20, 24 and 28 teeth. The low-gear combination using the 40-tooth chainwheel and the 28-tooth rear cog is not what I would call a low low gear at all, and certainly would not have gotten me up many of the hills I hit in Vermont and in Europe, where I met grades up to 15 percent.

Before we get into specific recommendations for gear selections, let's first become acquainted with what gear ratios and gear "inch" tables are all about, a subject you should at least have a nodding acquaintance with.

Gear ratio is simply the number of times the rear wheel will turn for every turn of the chainwheel up front. For example, my touring bike has a low-gear combination of 32 teeth on the freewheel cog and 24 teeth on the chainwheel, as noted above. That's a negative gear ratio, and extremely low. To find the gear ratio, simply divide the number of teeth on the chainwheel by the number of teeth of the freewheel. In this case 24 = .75. This means that the gear ratio between the chainwheel with 24 teeth and the freewheel cog with 32 teeth is 1 to 75 (1:75). Translated into action it means that for every revolution of the chainwheel 32-tooth ring, the rear wheel only turns ¾ of a revolution, which is why it is a negative gear ratio.

Going to the other extreme, my fifteen-speed bicycle has high gears of 50 teeth on the front chainwheel and 14 teeth on the freewheel cog in the rear, which gives a ratio of: 50 = 3.57, which means that for every turn of the chainwheel the rear wheel turns over a bit more than 3½ revolutions. So at a constant pedal cadence I am crawling in the low low "Granny" gear and going like mad in the high gear (if the road is flat and there's a thirty-mile-an-hour wind behind me). See discussion of cadence below. But first let's discuss the archaic term "gear inches," still in wide use. I would prefer the more meaningful concept of gear ratios instead of gear inches, but custom is a powerful inhibitor to progress. Besides, once you understand and get used to what gear inches mean, you develop a feel for the relative differences between different gear (inches) combinations and so will speak bicyclese to other bike experts.

EQUIVALENT WHEEL SIZE AND "GEARS"

As high-wheeler bicyclists of the 1880s soon realized, the larger the front wheel, the faster they could ride, up to a point beyond which the wheel became too big (i.e., the gear ratio too large and the pedals too far away) for them to pedal. The high-wheeler (Ordinary or Penny Farthing, as it was called) thus set the standard for gearing used today. You will hear modern cyclists on ten-speed bicycles talk about "the gear I'm in" or "what gear do you use to climb hills?" and if racing is involved, the "gear" the racer is using for a specific event. The "gear" shown in Table 6-5 (computed by your author) is simply a conversion table which converts gear ratio to the equivalent high-wheeler front-wheel diameter in inches. This is something like converting the thrust of an aircraft jet engine into the horsepower of a piston engine to find out how much power the aircraft has . . . sort of roundabout, to say the least. But the gear chart is in wide use; cyclists use it to compare gear ratios, so there it is and we're stuck with it.

Table 6-5   Gear Chart (27- and 700-centimeter wheels only)

Number of Teeth
in Chainwheel

		24	25	26	27	28	29	30
Number of	12	54	56.2	58.5	60.8	63	65.2	67.5
Teeth in Rear	13	49.8	51.9	54	56	58.2	60.2	62.3
Sprocket	14	46.3	48.2	50.1	52.1	54	55.9	57.9
	15	43.2	45	46.8	48.6	50.4	52.2	54
	16	40.5	42.2	43.9	45.6	47.3	48.9	50.6
	17	38.1	39.7	41.3	42.9	44.5	46.1	47.6
	18	36	37.5	39	40.5	42	43.5	45
	19	34.1	35.5	36.9	38.4	39.8	41.2	42.6
	20	32.4	33.8	35.1	36.5	37.8	39.2	40.5
	21	30.9	32.1	33.4	34.7	36	37.3	38.6
	22	29.5	30.7	31.9	33.1	34.4	35.6	36.8
	23	28.2	29.3	30.5	31.7	32.9	34	35.2
	24	27	28.1	29.2	30.4	31.5	32.6	33.8
	25	25.9	27	28.1	29.2	30.3	31.3	32.4
	26	24.9	26	27	28.0	29.1	30.1	31.2
	27	24	25	26	27	28	29	30
	28	23.1	24.1	25.1	26	27	28	28.9
	29	22.3	23.3	24.2	25.1	26.1	27	27.9
	30	21.6	22.5	23.4	24.3	25.2	26.1	27
	31	20.9	21.8	22.6	23.5	24.4	25.3	26.1
	32	20.3	21.1	21.9	22.8	23.6	24.5	25.3
	33	19.6	20.5	21.3	22.1	22.9	23.7	24.5
	34	19.1	19.9	20.6	21.4	22.2	23	23.8

31	*32*	*33*	*34*	*35*	*36*	*37*	*38*	*39*	*40*
69.7	72	74.3	76.5	78.7	81	83.2	85.5	87.8	90
64.4	66.5	68.5	70.6	72.7	74.8	76.8	78.9	81	83.1
59.8	61.7	63.6	65.6	67.5	69.4	71.4	73.3	75.2	77.1
55.8	57.6	59.4	61.2	63	64.8	66.6	68.4	70.2	72
52.3	54	55.7	57.4	59.1	60.8	62.4	64.1	65.8	67.5
49.2	50.8	52.4	54	55.6	57.2	58.8	60.4	61.9	63.5
46.5	48	49.5	51	52.5	54	55.5	57	58.5	60
44.1	45.5	46.9	48.3	49.7	51.2	52.6	54	55.4	56.8
41.9	43.2	44.6	45.9	47.3	48.6	50	51.3	52.7	54
39.9	41.1	42.4	43.7	45	46.3	47.6	48.9	50.1	51.4
38	39.3	40.5	41.7	43	44.2	45.4	46.6	47.9	49.1
36.4	37.6	38.7	39.9	41.1	42.3	43.4	44.6	45.8	47
34.9	36	37.1	38.3	39.4	40.5	41.6	42.8	43.9	45
33.5	34.6	35.6	36.7	37.8	38.9	40	41	42.1	43.2
32.2	33.2	34.3	35.3	36.3	37.4	38.4	39.5	40.5	41.5
31	32	33	34	35	36	37	38	39	40
29.9	30.9	31.8	32.9	33.8	34.7	35.7	36.6	37.6	38.6
28.9	29.8	30.7	31.7	32.6	33.5	34.4	35.4	36.3	37.2
27.9	28.8	29.7	30.6	31.5	32.4	33.3	34.2	35.1	36
27	27.9	28.7	29.6	30.5	31.4	32.2	33.1	34	34.8
26.2	27	27.8	28.7	29.5	30.4	31.2	32.1	32.9	33.8
25.4	26.2	27	27.8	28.6	29.5	30.3	31.1	31.9	32.7
24.6	25.4	26.2	27	27.8	28.6	29.4	30.2	31	31.8

Table 6-5   Gear Chart (continued)

Number of Teeth
in Chainwheel

		41	42	43	44	45	46	47	48	49	50
Rear	12	92.2	94.5	96.7	99	101.3	103.5	105.7	108	110.2	112.5
Teeth	13	85.2	87.2	89.3	91.4	93.5	95.5	97.6	99.7	101.8	103.8
	14	79.1	81	82.9	84.9	86.8	88.7	90.6	92.6	94.5	96.4
	15	73.8	75.6	77.4	79.2	81	82.8	84.6	86.4	88.2	90
	16	69.2	70.9	72.6	74.3	75.9	77.6	79.3	81	82.7	84.4
	17	65.1	66.7	68.3	69.9	71.5	73.1	74.6	76.2	77.8	79.4
	18	61.5	63	64.5	66.0	67.5	69	70.5	72	73.5	75
	19	58.3	59.7	61.1	62.5	63.9	65.4	66.8	68.2	69.6	71.1
	20	55.4	56.7	58.1	59.4	60.8	62.1	63.5	64.8	66.2	67.5
	21	52.7	54	55.3	56.6	57.9	59.1	60.4	61.7	63	64.3
	22	50.3	51.5	52.8	54	55.2	56.5	57.7	58.9	60.1	61.4
	23	48.1	49.3	50.5	51.7	52.8	54	55.2	56.3	57.5	58.7
	24	46.1	47.3	48.4	49.5	50.6	51.8	52.9	54	55.1	56.3
	25	44.3	45.4	46.4	47.5	48.6	49.7	50.8	51.8	52.9	54
	26	42.6	43.6	44.7	45.7	46.7	47.8	48.8	49.8	50.9	51.9
	27	41	42	43	44	45	46	47	48	49	50
	28	39.5	40.5	41.5	42.4	43.4	44.4	45.3	46.3	47.3	48.2
	29	38.2	39.1	40	41	41.9	42.8	43.8	44.7	45.6	46.6
	30	36.9	37.8	38.7	39.6	40.5	41.4	42.3	43.2	44.1	45
	31	35.7	36.6	37.5	39.3	39.2	40.1	40.9	41.8	42.7	43.5
	32	34.6	35.4	36.3	37.1	38	38.8	39.7	40.5	41.3	42.2
	33	33.5	34.4	35.2	36	36.8	37.6	38.5	39.3	40.1	40.9
	34	32.6	33.4	34.1	34.9	35.7	36.5	37.3	38.1	38.9	39.7

51	52	53	54	55	56	57	58	59	60
114.8	117	119.2	121.5	123.7	126	128.3	130.5	132.7	135
105.9	108	110.1	112.2	114.2	116.3	118.4	120.5	122.5	124.6
98.4	100.3	102.2	104.1	106.1	108	109.9	111.9	113.8	115.7
91.8	93.6	95.4	97.2	99	100.8	102.6	104.4	106.2	108
86.1	87.8	89.4	91.1	92.8	94.5	96.5	97.9	99.6	101.3
81	82.6	84.2	85.8	87.4	88.9	90.5	92.1	93.7	95.3
76.5	78	79.5	81	82.5	84	85.4	87	88.5	90
72.5	73.9	75.3	76.7	78.2	79.6	81	82.4	83.8	85.3
68.9	70.2	71.6	72.9	74.3	75.6	77	78.3	79.7	81
65.6	66.9	68.1	69.4	70.7	72	73.3	74.6	75.9	77.1
62.6	63.8	65	66.3	67.5	68.7	70	71.2	72.4	73.6
59.9	61	62.2	63.4	64.6	65.7	66.9	68.1	69.3	70.4
57.4	58.5	59.6	60.8	61.9	63	64.1	65.3	66.4	67.5
55.1	56.2	57.2	58.3	59.4	60.5	61.6	62.6	63.7	64.8
53	54	55	56.1	57.1	58.2	59.2	60.2	61.3	62.3
51	52	53	54	55	56	57	58	59	60
49.2	50.1	51.1	52.1	53	54	55	55.9	56.9	57.9
47.5	48.4	49.3	50.3	51.2	52.1	53	54	54.9	55.9
45.9	46.8	47.7	48.6	49.5	50.4	51.3	52.2	53.1	54
44.4	45.3	46.2	47	47.9	48.8	49.6	50.5	51.4	52.3
43	43.9	44.7	45.6	46.4	47.3	48.1	48.9	49.8	50.6
41.7	42.5	43.4	44.2	45	45.8	46.6	47.5	48.3	49.1
40.5	41.3	42.1	42.9	43.7	44.5	45.3	46.1	46.9	47.6

Table 6-5   Gear Chart (continued)

Number of Teeth
on Chainwheel

		61	62	63	64	65	66	67	68	69	70
Rear	12	137.2	139.5	141.8	144	146.2	148.5	150.7	153	155.3	157.5
Teeth	13	126.7	128.8	130.8	132.9	135	137.1	139.2	141.2	143.3	145.4
	14	117.6	119.6	121.5	123.4	125.4	127.3	129.2	131.1	133.1	135
	15	109.8	111.6	113.4	115.2	117	118.8	120.6	122.4	124.2	126
	16	102.9	104.6	106.3	108	109.7	111.4	113.1	114.8	116.4	118.1
	17	96.9	98.5	100.1	101.6	103.2	104.8	106.4	108	109.6	111.2
	18	91.5	93	94.5	96	97.5	99	100.4	102	103.5	105
	19	86.7	88.1	89.5	90.9	92.4	93.8	95.2	96.6	98.1	99.5
	20	82.4	83.7	85.1	86.4	87.8	89.1	90.5	91.8	93.2	94.5
	21	78.4	79.7	81	82.3	83.6	84.9	86.1	87.4	88.7	90
	22	74.9	76.1	77.3	78.5	79.8	81	82.2	83.5	84.7	85.9
	23	71.6	72.8	74	75.1	76.3	77.5	78.7	79.8	81	82.2
	24	68.6	69.8	70.9	72	73.1	74.3	75.4	76.5	77.6	78.8
	25	65.9	66.7	68	69.1	70.2	71.3	72.4	73.4	74.5	75.6
	26	63.3	64.4	65.4	66.5	67.5	68.5	69.6	70.6	71.7	72.7
	27	61	62	63	64	65	66	67	68	69	70
	28	58.8	59.8	60.6	61.7	62.7	63.6	64.6	65.6	66.5	67.5
	29	56.8	57.7	58.7	59.6	60.5	61.4	62.4	63.3	64.2	65.2
	30	54.9	55.8	56.7	57.6	58.5	59.4	60.3	61.2	62.1	63
	31	53.1	54	54.9	55.7	56.6	57.5	58.4	59.2	60.1	61
	32	51.5	52.3	53.2	54	54.8	55.7	56.5	57.4	58.2	59.1
	33	49.9	50.7	51.5	52.4	53.2	54	54.8	55.6	56.5	57.3
	34	48.4	49.2	50	50.8	51.6	52.4	53.2	54	54.8	55.6

The gear chart is derived very simply by multiplying the gear ratio by the diameter in inches of the rear wheel, which then converts the rear-wheel diameter to the equivalent diameter of a "high-wheeler." Take a low gear of 34 teeth rear, 36 front: $\frac{36}{34} \times 27 = 28.6$, or, this gear is equal to riding a high-wheeler with a pedal-driven front wheel of 28 inches diameter. To find out how *far* one turn of the chainwheel with this gear combination (or one turn of the front wheel on the "high-wheeler" equivalent) would take you, multiply the equivalent "gear" by pi, or 3.1416. In this case, one turn of a 36-tooth chainwheel connected to a 34-tooth rear gear ($\frac{36}{34} \times 27 \times 3.1416$) would cause the rear wheel to move forward 89.81 inches, or almost 7½ feet. You can check the "gear" for any combination of rear and front gear teeth by checking the chart. For example, find 14 teeth on the chart under "sprocket size" at left. Move along that line to the right to the 54 T column and you find 104.1, which multiplied by 3.1416 (*you'll* have to do it) tells that you will travel the 327 inches we came up with above (or $\frac{327}{12} = 27\frac{1}{4}$ feet).

HOW TO SELECT YOUR OWN GEARS

We've talked a lot, up to now, about gear ratios, gear inches, cadence and speed. Maybe you looked at your bike and discovered that the reason you couldn't make those hills was not advancing age, but simply because you did not have low enough gears. That's my excuse, anyway. But you have decided you want to change your gearing. What gears you should select is now the question.

Well, unless you're pretty good at math, coming up with a good selection of gears for where you live, your physical condition and the kind of cycling you do can be a difficult task. All I can do to help you is offer some rather general suggestions.

For example, you can conceive of a gearing system or combination of gears on a bike to fall within three groups, as shown in Figure 6-63. There's the low range, the intermediate or cruising range and the high range. As a general rule, you should take the low range, for hill climbing, in fairly large steps. You don't want to have to change through a bunch of gears to get to the low low on a steep hill. You need to change down as you approach the hill, not when you're climbing it. Otherwise, under high torque, gears change noisily, slip, or don't change at all but hang up on top of a cog or chainwheel tooth. When you're in the cruising range, on the flats or a moderate hill, or into a fairly strong wind on the flats, you need a wider selection of gears in smaller increments, clustered around the gear you normally use. And when you're tearing down a hill or riding fast before a high wind, you want a wide change between high gears, which you seldom otherwise use.

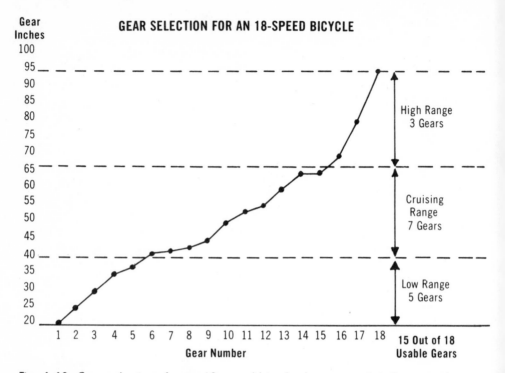

Fig. 6-63: Gear selections for an 18-speed bicycle. Low range has five speeds in larger increments. Intermediate range has seven speeds in closer increments and high range has 3 gears in still larger increments (than low range). Three gears are unusable, 8 and 9 because they are at extremes of the gears and 14 because it duplicates 15.

The curves in Figure 6-63 represent a selection of gears for an eighteen-speed bicycle. Table 6-6 represents the same selections in numerical format.

Of the eighteen speeds in column one in Table 6-6, and from the curve in Figure 6-63, you can see that three gears are unusable—two, gears 8 and 9, because each combines the smallest with the largest gears, which put the chain at a very great angle, that is, the chain is skewed way to the left in gear 8 because it is on the largest front chainwheel, which is the right-hand chainwheel, and on the largest rear freewheel cog, which is at the left-hand side of the freewheel. The opposite situation occurs in gear 9. Either way, with the chain skewed drastically, there is going to be much faster wear of the soft aluminum alloy (expensive) chainwheel and even of the steel freewheel cogs and the chain itself. And you will probably hear a lot of noise from the front derailleur because it's going to be hard to keep the chain from rubbing on the

Table 6-6   Gear Combinations for an 18-Speed Touring Bicycle

Gear No.	Number of Teeth in Freewheel	Number of Teeth in Chainwheel	Gear, Inches
1	32	24	20.3
2	26	24	24.9
3	22	24	29.5
4	32	40	33.8
5	19	24	34.1
6	16	24	40.5
7	26	40	41.5
8	32	50	42.2
9	14	24	46.3
10	22	40	49.1
11	26	50	51.9
12	19	40	56.8
13	22	50	58.7
14	16	40	67.5
15	19	50	67.5
16	14	40	77.1
17	16	50	84.4
18	14	50	96.4

inside of the front-derailleur side plates at these extreme chain angles.

Gear 15 is unusable because it duplicates 14. So out of eighteen gears (six-speed freewheel, triple chainwheel, 6 × 3 = 18) we wind up with fifteen usable gear selections, combinations of freewheel cogs and chainwheels. This is not at all bad for this many gears. Even a twelve- or fifteen-speed gear has two unusable combinations because of extreme angle of chainline, and one close gear duplication. The idea here is to select those gears that give you a quick downshift to the lower-lower gears without shifting through a lot of other gears along the way. Most of the total number of gear selections on a bike are in closer increments in the mid or cruising ranges in which you will usually be pedaling, and are farther apart as you move upward to higher gear ranges (for when there's a tail wind, or you're going downhill, or a dog is chasing you, etc.).

Figure 6-63 clearly shows that the basic criteria for gear selection are reasonably well met. I would probably opt for perhaps a wider spread in the lower ranges, but if you look at the curve you will see that the low and high ranges are fairly steep and that the cruising ranges are closer together. There are five usable gears in the low range, six in the cruising range and three in the high-speed range, which to me is a good combination for distance cyclo-touring. Again, gears 8, 9 and 14 (or 15) are not usable, as a practical matter.

Fig. 6-64: Handy computerized speed chart tells you how fast you are going, if you know your gear inches and your cadence (crank rpm's).

THE SPEED IN MPH EQUALS PI TIMES THE GEAR TIMES THE CRANK RPM TIMES 60 DIVIDED BY 63.360

GEAR	REVOLUTIONS PER MINUTE OF THE CRANK ARM											
	60	70	80	90	100	110	120	130	140	150	160	
26	4.64	5.41	6.19	6.96	7.73	8.51	9.28	10.06	10.83	11.60	12.38	MPH
27	4.82	5.62	6.43	7.23	8.03	8.84	9.64	10.44	11.25	12.05	12.85	MPH
28	5.00	5.83	6.66	7.50	8.33	9.16	10.00	10.83	11.66	12.49	13.33	MPH
29	5.18	6.04	6.90	7.76	8.63	9.49	10.35	11.22	12.08	12.94	13.80	MPH
30	5.35	6.25	7.14	8.03	8.92	9.82	10.71	11.60	12.49	13.39	14.28	MPH
31	5.53	6.46	7.38	8.30	9.22	10.14	11.07	11.99	12.91	13.83	14.76	MPH
32	5.71	6.66	7.62	8.57	9.52	10.47	11.42	12.38	13.33	14.28	15.23	MPH
33	5.89	6.87	7.85	8.84	9.82	10.80	11.78	12.76	13.74	14.73	15.71	MPH
34	6.07	7.08	8.09	9.10	10.11	11.13	12.14	13.15	14.16	15.17	16.18	MPH
35	6.25	7.29	8.33	9.37	10.41	11.45	12.49	13.54	14.58	15.62	16.66	MPH
36	6.43	7.50	8.57	9.64	10.71	11.78	12.85	13.92	14.99	16.06	17.14	MPH
37	6.60	7.71	8.81	9.91	11.01	12.11	13.21	14.31	15.41	16.51	17.61	MPH
38	6.78	7.91	9.04	10.17	11.30	12.44	13.57	14.70	15.83	16.96	18.09	MPH
39	6.96	8.12	9.28	10.44	11.60	12.76	13.92	15.08	16.24	17.40	18.56	MPH
40	7.14	8.33	9.52	10.71	11.90	13.09	14.28	15.47	16.66	17.85	19.04	MPH
41	7.32	8.54	9.76	10.98	12.20	13.42	14.64	15.86	17.08	18.30	19.52	MPH
42	7.50	8.75	10.00	11.25	12.49	13.74	14.99	16.24	17.49	18.74	19.99	MPH
43	7.68	8.95	10.23	11.51	12.79	14.07	15.35	16.63	17.91	19.19	20.47	MPH
44	7.85	9.16	10.47	11.78	13.09	14.40	15.71	17.02	18.33	19.63	20.94	MPH
45	8.03	9.37	10.71	12.05	13.39	14.73	16.06	17.40	18.74	20.08	21.42	MPH
46	8.21	9.58	10.95	12.32	13.68	15.05	16.42	17.79	19.16	20.53	21.90	MPH
47	8.39	9.79	11.19	12.58	13.98	15.38	16.78	18.18	19.58	20.97	22.37	MPH
48	8.57	10.00	11.42	12.85	14.28	15.71	17.14	18.56	19.99	21.42	22.85	MPH
49	8.75	10.20	11.66	13.12	14.58	16.04	17.49	18.95	20.41	21.87	23.32	MPH
50	8.92	10.41	11.90	13.39	14.87	16.36	17.85	19.34	20.82	22.31	23.80	MPH
51	9.10	10.62	12.14	13.66	15.17	16.69	18.21	19.72	21.24	22.76	24.28	MPH
52	9.28	10.83	12.38	13.92	15.47	17.02	18.56	20.11	21.66	23.20	24.75	MPH
53	9.46	11.04	12.61	14.19	15.77	17.34	18.92	20.50	22.07	23.65	25.23	MPH
54	9.64	11.25	12.85	14.46	16.06	17.67	19.28	20.88	22.49	24.10	25.70	MPH
55	9.82	11.45	13.09	14.73	16.36	18.00	19.63	21.27	22.91	24.54	26.18	MPH
56	10.00	11.66	13.33	14.99	16.66	18.33	19.99	21.66	23.32	24.99	26.66	MPH
57	10.17	11.87	13.57	15.26	16.96	18.65	20.35	22.04	23.74	25.44	27.13	MPH
58	10.35	12.08	13.80	15.53	17.25	18.98	20.71	22.43	24.16	25.88	27.61	MPH
59	10.53	12.29	14.04	15.80	17.55	19.31	21.06	22.82	24.57	26.33	28.08	MPH
60	10.71	12.49	14.28	16.06	17.85	19.63	21.42	23.20	24.99	26.77	28.56	MPH
61	10.89	12.70	14.52	16.33	18.15	19.96	21.78	23.59	25.41	27.22	29.04	MPH
62	11.07	12.91	14.76	16.60	18.44	20.29	22.13	23.98	25.82	27.67	29.51	MPH
63	11.25	13.12	14.99	16.87	18.74	20.62	22.49	24.37	26.24	28.11	29.99	MPH
64	11.42	13.33	15.23	17.14	19.04	20.94	22.85	24.75	26.66	28.56	30.46	MPH
65	11.60	13.54	15.47	17.40	19.34	21.27	23.20	25.14	27.07	29.01	30.94	MPH
66	11.78	13.74	15.71	17.67	19.63	21.60	23.56	25.53	27.49	29.45	31.42	MPH
67	11.96	13.95	15.95	17.94	19.93	21.93	23.92	25.91	27.91	29.90	31.89	MPH
68	12.14	14.16	16.18	18.21	20.23	22.25	24.28	26.30	28.32	30.34	32.37	MPH
69	12.32	14.37	16.42	18.47	20.53	22.58	24.63	26.69	28.74	30.79	32.84	MPH
70	12.49	14.58	16.66	18.74	20.82	22.91	24.99	27.07	29.15	31.24	33.32	MPH
71	12.67	14.79	16.90	19.01	21.12	23.23	25.35	27.46	29.57	31.68	33.80	MPH
72	12.85	14.99	17.14	19.28	21.42	23.56	25.70	27.85	29.99	32.13	34.27	MPH
73	13.03	15.20	17.37	19.55	21.72	23.89	26.06	28.23	30.40	32.58	34.75	MPH
74	13.21	15.41	17.61	19.81	22.01	24.22	26.42	28.62	30.82	33.02	35.22	MPH
75	13.39	15.62	17.85	20.08	22.31	24.54	26.77	29.01	31.24	33.47	35.70	MPH
76	13.57	15.83	18.09	20.35	22.61	24.87	27.13	29.39	31.65	33.91	36.18	MPH
77	13.74	16.04	18.33	20.62	22.91	25.20	27.49	29.78	32.07	34.36	36.65	MPH
78	13.92	16.24	18.56	20.88	23.20	25.53	27.85	30.17	32.49	34.81	37.13	MPH
79	14.10	16.45	18.80	21.15	23.50	25.85	28.20	30.55	32.90	35.25	37.60	MPH
80	14.28	16.66	19.04	21.42	23.80	26.18	28.56	30.94	33.32	35.70	38.08	MPH
81	14.46	16.87	19.28	21.69	24.10	26.51	28.92	31.33	33.74	36.15	38.56	MPH
82	14.64	17.08	19.52	21.96	24.39	26.83	29.27	31.71	34.15	36.59	39.03	MPH
83	14.82	17.28	19.75	22.22	24.69	27.16	29.63	32.10	34.57	37.04	39.51	MPH
84	14.99	17.49	19.99	22.49	24.99	27.49	29.99	32.49	34.99	37.48	39.98	MPH
85	15.17	17.70	20.23	22.76	25.29	27.82	30.34	32.87	35.40	37.93	40.46	MPH
86	15.35	17.91	20.47	23.03	25.58	28.14	30.70	33.26	35.82	38.38	40.94	MPH
87	15.53	18.12	20.71	23.29	25.88	28.47	31.06	33.65	36.24	38.82	41.41	MPH
88	15.71	18.33	20.94	23.56	26.18	28.80	31.42	34.03	36.65	39.27	41.89	MPH
89	15.89	18.53	21.18	23.83	26.48	29.13	31.77	34.42	37.07	39.72	42.36	MPH
90	16.06	18.74	21.42	24.10	26.77	29.45	32.13	34.81	37.48	40.16	42.84	MPH
91	16.24	18.95	21.66	24.37	27.07	29.78	32.49	35.19	37.90	40.61	43.32	MPH
92	16.42	19.16	21.90	24.63	27.37	30.11	32.84	35.58	38.32	41.05	43.79	MPH
93	16.60	19.37	22.13	24.90	27.67	30.43	33.20	35.97	38.73	41.50	44.27	MPH
94	16.78	19.58	22.37	25.17	27.96	30.76	33.56	36.35	39.15	41.95	44.74	MPH
95	16.96	19.78	22.61	25.44	28.26	31.09	33.91	36.74	39.57	42.39	45.22	MPH
96	17.14	19.99	22.85	25.70	28.56	31.42	34.27	37.13	39.98	42.84	45.70	MPH
97	17.31	20.20	23.09	25.97	28.86	31.74	34.63	37.51	40.40	43.29	46.17	MPH
98	17.49	20.41	23.32	26.24	29.15	32.07	34.99	37.90	40.82	43.73	46.65	MPH
99	17.67	20.62	23.56	26.51	29.45	32.40	35.34	38.29	41.23	44.18	47.12	MPH
100	17.85	20.82	23.80	26.77	29.75	32.72	35.70	38.67	41.65	44.62	47.60	MPH
101	18.03	21.03	24.04	27.04	30.05	33.05	36.06	39.06	42.07	45.07	48.08	MPH
102	18.21	21.24	24.28	27.31	30.34	33.38	36.41	39.45	42.48	45.52	48.55	MPH
103	18.39	21.45	24.51	27.58	30.64	33.71	36.77	39.84	42.90	45.96	49.03	MPH
104	18.56	21.66	24.75	27.85	30.94	34.03	37.13	40.22	43.32	46.41	49.50	MPH
105	18.74	21.87	24.99	28.11	31.24	34.36	37.48	40.61	43.73	46.86	49.98	MPH
106	18.92	22.07	25.23	28.38	31.53	34.69	37.84	41.00	44.15	47.30	50.46	MPH
107	19.10	22.28	25.47	28.65	31.83	35.02	38.20	41.38	44.57	47.75	50.93	MPH
108	19.28	22.49	25.70	28.92	32.13	35.34	38.56	41.77	44.98	48.19	51.41	MPH
109	19.46	22.70	25.94	29.18	32.43	35.67	38.91	42.16	45.40	48.64	51.88	MPH
110	19.63	22.91	26.18	29.45	32.72	36.00	39.27	42.54	45.81	49.09	52.36	MPH
111	19.81	23.12	26.42	29.72	33.02	36.32	39.63	42.93	46.23	49.53	52.84	MPH
112	19.99	23.32	26.66	29.99	33.32	36.65	39.98	43.32	46.65	49.98	53.31	MPH
113	20.17	23.53	26.89	30.26	33.62	36.98	40.34	43.70	47.06	50.43	53.79	MPH
114	20.35	23.74	27.13	30.52	33.91	37.31	40.70	44.09	47.48	50.87	54.26	MPH
115	20.53	23.95	27.37	30.79	34.21	37.63	41.05	44.48	47.90	51.32	54.74	MPH
116	20.71	24.16	27.61	31.06	34.51	37.96	41.41	44.86	48.31	51.76	55.22	MPH

CALIBRATED BY AN IBM 360 AND PROGRAMMED BY SAM RHOADS

How to Tell How Fast

All of these arithmetical shenanigans are fine, but they won't tell you how *fast* you are moving. We have to factor in another figure, which is the number of *times* you move the chainwheel one revolution in one minute. The formula to derive miles per hour at a given crank rpm (or chainwheel, or rear wheel rpm, it's all the same) is gear ratio times crank rpm, 3.1416×60 divided by $63,360$. All this work is saved for you, however, by the cadence chart (Fig. 6-64), which was kindly programmed on an IBM computer by Sam Rhoads of Boise, Idaho, who recognized the limitations of the conventional cadence chart.

Here's how to use this very convenient cadence chart. Let's say you're pedaling at 70 crank-revolutions per minute and your chain is on the small 14 T rear gear and the largest 54 T front gear. First, find your *gear* from the gear chart (Table 6-5), which will be 104.1. Then from the cadence chart, find 104 under the gear column (left) and, moving to the right under RPM of the crank arm of 70, you'll find you're moving at 21.66 miles per hour, which is a pretty good clip for anybody much over thirty. In the low-gear combination of 34 T rear and 36 T front, we have a *gear* of 28.6. From the cadence chart, at a *gear* of 27 (we fudge a little) you will travel at 5.62 mph (which is not fast but better than walking up a steep hill).

An easy (but not quite as accurate) way to figure speed is to use the speed chart (Fig. 6-65). To find speed, first find your gear from the gear chart, Table 6-5, and, knowing your crank rpm, follow the gear line to its intersection with the crank rpm line. For example, you're in a 100 gear at 75 crank rpm. Reading to the right from 100 intersection with curve 75, and upward to the speed line, you will be doing almost 23 mph. This chart has limitations in crank rpm selections and jumps up in fairly large chunks, but it's handy to copy and take along on the road.

One more point. You can use a stopwatch fastened to your handlebars to keep tabs on crank rpms. But this means you have to take your eyes off the road momentarily to look at the stopwatch, hardly a safe procedure. A better way is an ingenious little transistorized metronome, which costs about half the price of a good stopwatch, and which you can carry in your breast pocket. It weighs only nine ounces, has a neck strap, and can be adjusted from 40 to 208 beats per minute. The click is audible enough to hear above normal street traffic even when the unit, called a Mininome, is in your breast pocket. The Mininome is available from Hartley Alley's Touring Cyclist Shop (see Appendix and also Figure 6-66).

It's also a good idea to make up a cadence chart for your own particular

SPEED IN MILES PER HOUR

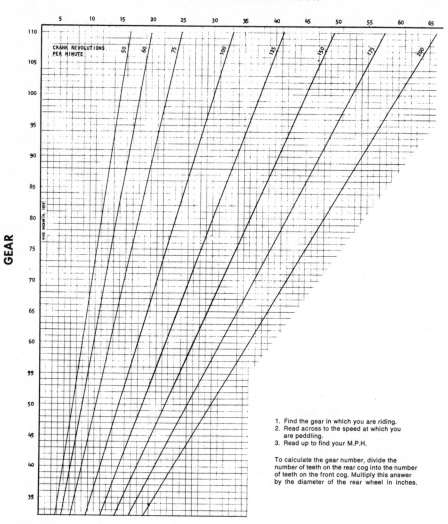

Fig. 6-65: Another way to compute speed is to use this nomogram, following instructions at the right of the graph.

combination of gears, so you always know how fast you are traveling at any crank rpm (see Table 6-7). This is one way to train yourself to work harder at pedaling, for better health. Also, because you can accurately predict how fast you can pedal (once you find your limitations), you can be quite accurate in estimating arrival times (but don't forget to consider hills).

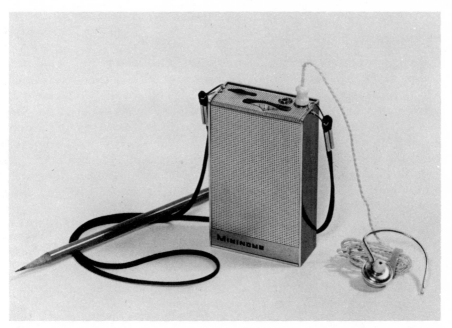

Fig. 6-66: A handy guide to training yourself to maintain a steady cadence, shifting gears so you can hold it comfortably, is a transistorized metronome, called the Mininome, which is the size of a cigarette pack. It has a range of from 40 to 208 beats a minute, with adjustable volume, and weighs nine ounces.

Table 6-7 Sample Individualized Speed Chart*

| | *Number of Teeth in Rear Sprocket* | | | | |
	14	*17*	*22*	*28*	*34*
Chainwheel T 54					
Gear (Inches Eq.)	104.1	85.8	66.3	52	42.9
MPH Speed	21.45	17.88	13.8	10.83	8.8
Chainwheel T 49					
Gear (Inches Eq.)	94.5	77.8	60.1	47.3	38.9
MPH Speed	19.35	16.8	12.5	9.8	8.0
Chainwheel T 36					
Gear (Inches Eq.)	69.4	57.1	44.2	34.7	28.6
MPH Speed	14.9	11.89	9.2	7.1	5.9

* Based on 72-rpm cadence. You'll probably be going a lot faster downhill, so you may want to gradually increase the cadence for fast runs downhill or before the wind. Or you can make up several charts, say one for a cadence of 72, one for 80, one for 85, etc., so you can pull out a 3- x 5-card for every road condition. And you may be pedaling a lot slower than 72 rpm up steep hills. Because the gear inches did not correspond exactly to the cadence chart, we made our own interpolations, which is why the speeds, or some of them, don't correspond exactly to speeds on the cadence chart.

The Meaning of Cadence

First, let's establish what cadence means. Cadence is the pedaling or turning of the crank arm at more or less constant revolutions. It is important to understand this concept, because a regular cadence is necessary for smooth long-distance cycling. You should try to pedal at the same rate of crank revolutions per minute all the time, varying your gear ratio to suit wind and road-grade conditions. For example, let's say you establish that a good cadence for you is between 60 and 75 turns of the crank per minute (for somebody with strong legs it may be 80 revolutions per minute and for a racing cyclist at high speed it may be 100 to 120, or more).

We all have different natural cadences, or pedaling revolutions per minute, at which we feel most comfortable. For most of us, from 65 to 85 pedal strokes per minute is the pace we can maintain most comfortably for the longest period. The reason for gear changes on a bicycle, then, is not only to help you climb hills or go down grades faster; they also help you maintain your natural pedaling cadence at all times.

Chapter Seven

HOW TO KEEP YOUR HEADSET TOGETHER

Like pedals, headsets take a terrific beating. Like pedals, most headsets use small ball bearings, 5/32 inch, and lots of them, usually 22 or 25 to a set. I think the most important requirement of a headset is that it be properly adjusted. *There should be absolutely no looseness in the headset!* To check for looseness, straddle the bike, lock the front brake, grab the handlebars and move them up and down and back and forth. If the headset is too loose, you will feel a slight looseness in the handlebars. If you have down-turned bars, grab them on the drops—the lower part—and twist that part up and down (not side to side). The reason you can't have looseness in the headset is that any "play" in the bearings will quickly flatten the bearings and gall the races, particularly the bottom set. Take a look at Figure 7-1. Reviewing the nomenclature, in Figure 7-1, parts are: (A) locknut; (B) washer (notice "tang" in the left side of washer); (C) screwed race; (D) upper pressed race; (E) lower pressed race; (F) upper bearings; (G) crown race; and (H) lower bearings (interchangeable with upper bearings). If you have "play" in the headset, the bearings, as noted, will take a terrific beating as you pound over the road. I might note here that when you disassemble the headset it's a good idea to replace these bearings anyhow, because they are bound to be somewhat distorted—if so, it will be difficult to get the silky smooth adjustment you deserve from a high-quality headset such as the Campagnolo or Shimano DuraAce designs. During the past few years component manufacturers have begun to furnish headset balls in retainers ("F" and "G" in Fig. 7-1). If you have an older bike, say one made around 1973 or before, your headset bearings will probably be loose, as

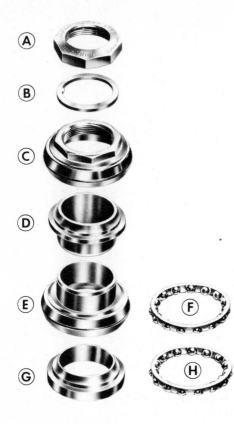

Fig. 7-1: Basic headset parts are: (A) locknut; (B) tanged washer; (C) screwed race; (D) top-pressed race; (E) bottom-pressed race; (F) bearings (in retainer); (G) crown race; and (H) bearings (in retainer).

Fig. 7-2: Some headsets come with loose balls, which offer greater support than bearings in a cage or retainer. This is how loose bearings should look when inserted back into the screwed race, held in place with grease.

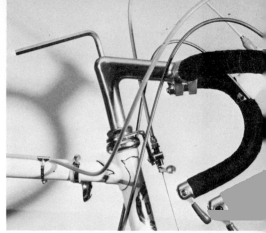

Fig. 7-3: To remove handlebars, unscrew binder bolt, at top, tap it down with plastic mallet to unseat wedge nut, pull bars out.

in Figure 7-2, which shows how these bearings should look when packed back in the race.

You really should clean and repack with grease the headset of any bike that has seen much use during the year. Here are the steps:

STEP ONE: Remove the stem (Fig. 7-3). If your stem has a recessed Allen bolt, it will probably take a 6-millimeter Allen wrench. When the bolt is turned enough so that it feels loose, the stem will still be tight in the steering tube, because this is a wedge type of bolt. Loosen the bolt enough to raise it about ¼ inch and then tap it down gently with a plastic mallet to loosen the wedge nut. Figure 7-4 shows the wedge nut (A) at the bottom of the stem. As you tighten the bolt, the wedge nut is forced up into the stem, where it expands the slit in the skirt (B) of the stem and holds it tightly against the inside of the steering tube. Remove the front wheel.

STEP TWO: Remove the headset locknut. Please use a tool that fits so you don't round off the edges. The latest model of Campagnolo locknut takes a 32-millimeter wrench; Shimano has their own special tool (Fig. 7-5) for their new headsets.

Fig. 7-4: Another version of stem binder bolt (arrow) uses an Allen wrench: (A) points to wedge nut; (B) to stem slit; (C) to binder bolt head.

Fig. 7-5: Shimano requires two special wrenches to remove, reinstall and adjust their new DuraAce headset.

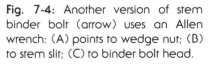

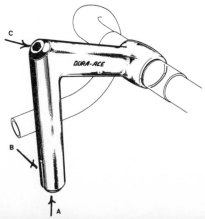

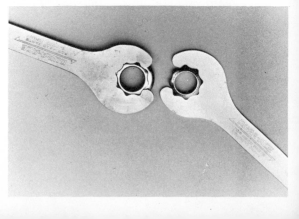

STEP THREE: Remove washer.

STEP FOUR: Remove the screwed cup, pull out the fork, discard the bearings or take them to your bike shop for a new, matching set. Do not replace old bearings, as noted above.

STEP FIVE: Clean and inspect top and bottom races. Look for galled spots, indicated by grooves or roughness. Replace any galled races with same make. In fact, if races are seriously damaged or worn, I would advise you not to try to replace them yourself. It's easy enough to drive the old bottom race out of the steering head tube with a drift, and to knock off the crown race, but replacing them is another matter. They must fit accurately, and there are special tools for this job that are costly and not practical as an investment. Take the fork and bike down to a good bike shop, the kind that specializes in high-priced bikes, and have their mechanic fit on a new headset. You can reassemble the headset yourself, after the races are fitted, of course. Here's how:

STEP SIX: Install new bearings in crown race and on upper pressed race and insert steering head from underneath. Bearings should be well greased with a good-quality lubricant such as Lubriplate.

STEP SEVEN: Screw on the screwed race by hand until tight. Replace washer. Washer tang (protuberance) should fit groove in steering tube. Some washers have a flat instead of a tang and slide over a ground flat on the steering tube.

STEP EIGHT: Screw on the locknut tightly. Turn fork to check for binding. Pull handlebars up and down to check for looseness. If the fork feels tight, or binds, loosen locknut and back off on screwed race about one-quarter turn, tighten locknut and check again. If the fork is too loose, and can be moved up and down by the handlebars, loosen locknut, tighten screwed race one-quarter turn, tighten locknut and check again. Repeat until there is zero play and the fork turns smoothly through 360 degrees.

STEP NINE: Reinstall the stem. Make sure the stem is in the steering tube so that at least two inches of the stem *above the split skirt* are in the steering tube. Newer bikes have stems with a mark that shows how high the stem can be. Never bring the stem up so high that the mark is above the locknut. Some stems have an angle cutoff at the bottom and

Fig. 7-6: Broken stem. Note binder bolt inside.

the wedge nut is cut to a matching angle so that as you tighten the stem bolt, the nut rides up on the stem bottom and wedges between it and the inside of the steering tube. If you bring the stem up too high above the two-inch limit, it can break off. You'd be mighty embarrassed to be barreling up a hill, honking on the bars, pulling the bars as you pedal and have the handlebars suddenly come off in your hands. Not the safest thing that could happen to you. Figure 7-6 shows a stem that did break off. This rider was lucky, I happen to know, because at least the bottom wedge bolt held and he could brake to a stop, although he did lose control and went into a ditch. But he braked as he went so that he was not injured by the impact.

HEADSET TROUBLESHOOTING

If after you have gone through all the bearing adjustments above and still can't get the fork to turn smoothly, here are some suggestions:

Fork Binds

- Too many balls (if loose balls are installed).
- Caged bearings in wrong-side-up. Retainer concave surface faces concave race, and should be vice versa, with concave retainer mating to convex curvature of race.
- Fork could be bent, so that crown race is out of alignment and binds on the lower pressed race.

- Steering tube or head tube could be bent so that they rub on each other or force races out of alignment.
- Headset adjusted properly but binds after handlebar is installed. This is because after tightening, the binder bolt expanding nut forces the stem out very slightly, and minutely alters the fit between bearings and races by "tilting" one side of the steering tube a thousandth or so of an inch. Just loosen the locknut and back off on the screwed race ⅛th turn, retighten locknut and all should be well. But check to make sure, and readjust screwed race as necessary.

Fork Too Loose

- If you can't adjust screwed cup to eliminate looseness, check for enough balls in bearing races (if balls are loose, not in retainers). Check also to make sure you are using mated parts that work together.

HEADSET SELECTION

The best headsets, such as the Campagnolo and Shimano DuraAce, have precisely mated races that fit very closely. Figure 7-7 shows a bicycle

Fig. 7-7: Better headsets, such as the Campagnolo installed on this bicycle, have the screwed race and the bottom pressed race overlapping to keep dust and dirt out of bearings.

fitted with a Campagnolo headset, and the arrows show that the screwed race plus the upper pressed race, and the lower pressed race and crown race, fit so that the top section fits over the bottom section. That is, the screwed race at the top projects down over the upper pressed race. This type of fit helps keep foreign matter out of the bearings.

If you do install your own headset, be aware of the national differences in threads. The English and Japanese steering heads are threaded 1 inch by 24 threads per inch. The French are threaded 24 × 1M and the Italian, 25.4 × 24F. Because the Italian thread diameter of 25.4 millimeters is equal to .999998 inch, and the threads per inch are the same, you might think they are interchangeable with English threads. Well, they are, almost, but I don't recommend forcing the two to mate. Italian threads are cut with a 5-degree pitch difference, from English threads, so the fit won't be accurate and you could have trouble adjusting the screwed race for a smooth fit. Also be aware of the locknut differences. The English will most likely have a 22.2-millimeter locknut; the French, a 22-millimeter locknut. Japanese bikes after 1975 will probably have a .833-inch locknut, which is 21.1582 millimeters and won't fit either the French or English steering head. Check your stem engraving to see if it's marked with a size. The measurements above refer to the I.D. (inside dimension) of the locknut

Headset Data

Campagnolo headsets still top my list (Fig. 7-8). The Campagnolo Super Record set is in alloy with a satin finish and with steel insert races. Not cheap at $41.98 but definitely a top-quality unit. Campy's conventional all-steel Record road set is also great, and costs $27.98. Both models are

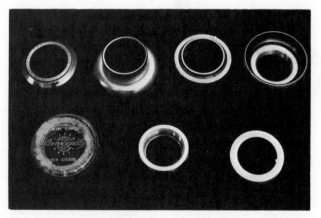

Fig. 7-8: Top-quality Campagnolo headset.

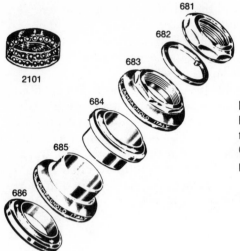

Fig. 7-9: Road type of Campagnolo headset. Parts are: (681) locknut; (682) tanged washer; (683) screwed race; (684) top pressed race; (685) bottom pressed race and (686) crown race.

Fig. 7-10: Campy track headset. Parts are in same sequence as in Figure 7-9.

Fig. 7-11: Shimano DuraAce headset

available in English, Italian and French threads. Figure 7-9 shows the Record road set; Figure 7-10, the track set, model 1040. Campy headsets for road come with ³⁄₁₆-inch balls; for track, with ⁵⁄₃₂-inch balls, both in retainers.

Shimano Headsets are another high-quality component priced some-what lower than Campy models. The finish is anodized, with steel in-serts in aluminum alloy races (Fig. 7-11). Figure 7-12 shows a detailed view of the DuraAce headset. Remember, the locknut and upper race take a special wrench (Fig. 7-5) shown earlier. You should have two wrenches. You're looking at around $24.50 for the DuraAce headset, $15 for the 600 EX.

Stronglight headsets are well known and have been proven in use over these many years. The V4 Competition model is available in French and English thread only, costs around $15.

Tange Levin headsets are modeled closely on Campagnolo designs, are chrome-plated steel, come in English thread, have an inside locknut diameter of 22.2 millimeters to fit a wide range of stems and cost around $10.

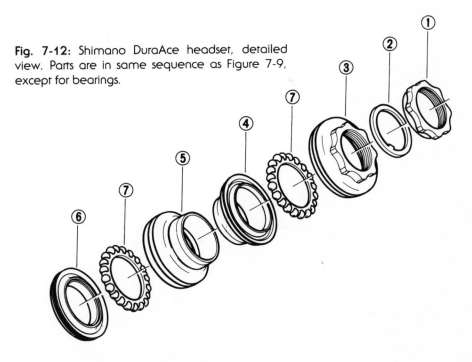

Fig. 7-12: Shimano DuraAce headset, detailed view. Parts are in same sequence as Figure 7-9, except for bearings.

Fig. 7-13: Avocet Professional headset, conventional design

Avocet makes two headsets. One is a good-quality unit, the Professional, that uses the conventional caged set of bearings and standard precision-ground races. The model is threaded for English, Italian and French threads, weighs 190 grams and costs around $18.90 (Fig. 7-13).

Another Avocet headset (Fig. 7-14) is a sealed-bearing unit that comes with a lifetime guarantee if properly installed. The unit is designed to take the heavy radial and lateral loads on headsets due to road shock, and should never require maintenance, according to Avocet. The entire headset, which uses alloy races and sealed bearings, is only 190 grams (6.7 oz.), making it one of the lightest on the market.

To install the new Avocet sealed-bearing headset, you will, of course,

Fig. 7-14: Avocet sealed-bearing headset

have to remove the old one on your current bike. Just follow the steps above as far as getting out the bearings is concerned, and add these steps:
- With a drift (tapered metal bar with a flat end), punch out the upper and lower pressed races.
- Invert the fork and tap off the crown race, moving the drift around as you tap.

To install the Avocet, all you do is push down the small flanged seal (see Fig. 7-14) where the crown race was located, and on top of that press down the bottom-bearing set. The tricky part here is that you must exert pressure *only on the inner part of the bearing* and be careful that whatever tool you are using you don't let it slip and hit the bearing seal, which could ruin it. Ideally you should use a Campy or VAR tool, which bike shops use. In discussing this problem with Avocet I suggested they supply a simple piece of pipe of the right diameter to fit over the steering tube and contact the inner-bearing race of the sealed-bearing set. Then pushing the bearing, which is a light drive fit, down over the steering tube would be a simple matter. Because steering tubes have an outside diameter of 25.4 millimeters if English, 25 millimeters if French, or 25.4 millimeters if Italian or American, a piece of straight pipe that's a bit bigger, say 1 inch, should do it. Twelve inches of 1-inch inside diameter of any kind of pipe of ferrous metal, say a gas pipe, would do just fine. Or, you can buy a crown race seating tool for about $5 (Fig. 7-15) from Phil Wood, made by Bicycle Research Products, which should work fine. That way, you can't hurt the bearing by banging on the outer retainer, the bearings themselves or the seal. The rest of the installation involves putting the rest of the stack in place—the lower and upper

Fig. 7-15: This crown-race seating tool can also be used to install the Avocet sealed bearing in place of the crown race. The tool costs around $5 from Phil Wood.

pressed fittings and the top bearing on the steering tube, and tightening down on the screwed race to drive fit the lower pieces. This set costs, at the moment, around $49.95, but it could go up, as all prices seem to be doing these days. Tightening down on the locknut completes the installation of this sealed-bearing headset. Now, with sealed hubs, pedals, rear-derailleur wheels and this new headset, the only unsealed component on your bike that requires maintenance would be the chain. Well, there is the saddle: If it's leather, it may need some attention from time to time.

SunTour (Maeda) makes a pair of excellent, high-quality headsets—one for track, Model HS-300, and one for road, Model HS-100. The track model is entirely of chrome-plated steel that takes loose balls and weighs 145 grams (5⅛ oz.); the road model is the same basic design but weighs 172 grams (6 oz.).

A Swiss Company, *Edouard & Cie*, S.A., CH-2108 Couvet, Switzerland, has introduced their line of Edco competition headsets in light alloy.

Replace Caged Bearings with Loose Ones

You can add two more balls to the races at each end if you discard the caged set and use just loose balls. The extra balls add considerably greater shock resistance than the fewer balls in the caged set. Just be careful to use balls of the same size as in the caged set (retainer). With loose balls your headset will last a lot longer.

More about Cone Fit

Although poor fit of the crown cone seems to be a plague of the less expensive bike, it should not be ruled out as a cause of steering assembly looseness, or tightness in a better bike either. Seating of the crown race is extremely critical, and if it's too loose, you can have a case of the "shakes" on a downhill run—the handlebars develop an uncontrollable "shimmy" that gets worse by the millisecond and will cause you to spill if you don't stop immediately. This type of front-wheel wobble can also be caused by loose front-wheel bearings and/or a bent fork. But the cone race must be seated very precisely in order to align the rest of the steering races and bearings. This race must seat perfectly square in the steering tube, and the lower and upper pressed races must also be exactly square with their mating crown race. It's easy to drive off the old parts, but darned difficult, without experience and costly shop tools, to get in new parts just exactly right. If you remove the fork and look at the races, you may find, particularly when caged bearings in a retainer are used, a series of symmetrically spaced dents in the raceways, corresponding to bearing location. If you see this condition, you must scrap the headset entirely, and chalk up the cost of a new headset to experience and to the certain knowledge that you will henceforth keep the headset properly adjusted. Or switch to the Avocet sealed set.

As you check headset bearing raceways, I advise you to use a good magnifying glass, such as a jeweler's loupe, and look for tiny, hairline cracks and for grooves cut into the raceways, either of which is cause for scrapping the headset. Remember, the road shock forces that impact on these small bearings can be on the order of thousands of pounds. On any day trip, if loose, the headset can receive a great many thousands of such blows, spread out among the bearings that absorb them. If the headset is adjusted for zero end play, the shock will be minimized.

Chapter Eight

PEDALS

Pedals are small. They use small ball bearings (most require $\frac{5}{32}$-in. balls) which take an awful lot of pressure and abuse for their small size. Pedals are right down there near the ground where they are exposed to considerable amounts of sand, dust and dirt, not to mention water.

Fortunately, pedals are quite simple in design and easy to take apart, clean, lubricate and reassemble. On a scheduled basis I recommend taking pedals down for maintenance at least once a year, more often if you ride a lot and certainly after every long tour.

The only way to avoid routine maintenance, aside from brushing off accumulated gunk from the outside, would be to use sealed-bearing pedals such as Hi-E, Phil Wood or Berthet which run from $85 to $100 a pair. Nonsealed, high-quality pedals can run you $50 or more a pair (a lot more if you go in for super lightweight parts, such as titanium pedals which list up to $108.98). Table 8-1 gives comparative specifications on most of the popular makes of pedals. What kind of pedals do I use? Well, I like maintenance-free bicycling, insofar as technology has it in its power to give it to me, so I use sealed-bearing pedals. I have Phil Woods on one bike, Hi-E on another. For road racing, the high-grade nonsealed bearings are preferable because they are much lighter in weight.

Because most bikes have conventional nonsealed ball-bearing pedals, and I imagine you would like to know how to maintain them, I'll cover this aspect first and then get into details on sealed-bearing and other exotic makes and designs of pedals.

As a starter, please look at Figure 8-1, a disassembled pedal with all the parts laid out on the table. Note that the tapered end of the spindle goes into the body of the pedal, from the crank side. You won't really have to worry about which way the spindle goes in; you can only do it

Table 8-1 Pedal Specifications

Make and Model	Pair Weight (grams)	Body	Spindle	Sealed Bearings	Precision Bearings	Price Pair
Campagnolo Record Road 1037	454	Steel	Steel	No	Yes	$ 46.98
Campagnolo Record Track 1038	404	Steel	Steel	No	Yes	46.98
Campagnolo Super Record Road	206	Alloy	Titanium	No	Yes	108.98
East Rochester Tool & Die Titanium	240	Alloy	Titanium	Yes	Yes	87.50
East Rochester Tool & Die	290	Alloy	Steel	Yes	Yes	62.50
Phil Wood	325	Alloy	Steel	Yes	Yes	51.00
KKT Pro Ace	460	Alloy	Steel	No	Yes	31.50
Hi-E	284	Alloy	Steel	Yes	Yes	41.00
KKT Pro Ace Track	431	Alloy	Steel	No	Yes	21.50
Barelli SS	410	Alloy	Steel	Yes	Yes	NA
Barelli B-10	NA	Alloy	Steel	Yes	Yes	NA
Shimano DD LA 100	346	Alloy	Steel	No	Yes	NA
SunTour PL 3000	335	Alloy	Steel	No	Yes	NA
SunTour PL 1000	353	Alloy	Steel	No	Yes	NA
SunTour Road VX	390	Alloy	Steel	No	Yes	NA
Lyotard 23	367	Steel	Steel	No	Yes	10.98
Lyotard 460D	325	Steel	Steel	No	No	5.98
Barelli SS	470	Stainless	Steel	Yes	Yes	54.50
Barelli B-10	350	Alloy	Steel	Yes	Yes	65.90

Fig. 8-1: Here are pedal parts: (A) body; (B) spindle; (C) bearings; (D) screwed race; (E) tanged washer; (F) locknut; (G) dust cap; (H) quill; (I) front plate.

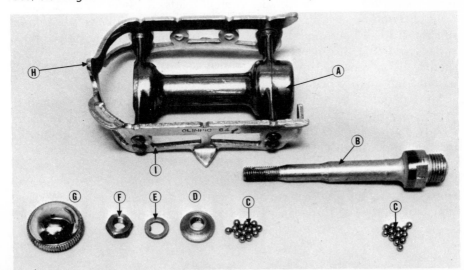

the right way for the pedal to screw back into the crank. Note that the washer (E) has a little tang. This is so the washer won't turn while you tighten the locknut (F). The washer tang fits into a groove cut into the spindle. Most pedals have twelve balls. They are loose. As you take the pedal apart, please follow the sequence below so you don't lose one or two. If one falls on the floor it will most likely never be found again, as I have pointed out earlier in this book. Take heart, however. Every bike shop worthy of the name stocks new ones.

PEDAL MAINTENANCE—STEP BY STEP

STEP ONE: *Remove pedals.* The left pedal threads off clockwise as you face it; the right threads off counterclockwise. The rule of thumb here is that pedals *always* go *on* the crank in the direction of crank rotation; *off*, opposite the direction of crank rotation. Here are pedal markings, if you are installing new ones, to tell you which is the left and right pedal:

Italian pedals: *D is right side: D stands for "Destro," or right.*
                S is left side: S stands for "Sinistro," or left.
French pedals: *D is right side: D stands for "Droit," or right.*
                G is left side: G stands for "Gauche," or left.
Spanish pedals: *D is right side: D stands for "Derecho," or right.*
                I is left side: I stands for "Izquierdo," or left.

And now for a word about pedal thread sizes. English and Italian pedal threads are $9/16 \times 20$ threads per inch (TPI). Italian thread is just a wee bit different from the English, however, so although it will fit English cut crank threads labeled $9/16 \times 20$, it will be a little tight, so you will have to use a little muscle. French cranks and pedals will probably be marked 14 mm. $\times$ 12.5 mm., which is what they are. French threads can be easily tapped out to the English $9/16 \times 20$ TPI, so don't hesitate to have this done, because the English threads are becoming standard. Some French bikes are even arriving in this country with cranks tapped the $9/16 \times 20$ TPI and pedals to match. But if you have a one-piece crank, be advised that the threads will be ½ inch by 20 TPI and the good-quality pedals are not available in this size. But then you would not install high-quality pedals on a one-piece crankset in any case.

Most pedals take a 15-millimeter thin steel wrench, long enough to exert some force, because pedals are going to be threaded in fairly tightly due to the fact that pedal rotation is in the same direction as the threads, and you will need muscle to remove them.

STEP TWO: Put the pedal in a vise (Fig. 8-2) gripping the *flats* of the axle sides on the crank side with dust cap end up. The pencil points to a dust cap. Don't grip the threads in the vise. Turn the dust cap with a small

Fig. 8-2: Step Two

screwdriver using the rattrap opening as a fulcrum, similar to where the pencil is located above. Be careful in removing the cap, so that you don't damage the knurled edges. There is a special wrench for dust cap removal; if you have a lot of bicycles to maintain it would pay to buy one. If you are working on the garden-variety rubber-steel pedal (Fig. 8-3), you can get at the locknut, etc., by removing the rubber-tread locknuts on the crank side and pulling off the entire rubber pedal assembly, after which follow the steps above and below, except the rubber treads should be replaced as above.

Fig. 8-3: Left, rattrap style of pedal with toe clip and strap. Right, conventional rubber-tread pedal. Pencil on rubber-tread pedal points to rubber-tread nut which must be removed from each tread so you can get at the bearings for maintenance.

Fig. 8-4: Step Three

Fig. 8-5: Step Four

Fig. 8-6: Step Five

STEP THREE: Remove the locknut, to which the pencil points in the photograph. On many pedals an 8-millimeter socket wrench will do the job; for others you will need a 9- or 10-millimeter wrench, or a small adjustable crescent wrench. I prefer wrenches that fit the nuts I am working on (Fig. 8-4).

STEP FOUR: Remove the splined washer (Fig. 8-5).

STEP FIVE: Remove the cone nut with a screwdriver. Count the balls so that you have the proper number to put back (Fig. 8-6).

STEP SIX: Holding the threaded portion of the pedal axle, loosen the vise and carefully pull the entire pedal out of the vise and hold it over a cloth rag on the bench top. If you are careful, you can remove the axle and leave the bearings in the races, and let them spill out on the cloth (Fig. 8-7).

Fig. 8-7: Step Six

STEP SEVEN: Clean the bearings, races, and axle in kerosene. Remove the toe strap from the toe clip, dunk the pedal body in kerosene, and clean off all road dirt, stuck-on tar, etc.

STEP EIGHT: Check the balls and races for cracks and rust. Replace balls as necessary.

STEP NINE: Put a light layer of grease, such as Lubriplate Type A (from auto supply stores) or Marine Lube grease (from boat stores), on races, and roll bearings around in a dab of grease till they're coated and clump together. Stick bearings back in the crank side of the pedal first. Make sure you have the correct count (see Step Five).

STEP TEN: Insert axle, threaded end first, into the crank side of the pedal; insert the remaining ball bearings in the dust-cap side; screw on the cone nut with a screwdriver until it's snug against the bearings (not tight), and back off about a quarter turn. Push on the splined washer and thread on the locknut. Put the pedal back in the vise, gripping the axle flats on the crank side as in Step One. Tighten the locknut. Remove from the vise and twirl the axle between thumb and forefinger to check for binding. Hold the pedal firmly and push the axle from side to side to check for looseness. If it is binding, loosen the locknut, back off the cone nut an eighth of a turn, retighten the locknut, and check again for binding. Repeat as necessary. If it is too loose so that you have sideplay, loosen the locknut, take up on cone nut an eighth of a turn, retighten the locknut, check again for sideplay, and repeat as necessary.

STEP ELEVEN: Put the pedals back on the cranks. Be careful to get the correct pedal on the correct crank, because the right side is threaded differently from the left, and if you're threading into a softer aluminum alloy crank you can strip threads easily. Also, be sure to thread on straight, using a drop or two of lube oil on threads. Don't get started cross-threaded. Alloy cranks are costly.

Remember that it has been estimated that most of us can easily exert 16 to 30 pounds of pressure on pedals, and if we learn how to lift up with one foot as we press down with the other (requires toe clips and straps) we can add another 25 pounds or so of pressure. If you are "honking" up a hill, you can add even more pressure, and if you are a trained athlete you can go up to 300 pounds.

The pedal is also vulnerable to damage if the bike falls or is knocked over. If your own bike is dumped, always check pedals for a bent spindle. Cranks are easily bent, too. You might also keep in mind that cheaper pedals do not have precision-ground races, so that they will have greater rotational friction, which makes pedaling a bit harder. Even the balls used in these pedals can be inferior.

TOE CLIPS AND STRAPS

Various tests have been made pedaling with and without toe straps and toe clips. Most of the test results show that with toe clips and straps (Fig. 8-8) you increase pedaling efficiency about 40 percent. My own experience bears this out. But just because you have toe clips and straps, and even cleats (Fig. 8-9) on your shoes (which you must have to achieve this added efficiency), you are by no means guaranteed this improved efficiency. Clips and straps alone, even with cleats, will do little for you unless you learn to pedal correctly, so that you pull *up* with one foot as you press *down* with the other. All clips, straps and cleats do for you is lock your feet in the pedals so that you can exert pedal action pretty nearly around the clock, except of course for the dead spots at 12 o'clock and 6 o'clock. There is a wide variety of shoe cleats on the market. I prefer leather ones because you can more or less walk on them without scratching anybody's floor or making a clanking sound. One problem with shoe cleats is getting them nailed onto bicycling shoes in the right location. The best rule I can give you is that you should cycle *without* them for at least 50 miles, and preferably 100 to 150 miles. This will give you time to find out the location that your feet naturally assume on the pedals. There will be a mark on your shoe soles made by the metal plate; this is the toe-to-heel location for the centerline of the tunnel of the shoe cleat. To determine how far inboard the cleat should be, center

Fig. 8-8: This is how the toe strap is threaded into a rattrap pedal with toe clip. Note that the strap adjuster is outboard of the pedal and far enough from clip top so it does not interfere with pedaling or rub on side of shoes.

Fig. 8-9: Underneath part of shoe, showing leather shoe cleat nailed to bottom, with a tunnel or groove that fits over the shoe plate. Notice also the twist of the strap, which keeps it in place.

the cleat on the pedal (have someone hold it there) and place your shoe on the cleat. (Have the bike next to a wall so you can hold yourself up.) The cleat tunnel should be right on the imprint made by the pedal on the sole of your shoe. Let your foot now assume the normal pedaling position, and have your helper then draw a line around the cleat with a white or other visible marker. Now you have the cleat more or less properly located, subject to later change if you find you are uncomfortable with this location of the cleat. Wherever I mention "shoes" I am referring to cycling shoes such as those made by Detto Pietro or by some other high-quality supplier of leather cycling shoes.

A better way to position pedals is to use shoes that already come with cleats that are adjustable in terms of location, but already fastened onto the shoes, such as the new Detto Pietro shoes from Italy. These cleats are adjustable laterally and lengthwise. As far as clips are concerned, I like the good old Christophe, or the newer Avocet Mod III, the latter of which cost $5.98 a pair and come in three sizes, small, medium and large.

Cleats come with nails, which never hold. I take mine to an Italian shoemaker who seems to understand these things, and I advise you to do the same. Then they will last. And, in the city, leave straps loose so you can get feet out fast. Tighten straps down only in the country, but loosen them if a dog appears.

Basic to this discussion of clips, straps and cleats is the proper size of toe clip. These clips come in small, medium and large lengths and you should get the size that gives you a little space, about ¼ inch at most, between the end of your shoe and the clip. A new pedal comes with an adjustable toe clip. This is the Shimano DuraAce EX Model VA-100. As you can see in Figures 8-10 and 8-11, there are three Phillips screws which, when loosened, permit the clip to move forward or backward. Maximum travel adjustment is 10 millimeters.

Fig. 8-10: The new Shimano pedal has a built-in toe clip that's adjustable fore and aft.

Fig. 8-11: Close-up of the new Shimano pedal, showing the three Phillips head screws which permit adjustment of the toe clip.

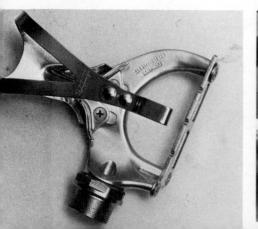

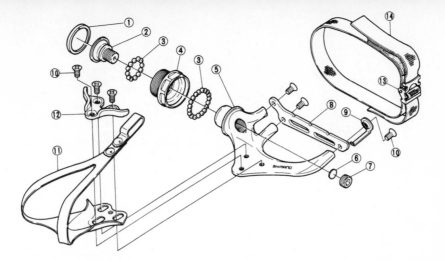

Fig. 8-12: Detailed drawing of the unique new Shimano pedal, Model VA-100. Parts are: (1) dust cap; (2) cone; (3) ⁵⁄₃₂-in. balls; (4) housing; (5) pedal body; (6) washer; (7) lock bolt; (8) side plate; (9) strap guide; (10) screw; (11) toe clip (comes in medium and large sizes); (12) front plate; (13) strap clip; (14) strap band.

These Shimano pedals have precision bearings and do not require a wrench to install. Instead you use a 6-millimeter Allen wrench, which simplifies life considerably. I should note, however, that using the new Shimano pedals requires that you install a new set of cranks on both sides, because the diameter of the spindle thread is 25 millimeters, versus 14 millimeters for conventional pedals. Chapter 6 compares these two cranks. I have used these pedals and find them quite comfortable. Bearings are sealed but easy to get at for maintenance, with very low friction. Figure 8-12 shows a detailed view.

DISASSEMBLING THE NEW SHIMANO PEDAL

Disassembling the new Shimano pedal is a fairly tedious operation; at least I found it so, compared with conventional pedals. However, this pedal does run exceptionally smoothly, and the design has a seal that although not as tightly fitting as on a conventional precision-sealed bearing, still will keep out a lot of fine, sandy, bearing-wearing stuff, without adding friction drag via the seal fit, so relubing need not be done as often as on conventional pedals. Now, here's how to disassemble the Shimano DD pedals.

STEP ONE: Remove the strap. Remove the toe clips by unscrewing the three Phillips head screws. There is just no way you are going to take this pedal apart conveniently without these steps. Figure 8-13 shows the toe clip removed.

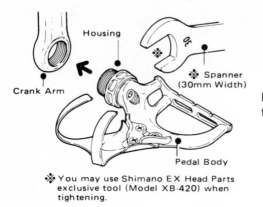

Housing

Crank Arm

✳ Spanner
(30mm Width)

Pedal Body

✳ You may use Shimano EX Head Parts
exclusive tool (Model XB-420) when
tightening.

Fig. 8-13: Removing Shimano pedal from crank

STEP TWO: Remove the pedal from the crank with a 30-millimeter wrench (Fig. 8-13). (You can install the pedal with the Allen wrench, but do not remove it with that wrench.)

STEP THREE: Before I forget, I counted 14 ⁵⁄₃₂-inch (2.5 mm.) balls in the inner cone and 18 in the outer cone. In case you lose one (or two or three). With a 5-millimeter Allen wrench in the locknut (refer to Fig. 8-12) and a 6-millimeter Allen wrench holding the cone (outer side), turn the locknut clockwise and remove it. Catch the tiny spacing washer (part 6 in Fig. 8-12) as the locknut comes out. Don't lose it; your dealer will have a tough time replacing it until Shimano stocks build up on this new pedal. If you do lose it, it will help if you ask for Shimano part number 461 0800.

STEP FOUR: The locknut, part 2 in Figure 8-12, holds the whole shebang together. Holding the cone with the 6-millimeter Allen wrench, turn the locknut counterclockwise one or two turns, just enough to take pressure off the cone threads (no. 4 in Fig. 8-12). Figure 8-14 illustrates the position of the two Allen wrenches. The locknut is going to be really tight, believe me, so use some muscle on it. You may have to put the 6-millimeter wrench in a vise. Once the locknut is loose, back out on the cone with the 6-millimeter Allen wrench, and the works will come apart (Fig. 8-15). Be ready to catch balls. Clean and regrease.

STEP FIVE: Stick balls back in a layer of grease in the right-side housing (part 4, Fig. 8-12). Now, you may think you can do the same with the left side of the housing, but you can't because the cone won't go in that way. You have to stick the balls back in a layer of grease on the cone itself and reassemble as follows:

STEP ONE: Refer to Figure 8-12 and to the set of fourteen balls at the left, next to the cone, part 4. These are the balls you have to stick on the

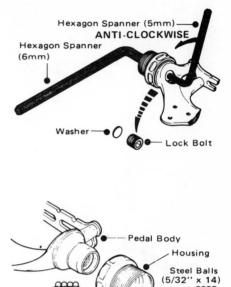

Fig. 8-14: Disassembling Shimano pedals requires two Allen wrenches.

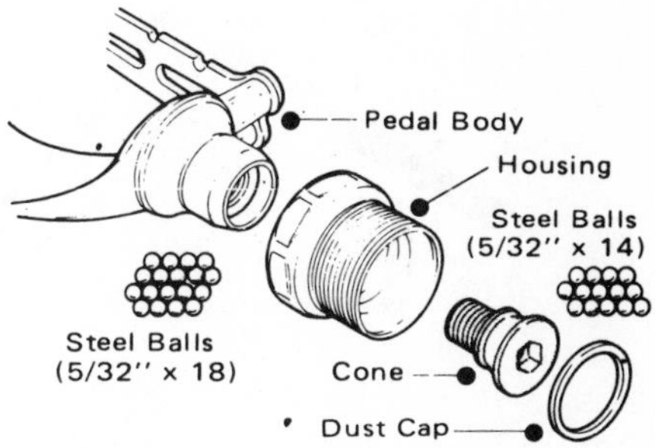

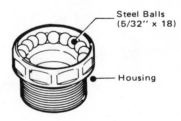

Fig. 8-15: Location of bearings and races in Shimano pedal

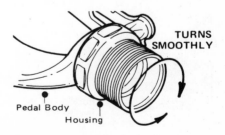

Fig. 8-16: Housing of Shimano pedal goes on inboard side of pedal.

Fig. 8-17: Check housing for binding on Shimano pedal.

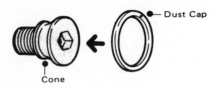

Dust Cap

Cone

Fig. 8-18: Installation of outer cone and dust cap.

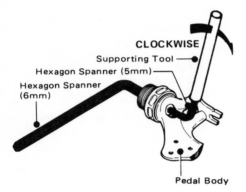

CLOCKWISE

Supporting Tool

Hexagon Spanner (5mm)

Hexagon Spanner (6mm)

Pedal Body

Fig. 8-19: Adjusting races on Shimano pedal.

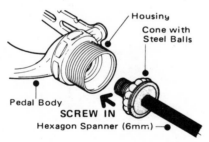

Housing

Cone with Steel Balls

Pedal Body

SCREW IN

Hexagon Spanner (6mm)

Fig. 8-20: Installing righthand (outboard) race requires that balls be held in place by grease on race, so that race can be installed in housing.

(Dia. 11)

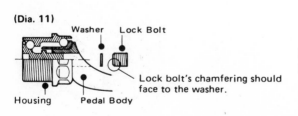

Washer   Lock Bolt

Lock bolt's chamfering should face to the washer.

Housing   Pedal Body

Fig. 8-21: Installing lock bolt in Shimano pedal

• Strap Use

1. Position the strap as shown in diagram. (Dia. 1)
   Ensure the "velcro" fixing system is facing outwards. (Dia. 2)

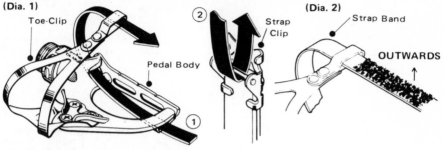

(Dia. 1) Toe-Clip Pedal Body
② Strap Clip Strap Band
(Dia. 2) OUTWARDS

Fig. 8-22: Installation of strap in Shimano pedal

cone. Okay, now we have balls inside the housing and on the cone. Fourteen on the cone, eighteen in the housing. Now, holding the pedal body (platform) in one hand (left hand if you are right-handed), put the left-side housing back onto the right-side housing, holding pedal upright with your other hand. Still holding the pedal, take the cone with balls held by grease, and with the flat washer on the end, held with grease, and put it inside the housing (part 4) and gently, by hand, turn the cone clockwise until it is hand tightened. With the Allen wrench (6 mm.) tighten the cone so that it is just snug. Then tighten the locknut. Check for binding or looseness. *Adjustment of the cone does not depend on adjustment of the lockbolt!* Adjust cone to remove binding or looseness, then tighten lockbolt. Shimano recommends tightening it to 55 to 77 feet pounds. No wonder it was so hard to get loose! The lockbolt holds whatever adjustment you have made on the cone. Reinstall toe clip.

STEP TWO: Install the toe strap. Figure 8-22 shows how. The strap should have its Velcro fixing system facing outward. Now, about this strap: I don't like it. There are kinder ways to say this, but I want to get to the point. It's hell to adjust, is stiff, and does not stay put. It rubs on the crank as the crank turns. I replaced this strap with a conventional leather strap with proper adjusting and all was well. I grant that the Velcro theory is nice, but in practice I just don't have the patience to fool with it. Figure 8-9, by the way, shows the leather strap twisted one turn. This avoids the strap "droop" shown in Figure 8-8. When you replace the top clip, remember that the front plate (part 12, Fig. 8-12) goes on top of the toe clip. If you lose one of these special beveled screws, reference to Shimano part number 000 1900 will help your dealer order more. Figures 8-13 to 8-22 illustrate major steps in assembly and disassembly. A final word about bearing adjustment: If you have binding or looseness, you have to back off on the lockbolt before making any adjustments. Then retighten the lockbolt.

Chapter Nine
FREEWHEEL MAINTENANCE

With the freewheel removed from the hub (in Chapter 5), you should do basic maintenance on it. With a toothbrush and kerosene, remove all old, accumulated, caked-on grease and dirt from the cogs. Then dunk the freewheel in *clean* kerosene and shake vigorously to get dirt out of its innards. If the freewheel has seals, you can skip the dunking step.

Then squirt on a *very* light oil, such as Chainlube (but do not use any aerosol lubricant that comes out depositing a layer of grease). Inside the freewheel (Fig. 9-1) are dozens of tiny balls that must rotate freely, and a layer of grease could cause them to bind. Further, the pawls must be free to turn or at least move (Fig. 9-1) so as to ratchet against the freewheel body ratchet gear (Fig. 9-2).

Sometimes, fairly rarely, you will start pedaling and nothing will happen. Pedals will spin but the bike stays put. What has happened, once you are sure the chain is on the cogs and not broken, is that a piece of dirt has gotten between the pawls and the ratchet body, so that the pawls are held closed. This lets the freewheel spin around uselessly. The purpose of the pawls is to let the freewheel turn in one direction, as when you are coasting, but not in the other direction, as when you are pedaling. If you are on the road and the pawls get stuck, causing this to happen, bum some kerosene or some sort of nonflammable solvent (well, I guess Listerine would work although it has alcohol in it, which makes it flammable, so be careful) and flush out the freewheel. Don't get any on the tire. I know I mentioned this earlier, but it bears repeating. Spin the freewheel as you dunk it until the pawls work free and

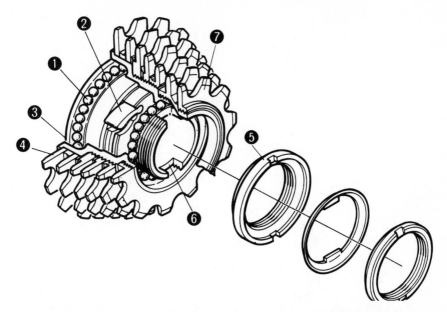

Fig. 9-1: Detailed view of the new SunTour Ultra-7 seven-speed freewheel. Parts are: (1) raceways on inner and outer ends; (2) ratcheted pawl (heat treated to withstand stress of reverse rotation when pedal torque is applied); (3) heat-treated body; (4) sprocket teeth are slant cut to help smoother, more precise chain shift from one cog to another; (5) adjusting cone nut (Note that this freewheel has **two** adjusting nuts [most have one], the cone nut and the locknut with lock washer.); (6) inner freewheel body with grooves for removal tool (Use SunTour tool designed for this freewheel.); (7) a 12-tooth high-gear cog is available for racing. Please also take note of the many small ball bearings that must be tucked back in place without benefit of grease to hold them. Disassembly of any freewheel requires a watchmaker's patience and dexterity.

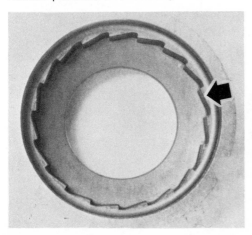

Fig. 9-2: Ratcheted teeth against which spring-loaded pawls open to keep freewheel from turning when you pedal, let the hub turn when you coast.

catch. If they don't work free, you may have a broken pawl spring. Some freewheels have only one spring, others have a tiny phosphor bronze spring behind each pawl. In any case, now you will need a replacement freewheel, if on the road, since it's unlikely you will find a replacement set of springs in the boonies. But if you are near a town of any size, the local bike shop can fix the freewheel for you or, of course, furnish a replacement.

I don't like freewheels with seals; they are almost always a drag, until worn in, at least. But on the other hand the seals do keep out dirt from the pawl mechanism, so perhaps the drag is worth the protection. I prefer freewheels with tightly fitting components so seals aren't all that necessary. Regina, SunTour, Atom, Normandy are a few of the brands that come to mind that are top-grade freewheels. Of those with wide gear ratios with cogs that go from 13 or 14 up to 34 teeth, I like the SunTour and the Shimano alternate-tooth sprocket type, in which every other tooth on the two lower gears is missing to make the chain jump to this extreme angle more efficient. Shimano also has a new approach involving what they call a "UniGlide" freewheel, on which the teeth are slightly twisted so as to guide the chain more accurately onto the gears. My experience with this model freewheel is that it works quite smoothly, is a bit quieter with shifting (less gear grind if you don't shift accurately the first time because the chain tends to go to a cog and not hang up in between) and a bit easier shifting to a lower gear if you forget and don't shift until the pedaling gets hard. You should always shift down before you have to, though. It's easier on the chain, chainwheel, derailleurs and your nerves. The UniGlide as of this writing goes to 32 teeth on the low-gear side.

Sprocket combinations for the Shimano FG-100 UniGlide freewheel are:

Type	Standard Sprocket Combinations (Teeth)				
5DS	15	17	19	21	24
5DW	14	17	20	24	28
5DUW	14	17	21	26	32

Sprocket combinations for the Shimano Alternate-Tooth Sprocket freewheel are:

Type	Standard Sprocket Combinations (Teeth)				
5AW	14	17	20	24	28*
5AUW	14	17	21	26*	32*
5AUS	14	17	22	28*	34*

* Alternate-tooth sprocket

You may have noticed that I have refrained from giving instructions about disassembling freewheels. To do so you will need special tools, an awful lot of patience sticking all those little balls back in without benefit of grease to hold them, and no reason outside of curiosity to undertake the project. If the pawls stick, you know how to clean them. If a pawl spring breaks, you won't be able to replace it on the road and so should buy a new freewheel. In all the thousands of miles I have traveled in this country and in Europe I have yet to have a pawl spring break on me. So this is a fairly remote possibility. All you need to do is clean out the freewheel itself, and spray a little *light* oil on it every month or so. Aim oil at the bearing area, on both sides.

OTHER FREEWHEELS

Regina makes a very interesting close-ratio seven-speed freewheel, the Titall, which requires 140 millimeters—well, perhaps 136 millimeters will fit if you have the right frame—between dropouts, and a correspondingly long locknut-to-locknut hub. The new freewheel weighs only 10.5 ounces, (297.7 grams) and has cogs of 13, 14, 15, 16, 18, 19 and 21 teeth. The first three cogs are titanium, the last three are aluminum, hence the name Titall. The first three cogs are threaded on, the rest fit over the splined body of the freewheel. You can also get 12-to-6-tooth cogs. The cost: $210 or so, depending on dealer markup.

Cog-to-cog width is 32 millimeters, so cogs are a little more closely spaced than a more conventional freewheel. I would recommend that you use the Regina Record chain with maximum width at the rivets of 7.9 millimeters or the SunTour 7.3-millimeter Ultra Six chain. Other chains can run to 9.5 or even 1 millimeter at the rivet, and could rub between cogs on this freewheel. The Titall requires a special remover, so buy one when you buy the unit.

If you change to any wider freewheel body, say going from a five- to a six- or seven-speed freewheel, you will have to re-dish the wheel slightly, as I noted earlier. This is because the rim must be centered between the locknuts (locknut-to-locknut distance) *not between the hub flanges.* (See Chapter 10 on wheel truing.) In other words, the rim, to be centered in the bicycle, must be centered between the dropout inside dimension or the locknut to locknut distance, which should be the same dimension. See Chapter 10 for dishing instructions, and Fig. 5-27 for locknut-to-locknut measurement. "Dishing" means pulling the wheel slightly to the right by tightening spoke nipples of the spokes on the right side, leading from hub flange to rim.

SunTour has a new freewheel, the Ultra Six, and, as noted above, a new narrower chain to go with it. Their six-speed freewheel will fit on a normal 120-millimeter locknut-to-locknut hub, made for a five-speed freewheel. This means you can switch over to a six-speed cluster with this freewheel without having to change to a longer axle, assuming of course that your dropouts will handle the longer width. Bikes built for five speeds have 120 millimeters between the inner surfaces of the drop-outs. Frames built for six speeds have 125- or 126-millimeter spacing, and frames built for seven-speed freewheels have a still wider distance, from 130 to 140 millimeters. These newer, narrower, freewheel-and-chain combinations now let you increase your choice of gears without having to buy a new frame. If you have a long touring frame you usually won't have to be concerned about chain clearance between the chain when on the high gear and the inside of the chainstay. On some bikes, the chainstay is rounded and not flattened, which will probably cause chain rub on the small (high-speed) cog. You can sometimes get by with a spacer: You simply remove the spacer from between the left-side lock-nut washer and cone nut and move it over to the freewheel side on the axle. If adding spacers to the axle means you have to force the stays apart so the axle will fit in, don't do it if you have a fine frame. And don't let anyone else do it. If the chainstay is flattened where the high-gear cog rotates (a very slight flattening), you will probably have clearance for the wider freewheel with more cogs. The SunTour Ultra-Six free-wheel is 26.5 millimeters between cogs, and this is a six-speed free-wheel, remember, so it will fit onto a 120-millimeter axle where your five-speed freewheel now resides. The Ultra-Six weighs 510 grams (18 oz.) and has cogs from 14 to 32 teeth. The model I tested has cogs of 13, 15, 17, 21, 26 and 32 teeth. Figure 9-3 shows that the six-speed free-wheel fits nicely on the five-speed hub, with only a 2-millimeter greater width than the five-speed; plenty of space for the chain.

If you have a six-speed hub and chainstay clearance to match an axle of 126 millimeters you can now go to a seven-speed freewheel without concern about chain clearance. The normal six-speed freewheel re-

Fig. 9-3: SunTour's new Ultra-6 freewheel fits onto a five-speed hub, as shown.

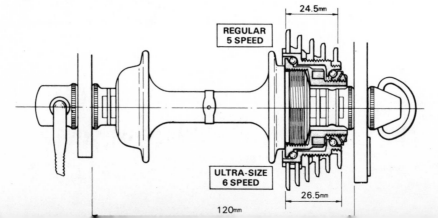

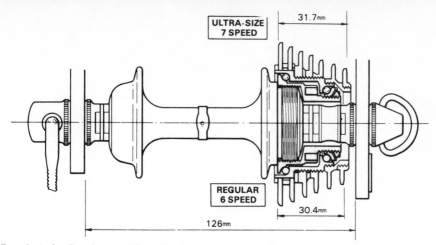

ULTRA-SIZE 7 SPEED

31.7mm

REGULAR 6 SPEED

30.4mm

126mm

Fig. 9-4: SunTour's new Ultra-7 **seven**-speed hub fits onto a six-speed hub. Now, if you have a triple chainwheel, you can be the only one in town with a 21-speed bicycle.

quires a 126-millimeter locknut-to-locknut distance. As Figure 9-4 shows, the Ultra Seven-Speed will fit the six-speed hub without adding more than 1.3 millimeters of width to the cluster, which should and most likely will give you plenty of chain clearance. For the close-ratio buff with big leg muscles and the cardiovascular system of a sixteen-year-old, these freewheels also come with cogs of 13, 14, 15, 16, 17 and 18 teeth, and the seven-speed model can accept a high gear of 12 teeth. Figure 9-1 shows a detailed view of a close-ratio version of the seven-speed model. See the caption for further details. Teeth on the new freewheels are "slant cut" which, according to SunTour, helps move the chain from one gear to another more smoothly and accurately. Shimano has a similar and more pronounced slant on a few of their freewheels.

A Warning about Threading Freewheels

From the footnote in Table 5-2, you will note the threading specifications for hubs threaded English, Italian and French. When you purchase a freewheel to mount on your good aluminum alloy hub, you need to remember two things. First, the hub boss, where the threads are located, is aluminum (see Fig. 9-5). Again, I repeat, these threads are a-l-u-m-i-n-u-m. They are very soft compared to the hardened steel of the free-wheel body. If when you thread the freewheel, it's cocked at even a very slight angle you may strip the threads on the hub. So be careful to thread the freewheel on straight.

Fig. 9-5: Threads on an aluminum alloy hub, even forged alloy, are a lot softer than the steel of a freewheel. So thread a freewheel on and off carefully, and make sure you don't use English threads on one piece and French threads on another. They don't mix and will ruin hub. Arrow points to threads.

About Interchangeability

From Table 5-2, you will note that the English-threaded hubs are 1.370 inches by 24 threads per inch, and that the Italian-threaded hubs are 35 millimeters by 24 threads per inch (TPI). Now if you multiply 1.370 × 25.4 to transform the English to metric, you come up with an English hub in metric terms of 34.799 millimeters, very close to the 35 millimeters of the Italian hub threading. Because the TPI is the same, but the Italian hub is 0.201 millimeters bigger than the English hub, it is reasonable to assume that an Italian-threaded freewheel will fit, albeit somewhat loosely, on the 0.201-millimeter smaller English threaded hub. It will fit and work okay.

Going the other way, if you bought an Italian bike on your last trip to Milan, and the *hub* is threaded Italian, and now you want to put an *English*-threaded freewheel on that hub, will it fit? The answer is, maybe. It's yes if you are terribly careful not to start threading the freewheel on cocked but get it on straight. You will have some slight forcing to do, because you will be cutting 0.201-millimeter deeper threads on the softer aluminum Italian-threaded hub with the hard steel of the slightly smaller English-threaded freewheel, but you can do it. I don't recommend the practice, but this is out of sheer perfectionism, not because it isn't fairly easy to do.

Worn Cogs and New Chains Don't Mix (and Vice Versa)

If you ride enough, eventually friction will wear freewheel and chainwheel cog teeth so they start to develop a slight "hangover," like a small inverted "L"—a tiny "lip" at the top of the tooth. This alone will cause the chain to be hard to shift or to jump from cog to cog. Even if the teeth are not worn down this far, though, a more subtle problem occurs when you install a new freewheel set of cogs (you can keep the old body, just change the cogs. We humans should be so lucky). The chain will have stretched and become worn, and with the new cogs, you can have the chain jumping from one freewheel cog to another, with a pronounced and very annoying jerk, especially when you strain on the pedals. I recommend that you install a new chain when you change cogs. After all, if the cogs are worn, it stands to reason that the chain is worn and stretched also, other things being equal.

How to Remove Your Freewheel

If you break a spoke on the freewheel side, you will need to take off your freewheel to remove that spoke.

Fig. 9-6: A few of the many styles of freewheel removers. Arrow points to the thin-walled Phil Wood splined remover that removes freewheels without having to remove the locknut on the freewheel side.

STEP ONE: Make sure that you have the proper tool for your freewheel. The bike shop will need to know the make and model. Don't use a tool that has the two teeth chewed up. The tool must fit exactly and snugly into the two notches of the freewheel. If you round off one of the gripping edges on the tool, file it down flat or, using a sharp chisel, with the tool in a vise, try chipping the gripping edges off square. Or buy a new tool. Figure 9-6 shows just some of the great variety of freewheel removers. There's no standardization at all among freewheel manufacturers in this respect. If the tool won't fit over the lockring, remove it. See Chapter 5, Figs. 5-2 and 5-3.

STEP TWO: Insert the remover jaws in the freewheel, insert the quick-release skewer (or axle nuts) and tighten down the freewheel. Back off about a one-quarter turn so that you turn the wrench (Fig. 9-8). You will have room for the freewheel body to turn. With the wrench on the remover, turn counterclockwise until the freewheel is loose. You will have to turn hard. Then loosen the quick-release just a bit more, turn the remover and by now you should be able to remove the skewer and turn the tool by hand. Be careful as you approach the end of the hub freewheel boss threads. At this point, hold the freewheel weight in your hands so that as you unscrew those last two or three delicate aluminum threads on the boss, you don't damage them.

About Fitting a Freewheel

The arrow in Figure 9-7 points to a Phil Wood splined freewheel remover that fits mating splines in freewheels such as the splined Regina, Shimano and Zeus 2000. This is a neat tool, it's thin enough to fit right into the freewheel without having to remove the locknut on the free-

Fig. 9-7: To remove freewheel (nonsplined type) insert tool, hold in place with slightly loose quick-release, with other end in vise or cogs between wood in vise, and turn wrench counterclockwise.

Fig. 9-8: Here's a damaged freewheel remover. Damage can occur in two ways: (1) use of the wrong tool; (2) tool not held firmly enough by quick-release so it can pop out and tear off teeth. Freewheel can also be damaged the same way, except that if this happens you will have to tear down the freewheel all the way to the basic shell and remove it with a pipe wrench over cloth. If you go this route, do it over a large cloth to catch the tiny balls that will come spilling out of the freewheel.

wheel side. Also, you don't have to use the quick-release to hold it down. Just stick the remover in a vise, put the freewheel down over it, grasp the tire and twist counterclockwise and off it comes.

I found out the hard way never to put a freewheel on a hub unless I was sure I could get it off. Because once you pedal, you really tighten down on the freewheel where it threads onto the hub boss. For example, I blithely screwed a splined freewheel onto a Hi-E hub. Clearances are so tight between that hub's spacer and the inside of the freewheel that I could not get a remover in there. I had to dismantle the freewheel, remove everything, balls and all, right down to the basic freewheel shell, to get that baby off that hub. Never again! Now I check first to make sure I can get a tool in there to get the freewheel off before I go about threading it on tight. By the way, Figure 9-8 shows what happens to a remover that doesn't fit or is allowed to get too loose. You can also mangle the indents in the freewheel.

You also have to make sure that the freewheel will clear the shoulder of the hub flange. Some flange bosses have wider or deeper shoulders (the raised part just behind the threads) than others, and when you tighten down the freewheel it rubs on the shoulder, sometimes so tightly the freewheel can't turn. In any case, the freewheel *must* rotate freely and not rub on anything. Some combinations of freewheels and hubs just won't work for this reason. I can't give you particular combinations, there are too many; just be aware that the problem does exist.

To Remove Cogs from Freewheel

The cog remover in Figure 5-6 is simply a long piece of metal with about six inches of chain fastened at one end. To remove cogs from a freewheel mounted on a hub laced in a wheel, just put the left side of the hub, with the quick-release skewer removed, in a vise around the locknut. Use the tool, as shown in Figure 5-6, on the small (high-gear) cog, rotating it *clockwise* to remove the cog. On some freewheels the rest of the cogs fit onto a spline of the freewheel body and can be slid off after the first cog is removed. Others require unscrewing two or even *all* of the cogs. Keep track of any spacers between cogs; they must go back in the way they came out so that the correct distance between cogs is maintained. Otherwise the chain will hang up on any cog that's too close to the next one.

Chapter Ten

Wheel Lacing and Truing

For any of a number of reasons, you may want to "lace" up a wheel. Your rim may develop a flat spot after a hard jolt and rotate with an annoying "thump, thump, thump." You may wish to upgrade your wheels, change from steel to aluminum rims, change hubs, replace spokes or simply build up a new set of wheels. You may want tubular tires for local touring over good roads, and another set of clincher-tired wheels for long-distance touring over a variety of good and bad road conditions. So if you already have either a set of clinchers or tubulars, you can buy a pair of rims for one or the other, a set of good hubs, enough spokes and nipples and build your own wheels.

If you have a bike shop build your wheels, you'll pay from $15 to $30 for lacing and truing to commercial standards, exclusive of parts. For a more exacting job to professional European road-racing standards, you'll pay more, because to lace and true to those requirements takes at least three hours. Bicycle shops that cater to the racing trade in this country charge around $40 for labor alone just to lace and true a set of racing wheels. It would, of course, be courting disaster for a racing cyclist, especially one who in Europe depends on his equipment for his livelihood (as much as $150,000 a year), to have anything but the most painstakingly accurately laced and trued wheels. In fact, there is at least one reported instance of a professional wheel builder in England taking forty hours to build a pair of wheels for European racing! I will say, categorically, and this is going to raise a lot of eyebrows, that any bike mechanic who claims he can build and true a wheel in fifteen minutes, and some do, can't possibly be doing anything more than a minimum job. That's the kind of wheel building that will buy you wheels that go untrue quickly, cause permanent flat spots in the rim and ultimate spoke breakage. I urge you to learn how to lace and true your own wheels, then you can be as finicky as you please, take all the time you want and come up with wheels that will stay "true" to you indefinitely, with perhaps minor touching up after the first 200 miles.

We will discuss wheel lacing or building (they're synonymous terms) and truing, after which we will take up more exotic wheel building such as radial spoking, tying and soldering spokes and various spoking arrangements.

Wheel building seems difficult, but once you get the hang of it, it's really quite simple. I still recall the time I saw a math prof busy with compass, protractor and slide rule, figuring out all the spoke angles so he could lace a wheel; he computed spoke angles, but not how to lace. Then I recall the time I was taught by an old-timer (who was taught by *his* grandfather) to lace a wheel. The lesson took exactly ten minutes. I have taught a twelve-year-old boy to lace a wheel in ten minutes, and *he* can still lace a wheel. Remember just one thing while you're learning. Forget about the·maze and mess of loose spokes flopping around you as you lace, and learn to concentrate *only* on the spoke you're working with and its preceding spoke.

SPOKES

I've nothing against other brands, but I prefer French-made Robergel spokes because they're stronger and used by racing cyclists in this country and abroad. You can buy Robergel spokes from Bikecology if you can't find them locally (see Appendix for addresses). Robergel spokes come in three types: *Etoile,* of stainless steel, plain gauge (not thicker or "butted" at the ends). Etoile spokes have a tensile strength of 14,930 to 16,369 pounds per square inch. Robergel Sport spokes are butted stainless steel with a tensile strength of 19,900 to 21,300 lbs./sq. in. (Table 10-1). Trois Etoiles spokes are butted stainless chrome nickel, with a tensile strength of 17,068 to 18,500 lbs./sq. in. The Trois Etoiles spokes will stay better looking longer, but the Sport spokes are stronger and I prefer them. Other good spokes are Berg-Union, made in Germany.

I don't recommend mixing different brands of spokes in the same wheel. Spokes of different brands are made of different metals. High-quality spokes are of high-tensile-strength stainless steels; cheap spokes are little better than drawn wire. Mixing different spokes means that there will be variations in "modulus of elasticity" (stretch) and tensile strength at random places in your wheel, so it will be next to impossible to adjust spokes to keep wheel rim in perfect alignment, and even to keep the weaker spokes from breaking. And spoke nipples aren't always interchangeable either.

Table 10-1   Robergel Spoke Lengths

Inches	Millimeters
$10^{15}\!/_{16}$	278
11	280
$11\frac{1}{8}$	282
$11\frac{5}{8}$	295
$11\frac{3}{4}$	298
$11^{13}\!/_{16}$	300
$11\frac{7}{8}$	302
12	305
$12\frac{1}{16}$	306
$12\frac{1}{8}$	308

If you change to a low-flange from a high-flange hub, you may need longer spokes, unless you lace three cross, for example.

Table 10-2 gives spoke size in relation to hub size and spoke crossings —two, three or four. This table is fairly accurate. The problem of accurate selection of spoke size will never be solved by any table, however, because there are dozens of brands of hubs, and even so-called standard high- and low-flange hubs do not have spoke holes spaced the same distance from the hub-axle housing. The problem isn't particularly great, though, because as long as you can get at least half the spoke threads in the nipple, the spoke can be made to fit. I just want you to know that this table is more of a reasonable indication than an exact specification of which length of spoke to order to lace your particular combination of rim and hub. For example, a ferruled rim may take a slightly shorter spoke than a nonferruled rim using a washer over the spoke hole (see discussion of these rims below).

A wood-filled rim, such as a Milremo Weltmeister, uses a spoke about an eighth of an inch longer than a non-wood-filled rim, given the same hub; so you'd add an eighth of an inch to the spoke regardless of the number of spoke holes and crossing. This is because the nipple head seats on the rim section just underneath the tire, instead of in the center section of the rim (Fig. 10-1). Also, you will notice that the chart breaks down rims and hubs by country. Rims and hubs given for the U.S.A. are the common garden-variety all-steel rims and low-flange hubs used on one-, two-, and three-speed hubs with and without coaster brakes. The 27-inch wheels are, however, presented first because these are, I hope, the sizes you are mostly involved with. In addition, if by some quirk of the manufacturer, your spokes are too short or too long, Table 10-1 gives the size range of Robergel spokes in inches and millimeters so you can go up or down one size, as you need to. If, as is the case in the smaller

Table 10-2 Spoke Length Selection Chart

Rim (in.)		Hub	Holes	Cross	Spoke Length (in.) Front	Rear
Tubular Tires and 700C wired-on tires	$27 \times 1\frac{1}{8}$	Hi*	24	2	$11\frac{5}{8}$	$11\frac{5}{8}$
		Hi*	28	3	12	12
		Hi	28	3	12	$11\frac{15}{16}$
		Hi	32	3	$11\frac{13}{16}$	$11\frac{3}{4}$
		Hi	36	3	$11\frac{5}{8}$	$11\frac{1}{2}$
		Hi	36	4	12	12
		Hi*	36	4	$12\frac{1}{16}$	$12\frac{1}{16}$
		Lo	28	3	$12\frac{1}{16}$	$12\frac{1}{16}$
		Lo	32	3	$11\frac{13}{16}$	$11\frac{3}{4}$
		Lo	36	3	$11\frac{5}{8}$	$11\frac{1}{2}$
		Lo	36	4	$12\frac{1}{16}$	$12\frac{1}{16}$
		Lo	40	4	$11\frac{7}{8}$	$11\frac{13}{16}$
Tires, English Sizes	$26 \times 1\frac{3}{8}$ $26 \times 1\frac{1}{4}$		36	3	11	11
			36	4	$11\frac{1}{4}$	$11\frac{1}{4}$
			40	4	—	$11\frac{1}{8}$
			36	3	$11\frac{3}{16}$	$11\frac{3}{16}$
			32	3	$11\frac{13}{16}$	—
			40	4	—	$11\frac{3}{8}$
			36	3	$11\frac{1}{4}$	$11\frac{1}{4}$
			36	4	$11\frac{1}{2}$	$11\frac{1}{2}$
			40	3	—	$11\frac{1}{4}$
			40	4	$11\frac{7}{16}$	$11\frac{7}{16}$
Tires, Lightweight, Hi-Pressure	$27 \times 1\frac{1}{4}$	Hi	28	3	$12\frac{1}{16}$	12
		Hi	32	3	$11\frac{7}{8}$	$11\frac{13}{16}$
		Hi	36	3	$11\frac{3}{16}$	$11\frac{3}{4}$
		Hi	36	4	$12\frac{1}{8}$	$12\frac{1}{8}$
		Hi	40	3	$11\frac{5}{8}$	$11\frac{5}{8}$
		Hi	40	4	12	12
		Lo	28	3	$12\frac{1}{8}$	$12\frac{1}{8}$
		Lo	32	3	$12\frac{1}{16}$	12
		Lo	36	3	12	$11\frac{7}{8}$
		Lo	36	4	$12\frac{1}{8}$	$12\frac{1}{8}$
		Lo	40	3	$11\frac{13}{16}$	$11\frac{13}{16}$
		Lo	40	4	$12\frac{1}{16}$	$12\frac{1}{16}$
Tires, U.S.A. Sizes	26×2.125	CB	36	3	10	10
		CB	36	4	$10\frac{5}{8}$	$10\frac{5}{8}$
		3S	36	3	10	10
		3S	36	4	$10\frac{5}{8}$	$10\frac{5}{8}$
	26×1.35	3S				
		CB	36	4	$11\frac{7}{16}$	$11\frac{7}{16}$
	$26 \times 1\frac{3}{8}$	3S				
		CB	36	4	$10\frac{7}{8}$	$10\frac{7}{8}$
	26×1.75	3S	36	3	$10\frac{5}{8}$	$10\frac{5}{8}$
		CB	36	4	$10\frac{7}{8}$	$10\frac{7}{8}$
	$26\frac{1}{2} \times 1\frac{1}{2}$	3S/				
		CB	36	4	$11\frac{1}{8}$	$11\frac{1}{8}$

* Track rims: Hi = Hi Flange; Lo = Lo Flange.
3S is Three Speed; CB is Coaster Brake.

Fig. 10-1: As you look at a rim, you will note that every other spoke hole is near one side of the rim, as shown here. Some rims (very few) have spoke holes drilled at an angle, so nipples can follow spokes in tangential (cross 1, 2, 3 or 4) lacing, minimizing stress and the potential of spoke breakage. If rims don't have angled nipple holes, you can angle them yourself, if you're careful. Also some rims have the first hole to the right of the valve hole on top, others on the bottom. The direction in which you twist the rim after the first nine spokes depends on the location of the first hole to the right of valve hole. The objective is to twist the rim so as to keep the valve **between** groups of four spokes instead of within a group, where the valve will be harder to get at with a pump or air hose. But if you have laced up a wheel with the valve inside a group of four spokes, I would not relace, because the valve won't be **that** hard to get at. Experts can tell at a glance that you goofed, but 99 percent of bike riders won't know (until they get this far in this book).

wheel sizes, you must use other than Robergel spokes, I suggest Berg-Union or Torrington. I have left out wheels smaller than twenty-six inches since they would be mostly for the juvenile market.

STRENGTH OF WHEELS

Properly laced wheels, even the light tubular-tire rim type, are very strong. I ran into a parked car head-on at about twelve miles an hour once, and the front wheel never even varied from true, yet I hit with sufficient force to bend a very strong Reynolds butted '531' tubing fork. (I varied from "true" for about ten minutes.)

A 40-spoke wheel weighing only 27 ounces was tested for maximum axle loading. The wheel sustained an axle load of more then 1,200 pounds, after which the wheel showed a permanent slight buckle. Since the buckling occurred at a pressure more than 700 times the weight of the wheel, it can be said that this wheel can safely sustain a working load of about 700 pounds at smooth riding conditions. Because the *average* cyclist weighs certainly no more than 180 pounds, we can assume this wheel is amply strong enough for racing on smooth roads and for touring even on fairly rough roads, such as cobblestone streets. But don't count on not putting a permanent crimp in your rim if you hit a pothole! I recall two of my own accidents, one in which I hit a crack in a bridge and the other in which I hit a parked car once again. Both times I used the same 3½-ounce Hi-E aluminum alloy hub, 32 spokes crossed 3 with an alloy rim. The second accident did put a crimp in the rim but the hub held up fine (I wish I had).

WHEEL LACING STEPS

Let's start wheel building with a few basic observations about rims and hubs. First, to make life complicated, rims and hubs have spoke holes drilled off-center. Figure 10-1 shows that rim spoke holes are drilled so that every other hole is closer to one side of the rim than to the other side. Please keep that in mind as we proceed, because we'll come back to it. Next, study Figure 10-2; note that hub holes are also drilled off-center; that is, the hubs in one flange are offset from the holes in the facing flange. If you poke a spoke down a hub hole from the top flange, straight up and down, it will land *between* the spokes in the bottom flange of the hub. Check this for yourself and bury it in your memory. Finally, and this is also important, pick up your hub and look at the spoke holes closely. You'll notice, as in Figure 10-2, that if you have a fine hub such as a Campagnolo alloy Record, Phil Wood, or Hi-E, every other hub hole is countersunk. This countersinking is to permit the spoke to bend gradually and to eliminate a sharp corner that would stress the spoke at this point, and contribute to premature spoke break- age. At first, though, because we're used to putting screw heads in coun- tersunk holes, you may believe spoke heads should go into hub countersunk holes. Believe me, it's not so! You can bury spoke heads in countersunk holes for a sexier-looking hub, but you'll have busted spokes on the road if you do! Figure 10-3 illustrates this point. (Some hubs have *all* spoke holes countersunk.)

Before you start building a wheel, first make sure you have the right

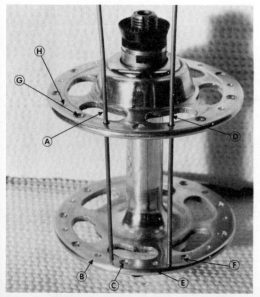

Fig. 10-2: All wheel hubs have holes drilled off-center with respect to holes in top and bottom flanges, as shown by spoke (A), which falls between spoke holes (B) and (C) below; and spoke (D), which falls midway between holes (E) and (F). Note also every other hole on **both** sides of the hub is coun- tersunk. Spoke head goes in noncountersunk hole. Countersinking minimizes spoke break- age by spreading stress at spoke head bend over greater area, instead of at sharp right angle. See Figure 10-3.

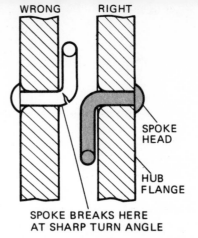

WRONG **RIGHT**

SPOKE
HEAD

HUB
FLANGE

SPOKE BREAKS HERE
AT SHARP TURN ANGLE

Fig. 10-3: Left, wrong way to put spoke in wheel hub, which stresses spoke at sharp non-countersunk hole. Right, correct way to insert spoke so that head is flush against rim and spoke shaft angles out against countersunk side of hole, which reduces stress and breakage at this point.

length spokes. Refer to the spoke chart in this chapter if you're not sure. Also, remove the freewheel gear cluster from rear wheels; you can't poke spokes in the rear hub with the freewheel in the way (which is why you should take a freewheel-removing tool as well as spare spokes on trips). You may also find it difficult or next to impossible to poke spokes through hub holes if they are drilled too small to accommodate the spoke. Most dealers, if they stock Robergel Sport spokes, only have them in .080–.072 gauge. This means the butted ends are .080, and the rest of the spoke is .072 inches. The nearest fraction equivalent to .080 is 3/32-inch (or 2.032 millimeters). So you would drill out a too small hole with a 3/32-inch drill. Actually, I'd rather see you use a metric drill, 2.05 millimeters, to be exact, which gives you a more snugly fitting hole only .018 millimeters larger than the butted section of the spoke. Be sure to drill straight, and remember, once you've drilled out your hub, always replace spokes with ones of the same diameter. If you use a smaller-gauge spoke you will invite spoke breakage, as the spoke bounces around in the larger spoke hole under stress. If you have a drill press you should recountersink holes, or countersink every other one on both sides if not already so countersunk.

A few definitions, so we're talking in the same language:

- *Rim* is the round steel or alloy part that the tire goes on.
- *Spoke head* is the section of the spoke with the curved area and flat head (flat on the bottom). The other end of the spoke is threaded.
- *Spoke nipple* is the short, tubular, internally threaded piece that holds the spoke on the rim and threads onto the spoke.
- *"Spoke head up"* means that in referring to the hub, the spoke head faces up, as shown in the Step One drawing (Fig. 10-4).
- *"Top rim hole"* means rim hole closest to upper edge of rim.

Before you start, you might consider drilling a one-inch hole in your wooden workbench to fit the axle of the hub so the hub assembly will stay put as you stick spokes in the wheel. And, while I'm thinking of it and before you despair, remember that, as I said, lacing a wheel is simple. It just *seems* difficult; it surely is hard to write about how to do it so that it comes out sounding as easy as it really is.

Since most wheels on ten-speed bikes have 36 spokes front and rear, I'll assume this is what you're about to lace. You have a naked hub and rim, and a fistful of spokes and nipples of the right diameter and length. You can get fancy later on and lace up 24-, 28-, 33-, or 40-spoked rims and hubs, and lace them radically or 3 or 4 cross as your heart desires. For now, we'll stick to 36 holes, crossed 4.

STEP ONE: Grab 9 spokes, threaded ends down. Hold the hub in one hand, the spokes in the other, and stuff a spoke down every other hole. The spoke head must be on the now countersunk side of the hub flange. Do the same for the bottom flange, with the hub in the same position as when you started. You should now have a hub that looks like Figure 10-4.

STEP TWO: Sweep up all the spokes on both flanges into two bundles, hold them so they don't fall out, turn the hub over and repeat Step One. When you're through, the hub will have all 36 spokes in it, with every other spoke head alternating, on each side of both hub flanges as shown in Figure 10-5.

STEP THREE: Sweep all the spokes as far away from the spoke hole as possible. Take any head-up spoke from the top flange (spoke head up means the spoke head is facing upward, on top of the flange) and put it in the first hole to the *right* of the valve hole. This rim hole must be a top rim hole (a top rim hole is the hole closest to the top of the rim); however, some rims are drilled so that the first hole to the right of the valve is a bottom rim hole (hole closest to the bottom of the rim). If so, start lacing with the first hole to the *left* of the valve hole. On this spoke and from here on thread a nipple four turns on each spoke as you lace it into the rim (Fig. 10-6).

STEP FOUR: Count off five spokes to the right (not counting the valve hole), including the hole you spoked in Step Three. This must also be a top rim hole. Into this hole put the next head-up spoke to the right of the one you spoked in Step Three. Continue this sequence until you have laced all head-up spokes in the top hub flange. The wheel will

Fig. 10-4: Step One   **Fig. 10-5:** Step Two

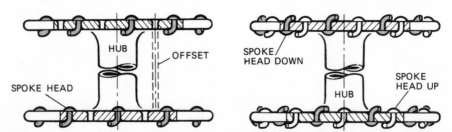

Fig. 10-6: Step Three

now look like Figure 10-7, with three holes between each spoke, the center of three empty holes being a rim-top hole, the other two, rim-bottom holes. (This happens to be a 32-hole rim and hub so only 8 spokes are showing. You should show 9 spokes.)

STEP FIVE: This is a critical step, so take it slowly and repeat it if you don't get it at first. Take the partially spoked rim and hub, and, keeping the same side up, *twist* the rim so the spokes are at an acute angle, just grazing the outside of their adjacent spoke holes. Depending on how the rim has been drilled, twist the rim either left or right, just so no spoke crosses over the valve hole (Figs. 10-8 and 10-1). Hold the hub as you twist the rim.

Fig. 10-7: Step Four

Fig. 10-8: Step Five

STEP SIX: Another critical step. Take any head-down spoke from the top-hub flange (the wheel should still be in the same position as when you started) and, going in the *opposite direction* from the spokes laced so far, cross *over* three and *under* the fourth spoke, as shown above, then stick it in the rim and thread on a nipple four turns. Remember Step Four? You had three empty spoke holes between each spoke. Right? I hope you did, anyway. If not, stop now and go over the preceding steps to check what you did wrong. Let's assume all is well. The spoke we are lacing in Step Six should go into a center rim hole (top rim hole) (Fig. 10-9). You are lacing Spoke "A." Note that it crosses *over* spokes "B," "C," "D" and *under* "E," and winds up in a top-rim hole. Continue lacing all head-down spokes in the top flange, cross *over* three and *under* the fourth spoke, as above. When you are finished, spokes will be in groups of two, with one bottom-rim spoke between each group of two. (If you wish to lace in a "cross three" pattern, pass the spoke *over* two and *under* the third spoke. A three-cross pattern uses shorter spokes.)

STEP SEVEN: This is a most critical step. Turn the wheel over, with all unlaced spokes in the top flange. Straighten spokes out, sweep all but one out of your way. Take an old spoke, put it straight up alongside any head-up spoke in the top flange, with the threaded end resting on the bottom flange facing you. Notice that just to the left of this trial· spoke is another head-up spoke, offset, to the left (naturally) in the bottom flange (See Fig. 10-2). We will call the bottom reference spoke in the bottom flange Spoke "A" and the spoke above and to its right, Spoke "B." Bring spoke "B" parallel but angled to the left of spoke "A" below it. Refer to Figure 10-10. Put spoke "B" in the first empty rim hole to the left of spoke "A," thread on a nipple. Now you will have (you'd *better* have) your first group of three spokes, with one empty spoke hole on either side. Step Seven is so critical I have taken extra photos from various angles to demonstrate it. Figure 10-11 shows a close-up of the hub, with

Fig. 10-9: Step Six

Fig. 10-10: Step Seven

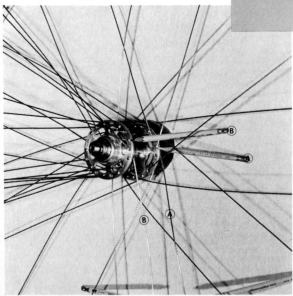

Fig. 10-11: Step Seven

Fig. 10-12: Step Seven

key spoke "A" at the bottom of the hub and key spoke "B" at the top of the hub. Figure 10-12 shows key spokes "A" and "B" as they enter the rim. Figure 10-13 is another view of Step Seven, with pencils on spokes "A" and "B." An important point to remember is that spoke "B" is parallel to spoke "A," is offset to it, and goes next to it in the rim, just above (to the left of) spoke "A."

STEP EIGHT: Now, if all has gone well so far, the rest is simple. Just take the next head-up spoke, count off two *empty (EMPTY)* spoke holes to the *left (LEFT)*, stick this spoke into *that* top rim hole and thread on nipple four turns. Repeat until all head-up spokes are in the rim with nipples on. Now you will have all spokes in groups of three (Fig. 10-14) and are ready for the final step.

STEP NINE: Take any one of the remaining spokes (they will all be head down, with heads *under* the top flange) and bring it around to the right, crossing *over* three and *under* the fourth spoke and stick it in the only hole it will fit into. If you're not sure which hole this is, please repeat Step Seven, only with head-down spokes, referencing a head-down spoke in the bottom flange and being sure that the parallel head-down spoke in the top flange also goes in a direction opposite to *its* reference spoke below. Confused? Well, actually I don't blame you. Let's take it from the top. First, find any head-down spoke in the bottom flange. Then find the first head-down spoke in the top flange offset to the right (counterclockwise) of your reference head-down spoke below, and put it in the first empty spoke hole to the right (counterclockwise) of spoke "A." Refer to the drawing of Step Six to refresh your memory as to what crossing over three and under four is all about. Continue as above, lacing up the remaining head-down spokes. Now the wheel is laced, spokes are in groups of four as shown above, and we are ready for the exacting job of "truing" the rim. Finished wheel is shown in Figure 10-15.

Fig. 10-13: Step Seven

Fig. 10-14: Step Eight

Step 10-15: Step Nine. Voila!

Varieties of Wheels

As you will note from Table 10-2, wheels can be laced with various spoking configurations. You can buy tubular tire rims and hubs drilled in multiples of 4, from 24 to 40 holes. And spokes can be crossed over three or even two, or not crossed tangentially at all but spoked radially, that is, straight up and down. They can even be laced tangentially on the driving side (the freewheel side) and radially on the other side; some racing cyclists prefer this combination, with 24 spokes, although it's rare in this country.

Wheels can also be tied and soldered, with 40 or 50 turns of thin steel wire wrapped around spoke intersections, and the wire soldered. Tying spokes in this manner makes a stiffer wheel and reduces spoke breakage by cutting spoke "whip" under stress.

Radial Lacing

Some cyclists prefer a radially laced front wheel and a tangentially (conventionally) laced rear wheel. Because radial spoking offers little resistance to forward power thrust, it's not practical for rear wheels. Radial spoking does offer less wind resistance because the spokes are in line behind each other, whereas tangentially laced spokes angle out more and so offer greater wind resistance. Radial spoking gives you a strong, rigid wheel for a front wheel only.

Crossing three instead of four spokes means that spokes are shorter and, again, offers a stiffer ride on any wheel.

High-Flange Versus Low-Flange Hubs

High-flange hubs provide a stiffer ride than low-flange hubs because they take shorter spokes. There's less spoke to absorb road shock. But I do not recommend using a 40-hole lacing with low-flange hubs, because this would put holes too close together and make a weaker hub. But that's my opinion, and if you wish to lace up a 40-hole rim and low-flange hub, by all mans try it out. If you're a 200-pounder carrying 26 or 30 pounds of gear on tour over rough roads, I definitely would use a 40-hole rear wheel with *high*-flange hub, and a 36-hole *low*-flange front wheel and hub. If you're lighter, say from 150 to 180 pounds, on tour with normal camping gear of about 30–35 pounds, I'd stick to a 36-hole high-flange rear and a 36-hole low-flange front arrangement. If you're lighter, a 32-hole front and rear low-flange hub should hold up. This assumes all the wheels recommended above are cross four. If you're a real lightweight, say 100 to 115 pounds, you may get by with a 28-hole, crossed-four, low-flange hub front, and a 32-hole, crossed-four, low-flange hub rear. Spoke breakage isn't just attributable to spoke configuration, though. It's also a matter of how even spoke tension is, and how much tension is applied. Too little tension permits excessive spoke play in the hub, and whipsawing can break spokes at the bend near the hub hole. If you're lacing a 36-hole rim, cross four, in a low-flange hub, and *rim* holes are not drilled at an acute enough angle to permit the nipple to follow the spoke line, you will have stress and possible breakage at the nipple. If, as you apply tension, the spoke winds up with a twist, you can have spoke breakage at the twist. As you apply spoke tension in truing, watch that spokes stay put. If not, hold spokes with a smooth-jawed pair of pliers as you tighten the nipple.

Speaking of nipples, use short nipples for lightweight rims and long nipples for heavier rims, such as clinchers and touring tubular rims.

Here is a rather general recommendation for wheel-lacing configuration, subject to modification as personal experience warrants, and as to weight and style of riding:

Table 10-3   Wheel-Lacing Configuration

Type of Riding	Front Wheel	Rear Wheel
Massed-Start Racing	28	36
Track Sprints	36 or 32	36
Distance Time Trials	36	36
Short Time Trials	28 or 32	28 or 32
Pursuit	28 or 32	28 or 32
General Riding	36	36
Touring, Heavy Rider, with Luggage	36	40

Remember, as one final observation, that reliability is more important than lightness, particularly when it comes to racing.

HOW TO "TRUE" A WHEEL

When we finished instructions for wheel lacing, you were left with spokes hanging loose. An accurately trued and tensioned wheel is vital to spoke life, for all the reasons noted above. You should also know how to true a wheel that has come untrue, because continued riding of an out-of-line wheel can put a permanent crimp or flat spot in the rim, and eventually you will need a new rim. Braking is also safer with true rims because brake shoes can grab the rim evenly all the way around, and because brake shoes can be adjusted closer to the rim for minimum

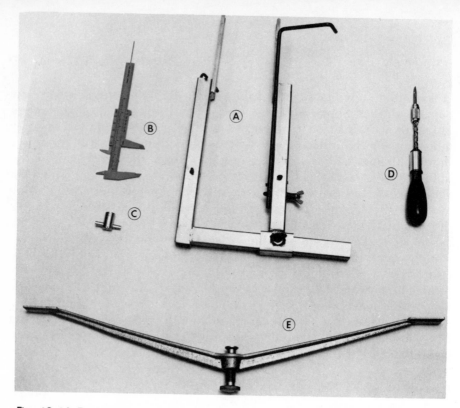

Fig. 10-16: Tools for truing include: (A) wheel-truing stand; (B) inch-metric vernier caliper and depth gauge; (C) spoke wrench; (D) ratchet screwdriver; and (E) rim-centering gauge.

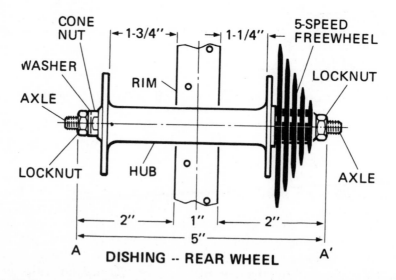

Fig. 10-17: Rear wheel must be "dished," or moved to the right, so that the rim is centered over the axle locknuts, as shown. Note that the distance on both sides of rim is equal (2 inches), yet hub is 1¾ inches on left and 1¼ on right side of rim. Rear wheel left-side spokes will be about ⅛th inch (2 mm. or so) longer than spokes on right (freewheel) side.

brake-lever travel and maximum stopping power. In other words, never ride very far with untrue rims; they're bound to be unfaithful.

Tools you will need for truing a wheel are shown in Figure 10-16. They are: "A," truing stand; "B," vernier caliper gauge; "C," spoke wrench; "D," ratchet screwdriver; and "E," rim-centering gauge.

It will be helpful before starting step-by-step truing instructions to establish a common vocabulary of truing terms, so we all talk the same language:

- *Concentricity* is the degree to which the wheel is perfectly round.
- *Lateral trueness* is the degree to which the wheel is centered over a point on the axle and remains on that point, with no side-to-side untrueness.
- *"Dishing"* applies to the rear wheel only, and means that the rim is "dished" or moved to the right so as to be centered *between* axle locknuts rather than on the hub alone. "Dishing" is well illustrated in Figure 10-17. The rim is centered between A and A', and you will notice that the space between the axle locknuts is the same on *both* sides of the rim. Notice also that the rim is *not* centered on the hub alone, as evidenced by the fact that more of the hub is on the left than on the right side of the rim. "Dishing" is vital not only to rear-wheel alignment, but also to the alignment of the rear wheel with respect to the frame and to the front wheel. Please study Figure 10-17 until you are sure you understand the concept of "dishing." Remember that dishing is necessary because the extra width of the freewheel gear cluster adds a dimension to the rear wheel which the front wheel doesn't have; and so the rim must be centered on the total dimension, which *includes* the freewheel, just as the front wheel must be centered on *its* total width, which includes only the hub and axle locknuts. The new Shimano "free-hub" designs are said to require little or no dishing, however. Measure just to make sure.
- *"Centering"* is what you do to the front wheel; although, of course, it's done to the rear wheel too, only we use the word "dishing" for the latter to stress that the rim is moved to the right side of the hub. The front wheel is centered on its hub. See Figure 10-18; note that the rim is centered on the hub.

Fig. 10-18: Unlike rear wheel, front wheel is centered on hub and between axle locknuts. Dimensions here and in Figure 10-17 are illustrative only and do not necessarily apply to your wheels.

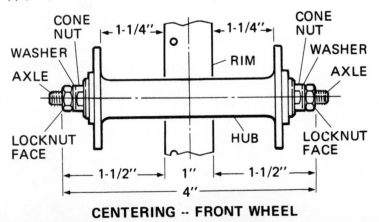

CENTERING -- FRONT WHEEL

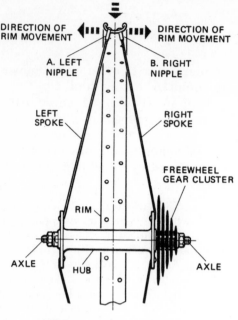

DIRECTION OF RIM MOVEMENT

DIRECTION OF RIM MOVEMENT

A. LEFT NIPPLE

B. RIGHT NIPPLE

LEFT SPOKE

RIGHT SPOKE

FREEWHEEL GEAR CLUSTER

RIM

AXLE

HUB

AXLE

DIRECTION OF RIM MOVEMENT

Fig. 10-19: Arrows show which way rim moves as spokes are tightened. Rim moves opposite way if spokes are loosened. Note that to remove out-of-roundness, **two** spokes must be tightened, spokes "A" and "B." If spoke "A" alone is tightened, rim moves to left. If spoke "B" is tightened, rim moves to right. If both spokes "A" and "B" are tightened to the same degree, rim moves only downward.

- *"Tension"* is the degree to which spokes are tightened. Too much tension can cause broken spokes; so can too little. Tension of *front*-wheel spokes should be equal on all spokes; on *rear* wheels, tension of right-side spokes is a bit more than left side because the rim is pulled (dished) over to the right.
- *The rim gauge* (see Fig. 10-16) helps you center the rim, or "dish" it accurately.
- *Direction of rim movement* is the way the rim moves (left or right, up or down, with respect to the hub centerline) as you tighten or loosen a spoke nipple. Please study Fig. 10-19 until you understand in which direction the rim will move as you tighten a particular spoke nipple. Remember that the rim will move the opposite way as you *loosen* a spoke nipple.

HOW TO TRUE A WHEEL

STEP ONE: We will start with the rear wheel, because it's the most difficult. Except for "dishing," the front wheel is trued up the same way as the rear wheel. If they're still on, remove the quick-release skewers. Put the wheel in the truing stand (or in an old fork held in a vise). The freewheel side should be on your right (Fig. 10-20).

STEP TWO: Start at the valve hole. With the ratchet screwdriver, speed-turn all the nipples on the right side down to where the spoke threads disappear under the nipple, and stop. Screw down the left-side nipples until the last four threads are visible on the spoke, under the nipple. When you do the front wheel, screw down all the nipples until the threads are just covered.

Fig. 10-20: Step One   Fig. 10-21: Step Two

STEP THREE: Measure the distance between axle locknuts. Now is when we learn to use the rim-centering gauge. Please study Figure 10-17 again. (Dimensions are illustrative only, and do not necessarily apply to your rim.) You will see that the measurement between axle locknuts is 5 inches. The rim is 1 inch wide. There are 2 inches on either side of the rim, between the locknut faces and the edges of the rim. Two plus 2 plus 1 equals 5 inches. So you can see the rim is *not* centered between the hub flanges, because there are 1¾ inches between the left hub flange and the left rim edge, and only 1¼ inches between the right rim edge and the right hub flange. The rear wheel is "dished" to the right. To adjust the rim-centering gauge to your rear wheel, measure the distance between axle locknuts with the vernier calipers. You can buy a surprisingly accurate pair of these calipers for around $3.50 from a metric supply house. I prefer the one from Ametric. They are inside, outside, and depth vernier calipers, in both inch and metric. Metric measurements are so much easier to use that I also urge you to convert your thinking to that system. Let's say the distance between locknut faces is 120.3 millimeters (for inch comparison, see Step Five) (Fig. 10-21).

STEP FOUR: Measure the width of the rim with the vernier gauge. Let's say it's 19.4 millimeters wide.

STEP FIVE: Subtract the first measurement from the second and divide the answer by 2. For example:

Table 10-4 Measuring Hub Width

	Millimeters	Inches, Fraction	Inches, Decimal
Locknut to locknut width:	120.3	4¾	4.750
Hub width:	− 19.4	−4⁹⁄₆₄	− .76242
Subtracting:	100.9	3⁶³⁄₆₄	3.988
Dividing by two:	50.45	1¹²⁷⁄₁₂₈	1.994

As you can see, the metric system is much easier to work with and more accurate. Good bikes are almost all made to metric measurements. A reminder: The measurements above are hypothetical, and may or may not apply to your wheel and hub. You will have to measure the ones you are working with.

STEP SIX: Put a reasonably flat strip over the rim-centering gauge, and with the vernier depth gauge set to 50.45 millimeters (or 1¹²⁷⁄₁₂₈ in.) adjust the rim-gauge centering screw to 50.45 millimeters. If you can't find a flat metal strip, set the gauge on a flat surface and look at the setting, as in Figure 10-22.

STEP SEVEN: Put the rim gauge on *both* sides of the rim to check how far off you are on dishing the rim to the right. Remove the wheel from the truing stand for checking, and then put it back. The rim-gauge screw is hollow, so it fits over the axle and axle locknut and permits the rim-gauge set screw flat to rest on the axle locknut face (Fig. 10-23).

STEP EIGHT: Set the lateral-movement indicator on the truing stand so it touches the worst bump on the left side of the rim. (Or, if you're using an old fork, anything that will stay still and indicate will do, such as a pipe cleaner wrapped around the fork blade.) When you find the worst left-side bump, stop there and find the spoke nipple just to the *right* of the bump. (Also at this point, study Figure 10-19 to review the direction of rim movement. Note that when spoke "B" is tightened, the rim moves to the right, and vice versa when spoke "A" is tightened.) Tighten this spoke nipple one turn to pull rim to the right. Then find the next worst bump and tighten the spoke nipple to the right of *that* bump one turn. Repeat this process once around the left side of the rim. Fine truing will come later.

Fig. 10-22: Step Six

Fig. 10-23: Step Seven

STEP NINE: Move the indicator so it touches the right side of the rim, and repeat Step Eight. Continue until you have removed all the right-side bumps.

STEP TEN: Check rim centering with the rim gauge, as in Step Seven. If the rim is too far to the left, tighten *all* the spoke nipples, on the *right* side one-half turn; if the rim is too far to the right, tighten all the spoke nipples on the left side one-half turn (Fig. 10-24).

STEP ELEVEN: With wheel in truing stand, repeat Steps Eight and Nine, except this time turn the spoke nipples one-quarter turn as you continue to pull out major lateral untrueness once around; one-quarter turn the second time around; one-eighth turn succeeding times around.

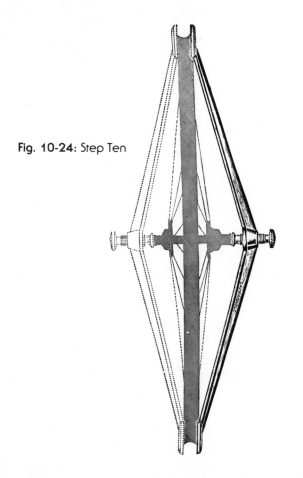

Fig. 10-24: Step Ten

STEP TWELVE: Now, with the wheel back in the truing stand, move the indicator so it touches the *outside circumference of the rim,* so we can remove out-of-roundness. Referring again to Figure 10-19, notice that when spokes "A" *and* "B" are tightened, the rim moves toward the hub; this is also true when spokes "C" *and* "D" are tightened. In other words, in removing concentric untrueness, *both* spokes at the points of major concentric highs must be tightened to pull the rim down. Rotate the rim, watch the indicator till you find the highest out-of-round spot, and tighten both left and right spokes at that spot one-half turn the first time; one-quarter turn the second time around; one-eighth turn third and succeeding times around.

STEP THIRTEEN: Repeat Step Seven, except turn the nipples one-eighth turn.

STEP FOURTEEN: Remove the wheel from the truing stand, and put the axle end on a wooden bench, holding the rim with both hands on either side of the rim. Press the rim sharply and hard down on the bench, to stress the rim, and seat in the spoke heads and nipples. You may hear popping sounds as spokes seat in. Rotate rim one-quarter turn, change grip, repeat rim press, and go around the rim twice.

STEP FIFTEEN: With the wheel in the truing stand, touch up lateral and concentric untrueness, turning nipples one-eighth turn. If you can't move a nipple, loosen the spoke nipple on the *opposite* side. Example 1: If you find a small lateral bump on the left side, and the right-side nipple is too tight to move, *loosen* the left-side nipple at the bump one-eighth turn. Example 2: You have a concentric high bump and both nipples at the bump can't be tightened any more. Instead, loosen both nipples at the point on the rim *opposite* the bump one-eighth turn (on the other side of the rim). On a rear wheel, as stated earlier, right-side spokes should all be slightly tighter than left-side spokes. Spokes on each side should show the same tension as other spokes on the same side. Don't try to pull a high or low spot out by tightening a nipple all at once; you'll have a highly stressed spoke that will very likely be short-lived and break, perhaps when you're careening downhill. Later, as you ride on your trued wheels, you may hear "twanging" sounds as the spokes seat in more. Or you'll likely hear that sound on a new bicycle, no matter what the price. Your rims will need touch-up truing for each 50 miles until you hit about 150 miles, after which rims should remain true, barring accident.

Chapter Eleven

Frame Alignment and Refinishing

It's a lovely spring day in the south of Austria, and you're going lickety-split, full tilt, wide open, down a winding mountain road. Suddenly, the handlebars begin to shake, and with each shake the bars swing wider and faster. You are out of control. This happened to me. I was able to stop because I knew I had no choice. This dangerous front-wheel shimmy is like a bad cold: There are so many reasons for it that almost anything could cause it, such as an unbalanced load, loose head or wheel bearings . . . or a slightly bent fork blade. The latter proved to be the case, thanks to the tender ministrations of the Austrian airline that transported it. Sometimes the fork blade can be so minutely bent out of line that it is almost undetectable to the naked eye; certainly it won't be seen at a casual glance—which is one good reason to block dropouts with a dummy spindle or piece of wood when shipping a bike with wheels removed.

I guess what I'm saying here is that an out-of-line bike frame can be a dangerous thing . . . a bike that can whip into a frenzy of front-wheel shimmy at high speed . . . a bike that will steer inaccurately and waste pedaling energy . . . a bike that in many instances can be saved through judicious application of muscle at the right tube member. Let's review how to check your frame for accurate alignment, and what to do about a misalignment of any of the tubes.

STEP ONE: *Check wheel tracking.* I use a five- or six-foot length of steel angle as a straightedge, which comes straight as stocked in a hardware store. Lay this straightedge (Fig. 11-1) against the front- and rear-wheel

278

Fig. 11-1: Step One: Wheel-tracking alignment (*Schwinn Bicycle Company*)

rim flats (remove tire if necessary). Both wheels should be in the drop-outs straight and should have been trued (see Chapter 10 for wheel-truing instructions). Wheels should track straight, with no more than a millimeter or so (1/16-to-1/8-inch max) difference. Try riding no hands and see if the bike pulls to one side or the other. If it does, or if the wheels are not tracking, go through the entire sequence of frame alignment checks that follow.

STEP TWO: *Rim centering check.* Check to make sure both wheels track true between frame members. Check rear wheel against *both* seat stays (Fig. 11-2) and chainstays (Fig. 11-3) and front wheel against both sides of fork (Fig. 11-4). Wheels should be equidistant from frame members. I'm unhappy with a 1-millimeter difference, but I can live with it. I'd rather see the rims absolutely centered This test won't work unless the wheels are trued and the rear wheel correctly dished (see Chapter 10). If the rear wheel is consistently too far to one side as measured on both sides from both seat and chainstays, it is incorrectly dished. Go to Step Three.

Fig. 11-2: Step Two: Wheel-centering check, rear wheel

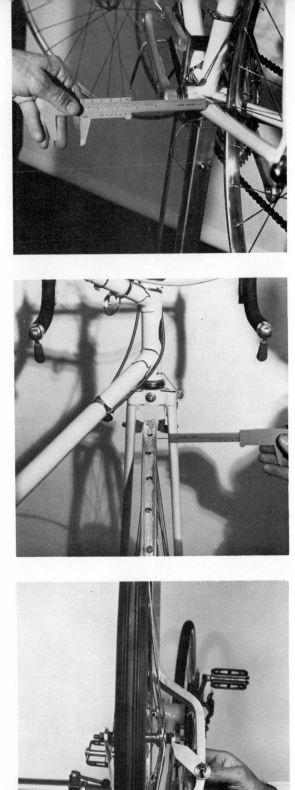

Fig. 11-3: Step Two: Wheel-centering check, rear wheel

Fig. 11-4: Step Two: Wheel-centering check, front wheel

Fig. 11-5: Step Three: Check rear wheel dish. *(Schwinn Bicycle Company)*

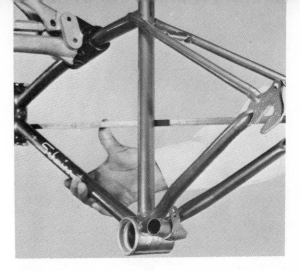

Fig. 11-6: Step Four: Check alignment of rear dropouts and stays. (*Schwinn Bicycle Company*)

STEP THREE: *Check rear-wheel dish* with a wheel-dishing gauge, such as the one shown in Figure 11-5. If the rim is not centered or dished accurately between axle locknuts, remove wheel and re-dish, following truing instructions in Chapter 10. If, however, the rear wheel *is* correctly dished, then we have a frame problem such as bent stays, bent dropouts, unparalleled dropouts, buckled main frame tube. So now . . .

STEP FOUR: *Check alignment of rear dropouts and stays.* Put a straightedge between steering head tube, seat tube and against the dropout (Fig. 11-6). You will have, if the straightedge is on the right side, a clearance between the right side of the straightedge and the dropout. Measure this distance. Now move the straightedge to the *left* side of the tubes and measure that clearance from the left side of the straightedge to the dropout. Both measurements should be the same. If not, the chainstay or seat stay could be bent, or the dropouts might not be parallel.

STEP FIVE: *Check dropouts for parallel alignment* with seat or head tube and with each other. Measure distance between dropouts in several places. Measurements should be the same (Fig. 11-7). Also measure dropouts between points "A" and "A¹" and "B" and "B¹"; measurements should be the same if dropouts are parallel. Also check seat stays

Fig. 11-7: Step Four: Check alignment of dropouts and stays.

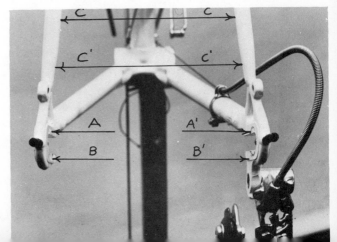

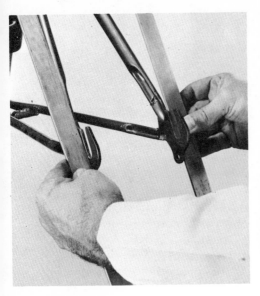

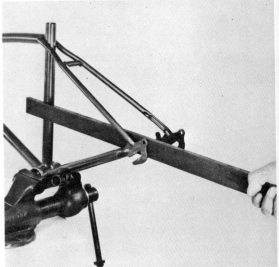

Fig. 11-8: Step Five: Check dropout parallel alignment. *(Schwinn Bicycle Company)*

Fig. 11-9: Step Five: Straighten dropouts if not parallel, or if stays are bent. *(Schwinn Bicycle Company)*

Fig. 11-10: Step Five: Remove kinks from stays if necessary. *(Schwinn Bicycle Company)*

Fig. 11-11: Step Five: These dropouts, of stamped steel, are easier to bend.

at points "C" and "C¹"—the difference between the tube angles should be the same on both sides. Another way to check dropouts is to put a straightedge on both sides, as in Figure 11-8, and measure the distance in several places on the straightedge. The measurements should be the same. This is going to take a helper, of course, because three hands are needed, or four. If the dropouts are not parallel, straighten, as shown in Figure 11-9, or by using a large crescent wrench on the dropout. Sometimes a framestay or chainstay can be bent. If so, straighten by using a hollowed-out block of steel or wood over the bent portion (Fig. 11-10) and tapping gently and carefully with a hammer. Wrap the stay to prevent damage to finish. Dropouts on less expensive bikes (Fig. 11-11) are just stamped pieces of metal and can easily be bent. The dropouts in Figure 11-7 are high-grade forged steel, and are much sturdier.

STEP SIX: *Check fork-blade alignment.* The fork is right up there where it or the steering head and head tube that it fits into can easily be bent in an accident. First, though, if you have been in an accident, visually check the area around where the top and downtubes join the steering head (Fig. 11-12). Look for wrinkled paint, indicating stress, particularly at the top of the downtube lug and where the top-tube lug joins the steering head. I'm not sure if the printed version of this photo shows the damage, but this is the bike I hit a Cadillac rear bumper with, at about 16 miles an hour. (The Caddy was black, parked on the forbidden side of the street; it was dark and streetlights were dim. So was I.) The fork steering tube was bent and straightened cold, but you can see some paint wrinkling at these two spots if you look closely. Figure 11-13 is a nonlugged frame, undamaged, brand new, but the arrows point to where to look if damage is suspected. By the way, on neither of these excellent frames will you be able to detect whether or not the frame tubes are

Fig. 11-12: Step Six: Check fork-blade alignment. But first check for bent tubes at intersections of tubing (arrows). Look for wrinkled paint, evidence of minor tube-bending accident.

Fig. 11-13: Step Six: On a nonlugged frame, look for paint wrinkling at locations where tubes join, as at arrows.

Fig. 11-14: Step Six: An unmitered joint is weaker.

unmitered

mitered

Fig. 11-15: Step Six: A mitered joint is stronger.

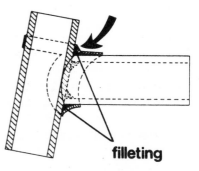

filleting

Fig. 11-16: Step Six: Filleting can hide an unmitered joint or strengthen a mitered one.

Fig. 11-17: Step Six: A filleted joint, not beautiful but at least strong. Arrows point to filleted areas.

mitered so they fit snugly against the rounded surface of the tube they fit or lie next to. Figure 11-14 shows a drawing of an unmitered joint. The flat edges of the tube leave a lot of air, and only a small part of the tube actually lies against the adjoining tube (arrow). The black section shows where a fillet of brass was put to disguise the unmitered tube joints. This is a very weak joint indeed. Figure 11-15 shows a mitered joint where the tube butts up more securely, with greater surface against the adjoining tube. A filleted joint is shown in Figure 11-16, and another in Figure 11-17, although the latter is not well finished.

Okay, now back to the fork-alignment check. This is to check the fork blades. Put a straightedge along the rim flat of the *trued* front wheel and the steering head and eyeball the clearance, or measure it. The clearance should not change from top to bottom. This will show a bent steering tube or steering head, or twisted steering head (Fig. 11-18). To check fork blades really requires a special jig, but another way to check blades requires removal of the fork. Lay the fork down on a flat surface and with a carpenter's bubble level, check alignment by moving the level from dropouts to crown. If you start level, the bubble should not have moved when you reach the crown. A rougher check is simply to lean the bike against the wall, squat down and eyeball the blade closest to you against the adjacent blade; you will pick up a gross misalignment that way. If fork blades are out of alignment, remove the fork and straighten them cold. Or buy a new fork if the old one is badly bent. Cold straightening is for *minor misalignment only*.

Fig. 11-18: Step Six: Checking fork alignment

Fig. 11-19: Step Seven: Check here for steering-head alignment. *(Schwinn Bicycle Company)*

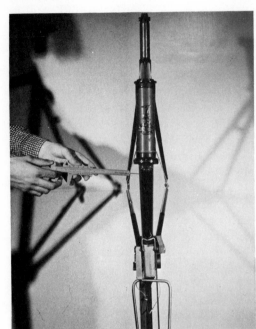

Fig. 11-20: Step Seven: Checking steering-head alignment, front view

Fig. 11-21: Step Seven: Straighten the steering head as necessary. *(Schwinn Bicycle Company)*

STEP SEVEN: *Check alignment of steering head.* Take a ten-foot-long piece of string. Tie one end to a rear dropout. Run the string around the steering head back to the other dropout and tie in the same place on *that* dropout as on the facing dropout. There will be clearance between the string and the seat tube (Fig. 11-19). Measure that clearance between the string on *both* sides of the seat tube. Both measurements should be alike. Figure 11-20 shows another view of this measurement technique. If the measurement is not the same, straighten cold as in Figure 11-21.

STEP EIGHT: *Check for steering-head twist.* Leaving string in place as in Figure 11-19, move it to the bottom of the steering head and then to the top of the steering head and measure distance from seat tube to the string on both sides when the string is in each position. Figure 11-22 shows the string in *both* positions. This check involves four measurements, all of which should show the same clearance on both sides of the seat tube. If the steering head has been twisted, realign as in Figure 11-21 or 11-23.

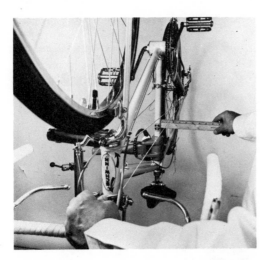

Fig. 11-22: Step Eight: Check for steering-head twist. (*Schwinn Bicycle Company*)

Fig. 11-23: Step Eight: Realign twisted steering head as necessary. (*Schwinn Bicycle Company*)

STEP NINE: *Check for steering-head centering* by placing straightedge against the side of the bottom bracket and steering head. Measure from the center of the steering head to the straightedge (Fig. 11-24) and repeat the same measurement on the other side of the steering head. Both should be the same.

STEP TEN: *Check alignment of seat tube.* Put the straightedge against the bottom-bracket shell and parallel to the seat tube. Measure at top and bottom of clearances between the seat tube and the straightedge (Fig. 11-25). Measurements must be the same. You can align the seat tube, if you're lucky, without undue damage by straightening cold as shown in Figure 11-26.

Just a word of caution: The alignment procedures you see in these photos are being made on an inexpensive frameset. You should carefully wrap all tools so as to prevent damage to finish, and if you use a vise be sure you use copper plates in the jaws. If you straighten cold, do it ⅟₆₄th of an inch at a time, or less, and recheck alignment as you do. *Do not use a torch* under any circumstances unless you are willing to ruin the paint finish and risk removing the heat treatment or temper in the tube, and so weaken that tube. A torch is for expert frame builders only.

STEP ELEVEN: *Check gear alignment* by putting the straightedge between the appropriate gears. See Chapters 4, 5 and 6 for chainlines. The straightedge should lie flat on the appropriate front and rear gear (Fig. 11-21) (e.g., on a ten-speed, flat against the No. 3 rear cog and on the centerline between the two front chainwheels).

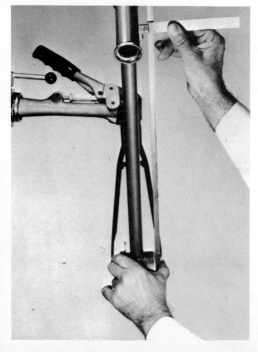

Fig. 11-24: Step Nine: Check steering-head centering. *(Schwinn Bicycle Company)*

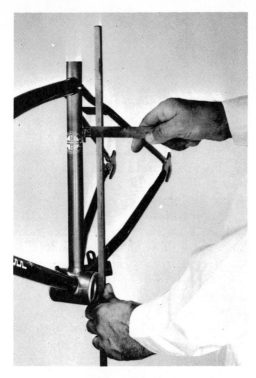

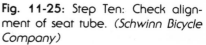

Fig. 11-25: Step Ten: Check alignment of seat tube. (*Schwinn Bicycle Company*)

Fig. 11-26: Step Ten: Straighten seat tube as necessary. (*Schwinn Bicycle Company*)

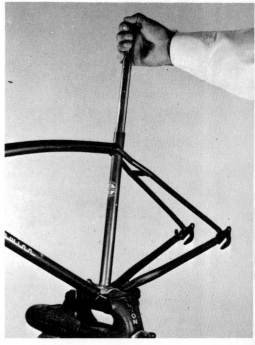

Fig. 11-27: Step Eleven: Check chainline.

FRAME TOUCH-UP AND PAINTING

If you have a really fine bicycle, it will pain you to see the finish become nicked, scratched and marred. Unless you keep your bicycle wrapped in cotton batting in your bedroom, nicks, scratches or mars are the inevitable concomitants of use. Perhaps you will feel better if we call these indications of healthy use "battle scars." And I know you will feel a lot better if these flaws on your beautiful, peerless machine can be removed and the finish brought back to perfection.

Removing scratches and nicks in the finish of a bicycle is virtually a fine art, and one, I must quickly admit, I am congenitally unsuited to and find difficult to do. I have, however, followed the instructions of experts and, with a great deal of internal stress and many mistakes, succeeded eventually in removing battle scars from my good bikes. But then I am not good at fine digital movements . . . I have always hated building tiny little things such as airplane models out of balsa, or ships in a bottle, things like that. If it were not for the sneers of my more artistic friends, and their twinges of real pain as they view my bike's battle scars, I would probably be content to daub something approximating the original color over them, just to keep the rust away. But you, I am sure, have the fine digital touch, the artistic taste and the desire to bring your two-wheeled steed back to its original state. For the following instructions on scratch removal and frame finishing, I am indebted to Otis Childress, of Los Angeles, and to that highly recommended magazine *Bike World* in which the following material appeared in the October 1977 and January 1979 issues. These data are from Mr. Childress's articles in those issues, reprinted by permission of both Mr. Childress and *Bike World*.

Before quoting from these articles, however, let me note that matching paint on your bike is going to be a problem, unless it is a Schwinn, Raleigh or Nishiki. Puch furnishes a small bottle of finish with their top-line models. Otherwise, my solution is to wheel my bike into a large auto-supply store, right up to the display of pressure cans of touch-up paint, and try to select one from either the color on the top of the can (not always a reliable indication of what's inside) or from a color chart sometimes available and hanging on the rack next to the paint cans. My color-matching reliability is around 3 on a scale of 0 to 10, so I always ask a clerk or another shopper for help, and the consensus determines which can I buy. But I have never really precisely matched colors this way, although the match is close enough for my low-grade taste. Okay, Otis, the rest is all yours, I won't put it in quotes because it isn't necessary.

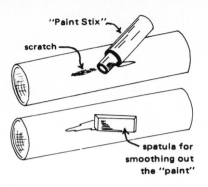

Fig. 11-28: Filling in small scratches

Scratch Removal and Refinishing

For a "quicky" repair of scratches so they won't show at a distance, at least, follow these steps:

STEP 1. Clean scratch with soap and water and grade "000" steel wool to remove loosened bits of clinging paint.

STEP 2. If bare metal shows, apply a layer or two of primer and let it dry between coats for at least one hour. Brush in direction of scratch.

STEP 3. Find matching paint. Schwinn bike stores market spray paints, as do Raleigh and bike stores selling Nishiki bikes. You can spray a small amount of paint into a clean small container or onto a small piece of lint-free paper, first shaking the can.

Then, with a small artist's brush, brush in the color coats. If it's just a spot dent, dab in a little paint. If the scratch is tiny, you can dabble some primer and color in it. You can also use paint sticks (Fig. 11-28) such as the ones marketed by Schwinn, rubbing the paint into the groove and then smoothing it out. Paint sticks are easier to use if softened with a match flame first. They won't work on a flat scrape where there is no groove to fill in.

Larger Scrapes—Blending In

You can fill in and blend larger scrapes with a technique known as vignetting and feathering. If you have darkroom experience you will recall how this is done to shade off areas in order to avoid abrupt changes in tone in the finished print.

You can mask off the damaged area with newspaper or masking tape. But unless you follow these steps you will have an abrupt ridge line (Fig 11-29) where the paint repair ends and the tape starts. These can be removed by 400-grade sandpaper or "000" steel wool and rubbing compound, but ridge lines may still show. Here are steps that will do the job:

Fig. 11-29: Ridge lines can form around edges of masking tape.

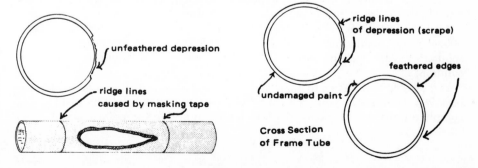

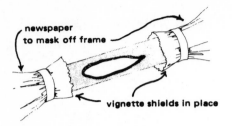

newspaper
to mask off frame

vignette shields in place

Fig. 11-30: Vignette shields can prevent ridge lines.

STEP 1. Sand the scraped area to eliminate the abrupt paint break or depression ridge; feather out the edges as shown in Figure 11-30. Use wet or dry sandpaper of a grade appropriate to the hardness and toughness of the old paint (grade 280 or 320), progressing to finer sandpaper, (400 or 600). Final sand with the paper wet to reduce its abrasive action. After final sanding, wash away all residue with clear water.

STEP 2. Mask off the area of the scrape and the rest of the bike to protect it from paint overspray. Don't follow the outline of the scrape. Instead, place one or two layers of masking tape around the frame tube, perpendicular to the tube axis and two or three inches from the edges of the scrape.

Use masking tape because it works well, is not so adhesive it pulls off the paint when you remove it, yet holds well enough to prevent paint seepage under the edges of the tape.

STEP 3. Build a "platform" around the masking tape already in place. Either wrap extra layers of tape or wrap a folded piece of paper around the tape, holding in place with a separate piece of tape. This platform should be ¼ to ½ inch thick.

STEP 4. Tear a piece of paper so it has an uneven and ragged edge, which then serves as a vignette shield. The shield should be long enough to encircle the frame tube, and should overlap about ½ inch. Use paper that is lint free and clean.

STEP 5. With the ragged edge toward the scrape, wrap the shield around the platform and secure it with a piece of tape as shown in Figure 11-30.

If the shields are placed too close to the frame surface (a low platform), the paint may not be fully vignetted, thus leaving a light paint line (though easily removed with steel wool). To be discussed later, but worth noting now, are such variables as paint temperature and spraying distance, which also can cause paint lines and paint "runs."

STEP 6. If bare metal is visible, apply two or three light coats of primer from a spray can. If only a small spot of metal is exposed, it may be covered by using a small brush. Spray, however, leaves a much smoother and more even surface.

After the last primer coat has completely dried, sand lightly with grade 400 or 600 wet-type sandpaper. Steel wool (grade "0000") may be used instead of sandpaper. After sanding or steel wooling, clean the area with a clear water solution.

You may find it easier to sand and clean the area with the vignette shields removed. In this way you are assured of clearing away all sanding residue and completely drying all traces of water before applying the color coats. Do not forget to reposition the vignette shields if you do remove them. Also, you may wish to sand each, or every other, primer coat instead of only the last.

STEP 7. If the original paint finish had an undercoat (which gives tone and depth to the outer color coats) apply two or three layers of an appropriately colored undercoat. This step will assure the fidelity of the final color coat with the original color. (To eliminate this step, especially with a large patching, would result in the repaired area being of a noticeably different shade, something that can still result if the original finish is badly weathered.) Sand or steel wool each layer of undercoat or only the last as instructed in Step 6.

Sanding a previous coat is necessary if it dries rough, even slightly so, as the next coat may amplify the roughness.

STEP 8. Spray on the outer color coats (four or so light ones). To assure a smooth final color coat, each previous coat should be wet-sanded (grade 400 or 600) or steel wooled (grade "0000"). The final color coat is, of course, left unsanded.

Spray paints generally function best at room temperature. Submerge spray cans in warm water for 10 minutes or so if necessary. If the paint temperature is too low, the spray will be relatively thick or instead of a spray, the paint will stream out; in either case, the paint will tend to run. The spray nozzle should be held 8–12 inches from the paint surface.

The closer to room temperature the spray is, the closer to the paint surface the nozzle may be held. This is particularly important when "shooting" tight spots in which the nozzle must be held very close to the surface, such as around the seat cluster.

When selecting paint, match it not only by color, but also by type: lacquer on lacquer, or enamel on enamel. Lacquer painted over enamel will lift the enamel off; enamel, however, can be painted over lacquer without damage.

STEP 9: After the final color coat has dried, remove all the shieldings, masking tape and so forth from the bike. After a few days to a week, and especially if the patched area shows any "powdered" or lightly rough spots, go over the area with steel wool (grade "0000") saturated with water. If the area is gone over with dry steel wool, the gloss of the area will be removed and even waxing will not return it to a gloss matching the rest of the frame. You may want to try rubbing compound instead of steel wool. At any rate, such rubbing should be at a minimum.

STEP 10. After the paint has completely dried (three weeks), apply wax.

If paint is not allowed to dry completely and equipment is clamped on, the clamps will make an imprint into the thickness of the paint leaving it to dry not flat and smooth, but bunched up. The reader will do well to consider that a frameset completely refinished requires not less than a month to dry before waxing or clamping on components. Paint may surely be dry to the touch within an hour or two, but only to the touch; it will not be thoroughly dry, nor will it be durable.

An alternate method of vignetting paint is to use a hand-held vignette shield (made by tearing an opening into a small piece of paper). The opening should be slightly larger than the size of the scrape and follow the general outline of the scrape.

In using, hold the shield half an inch to an inch away from the scrape to be repaired and spray with sweeping motions across the openings. This method is applicable to any flat, curving or irregular surface such as around the bottom-bracket shell.

An example of using a hand-held vignette shield is in repairing a deep scratch. Using touch-up paint and brush, fill in and build up the scratch above the level of the undamaged paint surface. Carefully sand until level down to the undamaged paint. Finally, after washing away the sanding residue, use the hand-held shield and spray across its opening.

Do not stop spraying while within the opening of the hand-held or taped-on vignette shield or you risk the paint running. Also, thick layering of paint into a deep scratch may take several days to build up to allow each lower layer to dry. Do not sand paint that is not dry or you will literally roll layers of paint off the area and create a gorge in the still-wet, dry-to-the-touch paint. Finally, by placing a strip of masking tape on the opposite side of the frame tube, opposite the scrape, this unprotected area would then be protected against any paint overspray. The result of overspray, when dry, is a rough texture.

Chrome Forks and Stays

The second use of vignetting techniques is in the refinishing of chrome forks and stays (if the frame as a whole is being refinished).

First, if chrome is to be painted, it must be sanded, the standard preparation for painting any surface, but especially important with chromed surfaces. Secondly, a primer coat is a particular necessity prior to any color coat.

Paint will absolutely not "take" to a shiny chrome surface, even one clean of wax. In such a case, the paint easily can be removed with the lightest grade of steel wool, or literally peeled off as you might peel an orange. Yet sanding need not be too harsh. In fact, the chrome under some factory-finished forks is so undamaged that with a little buffing and polishing you can have an all-chrome fork or at least one with more chrome and less paint, like a Raleigh Pro.

Basically, the same problem exists with masking tape in refinishing chrome forks and stays as in repairing scrapes and scratches: a piling up of paint into a ridge at the end of the tape. More importantly, in refinishing a frame more layers of paint are used, causing a tendency for the paint to "sheet-over" the edge of the masking tape, forming a continuous layer (or sheet) of paint. When the paint dries and the masking tape is removed, the effect is one like tearing a sheet of paper, leaving a torn and ragged edge (Fig. 11-31). Vignetting puts a stop to such problems before they start.

The following describes the refinishing of chrome forks and stays (for simplicity only one seat-stay is described and illustrated).

STEP 1. Measure off the amount of chrome to be painted (or not to be painted) by using a taut line anchored equidistant between the stays or fork blades. The brake anchor-bolt hole is suitable for this, unless the stays or fork blades are badly misaligned (Fig. 11-32). Pen or pencil is used to mark off the distance.

If the stays are misaligned, have them properly re-aligned (there are tools for this) before chroming, or if already chromed, before painting. Besides an ill-

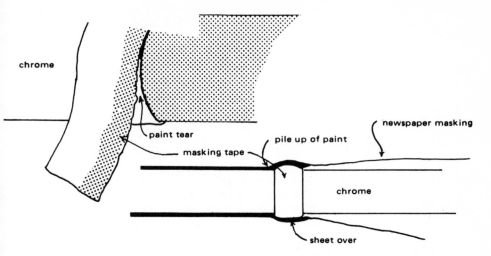

Fig. 11-31: Platform of masking tape at edge and paper shield over platform

tracking and ill-handling bike, the misalignment may throw the above measurements off (however, unnoticeably so).

If you are a bit daring, you might consider having chrome only on the right, drive-side chainstay, or the drive-side chain and seat-stays with the left side drop-out only showing chrome. Asymmetry, if well-balanced and thought out (in this case, using a dark color, particularly black) can have an unusual sort of attractiveness.

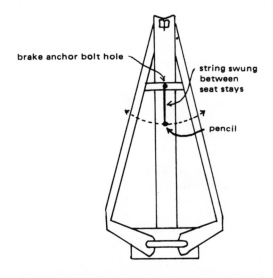

Fig. 11-32: Measuring chrome to be painted

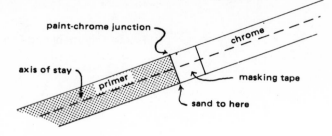

Fig. 11-33: Masking stays

STEP 2. Using masking tape, encircle each stay. Now, with grade 400 or 320 wet or dry paper (dry), sand the stays to the edge of the masking tape (to the paint-chrome juncture line, Fig. 11-33).

STEP 3. After sanding, remove and replace the tape with new tape. Using no more than three encirclements of tape around each stay, be certain that the tape is straight (perpendicular to the axis of the stay, Fig. 11-34). Using newspaper, mask off the chrome that is not to be painted. Mask off each stay individually, as the masking tape will be removed and replaced several times.

With modification, the same procedures are used to create "spearheads" (Fig. 11-34). Masking tape is flexible enough to conform to tapering stays and chain-wheel indentations.

STEP 4. Prime the complete frame (four or so light coats). After the last primer coat has dried, remove the masking tape and go over the immediate area of the juncture line with "0000" steel wool in addition to wet-sanding (grade 400 or 600) the rest of the frame.

Do not sand in the area of the juncture line, or you may remove too much edge paint and scratch the chrome. If you continually sand through paint to bare metal when sanding the frame in general, you might want to try "steel wooling" the frame with grade "000" or "0000" steel wool instead of sanding it.

STEP 5. Replace the masking tape (from Step 4) with a new strip. Apply an undercoating (three or so coats) to the frame if you have decided to use one over the primer coat. After the last undercoating has dried, remove the masking tape and steel wool the area of the juncture line (as in Step 4) to remove any hint of paint buildup as you sand the rest of the frame.

If at any time you suspect paint seepage under the masking tape, remove the tape and clear away the excess paint with steel wool.

STEP 6. Replace the masking tape (from Step 5) with new tape, but this time place it about one millimeter away from the juncture line (Fig. 11-35, top two figures).

Now, build a platform of masking tape or folded paper behind the strip of tape already in place (Fig. 11-35).

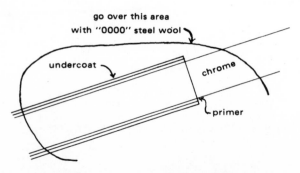

Fig. 11-34: Masking spearheads

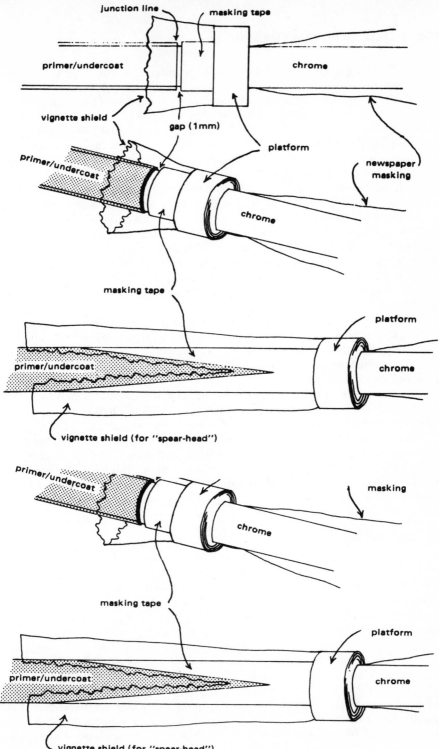

Fig. 11-35: Details of masking on stays and spearheads

STEP 7. Make a vignette shield from torn paper and shield off the juncture line about half an inch (Fig. 11-35).

STEP 8. Using your chosen finish color, spray the frame. The finish coats will be lightly layered (vignetted) under the vignette shield.

Before spraying the last two color coats, remove the shield permanently, but leave the masking tape in place (or replace it with a new tape, still with one-millimeter gap). The final two coats, sprayed with the shields removed, will cover the drop-off at each paint-chrome juncture.

When the frame is completely dry (about a month) apply wax.

After wet-sanding each color coat, it may be necessary to remove the shields in order to effectively clear away any sanding residue and water that may have "rolled" under the shields (to prevent fouling the next applied coat). This would also, with the shields removed, be a good time to smooth out the area of the juncture line with steel wool. Remember to replace the shields.

To vary the amount of spray being vignetted under a vignette shield, alter the shield's height above the paint surface or the amount that it overlaps the juncture line.

The number of coats suggested is simply that, a suggestion. Three or four coats may just as easily be five or eight light coats (but definitely no less than three). Vignette shields can be used with each coat of paint (from the first primer to the last color coat), or only with every second or third coat (be sure to remove paint buildup between coats).

An extra degree of protection may be added to the paint-chrome juncture by lining it with clear lacquer or enamel. First, using "000" steel wool, go over the juncture line (about one-eighth inch of paint and an equal amount of chrome). Next, using an artist's brush, trim the juncture line with two or three thin layers of the "clear" (which will "take" sufficiently to the chrome and be durable).

The value of all this seemingly unnecessary concern and preparation is in the results: smooth and sharply defined juncture lines, unlike some assembly line paint jobs that require a contrasting trim color to hide (unsuccessfully) hurried workmanship.

Color Contrasting

The third use of vignetting is in color contrasting the head-tube with the frame color (as the complete frame is being refinished).

The preliminary steps are no different from painting the frame in general—apply primer, then an undercoat. Next, select a color that is contrasting to the chosen frame color. For illustration, orange will be the frame color with gray as the head-tube color.

STEP 1. (After the primer and undercoatings are applied and completely dried.) Mask off the frame, using masking tape and newspaper, about two or three inches from the lugs on the head-tube.

Remove the headset before painting the frame. This will allow the inside of the head-tube to be cleaned thoroughly, particularly of rust. Secondly, if the headset is not removed, paint may seep into the thin gap between the headset and the head-tube and remain "wet" for quite a while. Finally, painting is easier with non-essentials removed.

STEP 2. Place vignette shields about the upper and about the lower lugs. The opening between the shields and the lugs should be about half an inch.

STEP 3. Spray about four light coats of the chosen contrast color (gray) onto the head-tube. (Always spray with a sweeping motion, horizontally or vertically.) When dry to the touch, remove the shields.

Schwinn aluminum undercoat is a silver-gray, perfect in this case as both an undercoat and a contrast color, thus allowing steps 1, 2 and 3 to be eliminated.

STEP 4. After the head-tube area is completely dry, mask off the head-tube only (leave the lugs unmasked).

If the head-tube is not allowed to dry completely (one or two weeks depending on the number and thickness of the coats), the masking tape will, when eventually removed, pull off the paint.

While the frame is completely stripped of paint, a "masking" should be made to fit the head-tube perfectly into the area between the lugs. A masking is made by placing overlapping strips of masking tape on a plastic or glass surface and, using a razor blade, cutting out the masking. This is a trial-and-error proposition. Be sure to get a good fit and make an extra one. (The masking should be only one layer thick except at the overlap.)

Small pieces of tape can be fitted on the head-tube along the lugs if necessary to completely mask off the head-tube. Use a fingernail (or whatever) to shape the masking into a perfect fit along the edge of the lugs where there should be no bunching.

STEP 5. Make a platform one-fourth to one-half inch high of masking tape or folded paper and place around the head-tube.

STEP 6. Make a vignette shield by tearing a newspaper to the contour of the head-tube, but about one-fourth of an inch larger.

Place the shield around the full circumference of the head-tube, and tape in place. The shield should not only overlap the lugs by at least one-fourth of an inch, but should "stand off" from the head-tube and lugs by the same amount. Some adjustment of the shield may be necessary at the rear of the head-tube (Fig. 11-36).

STEP 7. With the shield in place, apply the frame-color coats (orange). After the last coat is dry to touch, remove the shield, but do not remove the masking.

STEP 8. With the shield removed, examine the lug/head-tube juncture (where the gray and orange colors meet). If the frame paint at the edge of the lugs appears too thin, spray on an extra-light layer or two of the frame color about the lugs (with the shield still off, but with the masking in place).

STEP 9. If satisfied with the results thus far, and after about three days to a week, remove the head-tube masking. After at least a month, wax may be applied to the complete frame.

If contrasting the head-tube is an after-thought (after the frame has been painted one color), it may be necessary to sand away some of the paint from the lugs and head-tube before beginning Step 1. If not done, the extra paint of the contrast color on the head-tube and the extra frame paint applied to the lugs may be so thick that it would be difficult to distinguish the lug drop-off from the head-tube proper, especially with lugs thinned and tapered at the edges (Fig. 11-37).

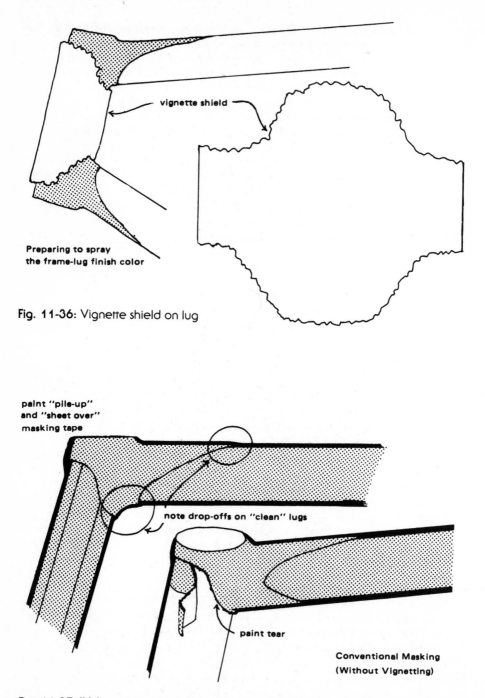

vignette shield

Preparing to spray
the frame-lug finish color

Fig. 11-36: Vignette shield on lug

paint "pile-up"
and "sheet over"
masking tape

note drop-offs on "clean" lugs

paint tear

Conventional Masking
(Without Vignetting)

Fig. 11-37: Without proper masking you can get paint pile-up and paint tear where shown.

As extra protection and as a "leveler," before waxing, you might want to line the lug/head-tube juncture with a clear lacquer or enamel using a small artist's brush.

If only the head-tube masking were used (without the vignette shield), the expected piling up and "sheeting-over" of paint at the lug/head-tube juncture would occur. The masking would, when removed, pull and tear the lug paint leaving a ragged edge (Fig. 11-37).

Attempting to smooth out ragged edges by sanding is frustrating at best, as it is easy to sand through to bare metal. Of course, the juncture line can be trimmed or lined with a third color and so, to a degree, can hide poor workmanship. Yet, steady hand or not, the trim line would just be a tacky reflection of tacky workmanship.

Tips to Inexpensive Frame Painting

More often than not, experience is acquired through costly mistakes and wasted time, often only to learn a few tips, a couple of shortcuts and several do's and don'ts. This holds true in the painting of your frame.

If you have decided to repair your frame this winter, but are without experience, the following may help guide you through inexpensively. Each set of tips has been placed under appropriate headings for easy reference.

SOLVENTS (REMOVERS)

You should apply semi-paste solvents with a paintbrush. Then, use coarse-grade steel wool to remove the solvent-loosened paint from the frame. Before rinsing the frame clean of solvent, however (in fact, before applying the solvent), plug up the bottom-bracket shell and the head-tube by tightly stuffing them with newspaper to keep water out of the frame tubes.

Keep in mind that newer paint generally dissolves more quickly and easily than older (cured) paint. Also, remember that warm, ambient temperatures will speed the dissolving action of solvents. Solvents burn, so cover exposed skin areas and have water nearby for rinsing off. Be careful. Although the fingertips may be somewhat insensitive to the "burning" of solvents, the sinuses, insides of the wrists and the eyes are not.

Use paint and lacquer thinners only secondarily, as they are not primary paint removers.

PREPARING THE FRAME

Strip off all the old paint, or at least repair all scratches, chips and scrapes. Consider well that the original paint can hide the "carelessness" of a frame builder. If it needs to be repainted, then it needs to be stripped.

File off all excess brazing material (which was hiding under the original paint). If necessary, reshape the dropouts and the dropout derailleur-attaching "lug" (or "boss"), and make any needed frame realignments before painting or chroming.

Remove all nonessentials (such as the headset) for ease and completeness in preparing the frame for painting and in the actual painting. Optionally, you may wish to remove the builder's head-tube "marque," replacing it later with rivets, or leaving it off and filling in the rivet holes with a filler such as one of the commercially available "liquid metals."

Forget about liquid "etchers." Sandpaper the bare frame to a smooth, but not slick finish. Use coarse or medium-grade emery cloth followed by "180" or "220" Wet-or-Dry sandpaper. (As you sand, remember to do it always in one direction.) If you sandblast the old paint, be sure to use the proper grade of blasting material and mask all chrome and repaint immediately. Sandblasted frames begin to rust *very* quickly. *Do not touch frame with bare hands.*

You will need to look for, and remove, rust. Many times it hides in areas such as inside the seat tube.

Mask all threads before painting. Shove rolled-up newspaper into, and sticking out both ends of, the bottom-bracket shell and head-tube. Removing paint from bottom-bracket threads, without damaging the outside frame finish, is not always easy. In addition, the front fork can and should be refinished separately from the main frame.

PAINTING CONDITIONS

If you are painting indoors, you should open all windows, clear the room of furniture (or cover everything with newspaper, including the floor) and close all closets. It might be wise to wear a "respirator"-type mask or breathe through a wet face towel held over your mouth and nose. Paint overspray should not be allowed to enter your lungs.

Use well-diffused lighting. In addition to opened window curtains, use ceiling lights, repositioned table lamps (with the shades removed), and a hand-held flashlight for checking tight areas.

Remove all dust from the frame between coat applications. A clean paint brush is adaptable for this purpose, because rags rarely are lint- or static-free. Dust particles caught under layers of paint will show through as paint "blisters."

Do not create static charges by rubbing the frame tubes unnecessarily, as this tends to attract dust particles. Besides, there is no such thing as clean, oil-free hands, so hands off between coats.

Do not spray onto a cold/damp frame or on cold/damp days. Water (dampness)) will bubble up or blister the paint, as I have sadly and expensively learned from personal experience. Spraying on a cold/damp night can cause the paint to dry to a dull, "frosty" finish even though a "glossy" finish color is used. Maintain spraying conditions as constantly as possible from one spraying session to the next, especially if respraying only a small section of the frame. Note such spraying instructions as "... material and surface temperature 65–95 degrees ... relative humidity 85% ... recoat at 70 degrees. ..." Keep in mind that instructions may vary among paint brands.

When cleaning up paint overspray, use a vacuum cleaner and a damp dusting cloth. Sweeping with a hand broom only will cause the overspray to become airborne and settle or resettle on furniture, shelves and you, and even worse, in your lungs.

When you finally are ready to start painting, practice on something first. Learn the spray characteristics of each spray can, and read all label instructions.

Hang the frame so that you easily can get to and spray all areas of it. A pipe, one end supported in a stable base and the other end inserted into the frame's seat tube (at about waist or head high), is even better. The frame should be easily rotatable on its "paint stand."

Always spray with sweeping motions, except when spraying tight areas or very small spots, which are "shot" with quick bursts of spray. Lightly spray hard-to-get-to areas before spraying the frame in general, assuring that easily missed areas such as the undersides of the frame tubes and around the seat and head-tube lugs are fully covered. Some manufacturers miss these areas, or the paint is so thinly applied that Comet cleanser, a dish towel and very little "elbow grease" are enough to rub away the finish completely. (Use a nonabrasive cleaner for cleaning the frame.) Additionally, extra paint also should be applied to the underside of the down tube and the backside of the seat tube as extra protection against kicked-up road gravel.

Shake the spray can often to keep the paint ingredients well mixed. Never start spraying directly onto the frame, as this may cause a paint "run." Begin spraying first into the air, then with a sweeping motion move onto the frame. Conversely, stop spraying by first sweeping from the frame into the air before releasing the spray nozzle.

At some point before applying the first color coat (preferably before the first primer coat), coat the insides of the frame tubes, chainstays and bottom-bracket shell with a rust inhibitor ("Penetrol" or "Rust-oleum" primer) to protect from the effects of rain and condensation. Plug up one end of a frame tube and, using a funnel, fill completely with the rust inhibitor and then empty. Do the same with the other tubes. Alternately, you might want to try using a sponge brush with a long, flexible handle.

The first two or so coats of primer, undercoat and color coats should be "misted" or "dusted" onto the frame. They will dry slightly rough, but with successive coats and with sanding, the coats will be smoothed out. Use grade "400" or "600" Wet-or-Dry paper.

A painting tip to remember is that several thin, light coats are better than one thick coat. However, spread the coat applications over time (one or two weeks). Each coat of paint will reflect the quality of the previous coat. So, prepare each coat for the next one.

Do not try to stop paint runs by wiping with a rag. Runs can be stopped by the following methods: soaking them up with a finger wrapped in a rag; by turning the frame over to reverse the run; by using quick sweeps of spray, undercutting the run (but without feeding it much more paint), thus sweeping and spreading out the run; or by blowing on the run to spread it out and prevent its running farther. (For a stream of "air" without paint, turn the spray can upside-down, aim just below the run and depress the nozzle.)

If all else fails, allow the run to dry completely, then sand and repaint. To lessen the time needed for a thick run to dry, cut away part of it (when partially dry) with a razor blade. Do not attempt to sand wet paint, as you will only create a gorge in the thickness of the paint surface. *Do not sand a wet paint run.*

A coat of paint being applied over a previously applied coat may rewet the previous coat, thus effectively acting as a solvent. This is one reason for not wiping away a paint run. You may wipe through the rewetted previous coat of paint to expose bare metal.

If your touch is too light, or the spray nozzle is held too far from the frame, the paint will "dust-on," creating a rough or "powdered" texture. To smooth it out, use "0000" steel wool. Keep your technique controlled.

Do not apply lacquer over enamel, as the former will lift off the latter. Enamel can be applied safely over lacquer without damage, but why confuse yourself? Stick with one or the other throughout.

If you are painting outdoors, do so on ideally windless, dry and warm days and in the shade. If you can outlast family objections, it is preferable to paint indoors in an empty, well-ventilated room in which control of dust and other conditions can be maintained.

If a bug lands on wet paint, remove it with a pin or needle. If the removal messes up the paint, allow the surface to dry, then sand and respray the area without masking it off.

If only a small amount of paint remains in the can, or if the nozzle is clogged, the paint will tend to spurt out, creating large paint globs ("toad skin") on the frame. Either throw away these cans, or use only with an artist's brush for small touch-up jobs. Besides, the "last" of the paint is never quite the same quality as the "first" of it. Clear the spray nozzle/siphon tube by turning the spray can upside down and depressing the nozzle. The nozzle itself also can be cleared by reaming it out with a pin or needle. Occasionally wipe clean the outside of the nozzle with a rag.

Epoxies and Exotics

"Exotics" such as epoxies and the like are up to you, but learn their limitations, special preparation and so forth. Again, practice on something first. Remember that if you choose an unusual frame color, and later must repair a large paint scrape, you may have difficulty in matching that color.

Clear lacquer (or enamel) applied over the frame color coat will give it a heightened gloss and, to a certain extent, act as a protective coat. However, a clear coat is not in the least bit necessary, and if improperly applied, may prove disastrous. If you do use a "clear," practice on something before applying it to the frame.

"Levelers," "surfacers" and rubbing compound all have the same basic function of smoothing out scratches in the primer and finish coats. These refinishing accessories are not especially necessary, however, and you can do just as well without them. You may, however, want to try rubbing compound on the finish coats.

Enamels require a different application procedure from lacquers, despite the fact that some manufacturers use the same label instructions regardless of whether the paint is lacquer or enamel.

Find and stay with one supplier who has a good, "no-hassle" refund policy and who is knowledgeable (a salesperson who gets all of his or her information by reading the back label of the spray can is not knowledgeable). Finally, do not lose that receipt.

Chroming Tips

The surface to be chromed must be absolutely smooth. Chrome plating does not fill in nor does it smooth out scratches (large, small or tiny), it just plates them. Sand out all scratches (grade 400 or 600 Wet-or-Dry paper).

Those parts of the frame not to be chromed should be masked with plastic electrician's tape, which will conform to just about any irregular shape. It may be to your advantage to mask the frame yourself. Talk to the plater first.

Even if you want only a few inches of the lower blades chromed, have the complete front fork chromed (chrome, properly sanded, can be painted). If chroming the rear stays, chrome each stay completely, from the dropout to the seat lug or bottom-bracket shell—in general, to any point where there is a bend or turn. Do so even if only partially chromed stays are desired, otherwise the chrome plating may form a "ridge" at the edge of the electrician's tape (depending on the thickness of the plating). Partially chromed stays (and forks) of commercially produced frames actually are completely chromed.

There are a few tight areas on a bike frame that are difficult for the plater to polish properly (a prerequisite to plating "bright" chrome). The result is that if you have these areas or the complete frame chromed, they may not be as bright as other areas of chrome.

Mask all threads. In general, mask anything in which a dimensional enlargement would cause a component "misfit" (such as the headset lower race platform, or shoulder, or the fork crown). Chrome plating is not at all easy to file off, so do not put it where it is not wanted.

Chrome plating has its disadvantages, such as the corrosive actions of the plating process (for example, rust forming on the insides of the frame tubes). Hydrogen embrittlement, another bugaboo of the plating process, is caused when hydrogen diffuses into the metal being plated during the chroming operation. Oven baking at a prescribed temperature/time setting will relieve the hydrogen. However, some platers will not do this, do not want to be bothered with it and simply do not care. The question is, do you? Some cyclists are very wary about riding with front forks weakened or made brittle by the plating process.

As soon as the frame is chromed, get it back from the plater and remove the rust formed during the plating process. Do not allow the frame to remain in the plater's shop longer than necessary.

The disadvantages of chroming (real, imagined or simply exaggerated) are enough to discourage many from having any frame part plated. It is your choice. If the plater becomes lazy during one of the steps of the plating process, you easily may end up with a shoddy plating job.

One plater, who assured me that he had experience in plating bike frames, returned a front fork to me that literally peeled. Yes, I was able to peel much of the chrome plating off the fork (just as you would peel the foil wrapping from a candy bar), exposing the copper base, or "under-plating." Collective opinion suggested that one probable cause was the plater's failure to keep the fork, while handling it, clean of dirt and/or grease. In any case, it was a shoddy job.

A verbal guarantee is just another way of saying, "maybe, but probably not." Get it in writing, and hang on to that payment receipt. A final consideration, for chromed (as with unchromed) frames, is to coat the insides of the tubes with a rust inhibitor/preventative.

Admittedly, the foregoing is less than complete. But with experience, you will no doubt add several tips of your own. In the meanwhile, the usual, but avoidable, "blunders of inexperience" hopefully will be minimized.

Chapter Twelve

Three-Speed and Coaster-Brake Hubs

There are four makes and a wide variety of one-, two-, three-, and five-speed integral rear hubs in common use on bicycles in this country. There is even an adapter kit to convert multi-speed integral rear hubs into a six- or nine-speed machine, using a derailleur. A Japanese manufacturer makes a twelve-speed combination rear hub and derailleur which, if used with a double front chainwheel, will give you twenty-four speeds, and with a triple front chainwheel, thirty-six speeds. I don't know what you'd do with more than twelve or fifteen speeds, but if you want them, they're available. More on these combinations later in this chapter.

I am not going to attempt to give you detailed take-apart and assembly instructions for all these hubs; there are simply too many makes and models to make this practical. Hubs are a rather complicated assemblage of gears and mechanisms. (If Fig. 12-1 doesn't scare you off, nothing will!) Many require special tools to assemble or disassemble, and the majority of bicycle dealers are competent to deal with most of them.

This chapter, therefore, will be limited to routine hub maintenance, adjustment, and tips on correct usage. If you follow these instructions, your hub should last the life of the bicycle and seldom, if ever, need to be taken apart. However, if you really want to disassemble your rear hub, either out of curiosity or because you can't find a bicycle mechanic who knows how to fix it, you can obtain step-by-step illustrated assembly and disassembly instructions, complete with a list of spare parts, from the hub manufacturer or the bicycle manufacturer.

BENDIX AUTOMATIC COASTER BRAKES

The Bendix automatic coaster brake is a two-speed unit which contains both coaster brakes and a set of internal gears. This type of hub permits the cyclist to change gears by backpedaling slightly, or to brake by backpedaling, both without removing hands from the handlebars. It is well suited for a young rider, up to age twelve. There is a 32 percent decrease in gear ratio between high and low gears on this hub—enough to enable a young rider to negotiate moderate hills fairly easily.

There are two types of Bendix coaster-brake two-speed hubs. The standard model is marked with three yellow bands around the hub shell. The other, which is marked with three blue bands around the hub shell, is the overdrive automatic unit. This has a direct drive and a high gear with a 47 percent gear ratio increase, which makes cycling a bit easier on hills.

Lubrication

Because all the working parts are inside the hub, these hubs don't require much maintenance, beyond regular lubrication about every month, and after long trips. Use a fairly light oil, equivalent to No. 20 SAE viscosity motor oil. Squirt about a teaspoonful into the hub through the hub hole provided for this purpose.

Also, once a year you should take the bicycle into the dealer and have him disassemble and regrease the hub and check for any worn or broken parts.

Because coaster brakes (*unlike* caliper brakes) need grease for proper operation and for long life, if you've made extensive tours in hilly country involving a lot of braking, it's a good idea to have your dealer disassemble the hub and regrease it when the tour is over, rather than wait until the year is up.

If the hub does not shift properly, makes grinding noises, shifts into low without back-pressure, or if the brakes fail, this means that new internal parts may be necessary. These can be installed by your bicycle dealer.

No routine operating adjustments are required on any Bendix hubs, making them even better for children and more child-proof than other hubs, which have wires attached to them.

All you need to remember, if you remove the rear wheel, is to refasten the coaster-brake clamp arm which clamps onto the rear fork stay.

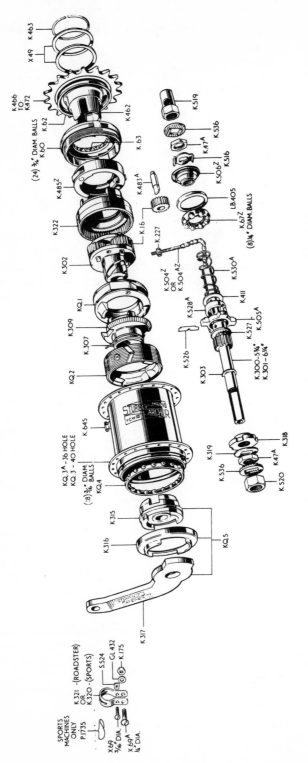

Fig. 12-1: Sturmey-Archer three-speed hub and coaster-brake combination. This drawing is shown here to convince you not to take any three-speed hub apart. Let your bicycle dealer fix these. Of course, if anything mechanical poses a challenge to you, go right ahead and take it apart, but save the pieces.

LEGEND

Part No.	Description
GL432	Shakeproof Washer
K16	Planet Pinion
K47A	Cone Locknut
K60	Right-Hand Ball-Ring
K62	Sprocket Dust Cap
K67Z	Ball Retainer—(8) 1/4" Ball
K175	Nut for X69A Bolt
K227	Locknut
K300	Axle 5¾"
K301	Axle 6¼"
K302	Planet Cage
K303	Axle Circlip
K307	Brake Actuating Spring
K309	Thrust Plate
K315	Left-Hand Cone
K316	(Chromium) Dust Cap for Left-Hand Cone
K317	Brake Arm
K318	Brake Arm Locknut
K319	Lock Washer
K320	Clip for Brake Arm (Sports)
K321	Clip for Brake Arm (Roadster)
K322	Gear Ring
K411	Thrust Washer
K462	Driver
K463	Driver Circlip
K466	Sprocket 16 Teeth
K472	Sprocket 22 Teeth
K483A	Planet Pinion Pin
K485Z	Gear Ring Pawl-Ring
K504Z	Gear Indicator Rod and Coupling. For 5¾" Axle
K504AZ	Gear Indicator Rod and Coupling. For 6¼" Axle.
K505A	Clutch
K506Z	Cone
K516	Right-Hand Cone Locking-Washer
K519	Right-Hand Axle Nut
K520	Left-Hand Axle Nut
K526	Key
K527	Clutch Sleeve
K528A	Thrust Ring
K530A	Clutch Spring
K536	Serrated Axle Washer
K645	Lubricator
KQ1	Planet Cage Pawl Ring
KQ2	Brake Band
KQ3	40-Hole Shell and Left-Hand Ball Cup Assembly
KQ3A	36-Hole Shell and Left-Hand Ball Cup Assembly
KQ4	Ball Retainer—(18) 3/16" Ball
KQ5	Brake Arm/Left-Hand Cone/and Dust Cap Assembly
LB405	Dustcap
S524	Nut for X 69 Bolt
P1735	Strengthening Pad—For Sports Machines only
X49	Sprocket spacing Washer (1/16")
X69	Clip Screw, 3/16" Diameter
X69A	Clip Screw, 1/4" Diameter

STURMEY-ARCHER MULTI-SPEED REAR HUBS

Sturmey-Archer multi-speed rear hubs are perhaps the most widely used of all hubs.

There are three- (Fig. 12-1), four-, five-speed and combination coaster-brake and three-speed Sturmey-Archer rear wheel hubs in use today. All of them have a number of things in common, one of which is that proper gear shifting is greatly dependent upon proper adjustment of working parts.

Lubrication is also very important. In fact, oil can evaporate from a hub between the time the bicycle leaves the factory and when you buy it, so be sure to have the dealer add a tablespoonful of *light* oil to the hub before you ride off.

When changing gears with any Sturmey-Archer hub, ease pedal pressure slightly, and change gears quickly.

Sturmey-Archer Troubleshooting

PROBLEM: Gears slip; they won't stay in the gear selected.
SOLUTION: Adjust the indicator rod. Check your hub so you know which type you have, and follow the instruction on the indicator rod adjustment for your particular hub.

TCW, AW, AB, AG, and SW Hub Indicator Rod Adjustment

STEP ONE: Put the gear-shift lever in No. 2 position (or S5 five-speed hubs in third gear) (Fig. 12-2).

STEP TWO: Unscrew the locknut (A, Fig. 12-2).

STEP THREE: Adjust the knurled section of the cable (B, Fig. 12-2) until the end of the indicator rod is exactly level with the end of the axle (B, Fig. 12-3). Check the location of the indicator rod through the "window" in the *right-hand* nut on the axle (B, Fig. 12-2).

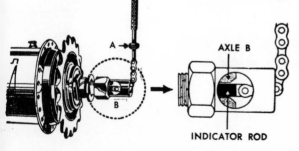

Fig. 12-2: Cable adjustments for SW-TCW hubs, including locknut (A), and knurled section of cable (B). Indicator rod should be where shown for proper hub operation. *(Courtesy of Raleigh Industries, Limited)*

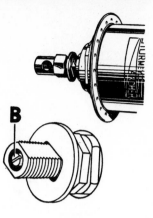

Fig. 12-3: Rod (B) on a Sturmey-Archer hub should line up with end of axle for proper cable adjustment of Sturmey-Archer hubs.

STEP FOUR: Tighten the locknut.

STEP FIVE: If you can't obtain enough adjustment with the cable connection at the hub, unscrew the nut and bolt holding the cable on the top tube (X 90, Fig. 12-4), and move the cable forward or rearward, as required. This step is known as "changing the fulcrum point" of the cable.

AM, ASC, and AC Sturmey-Archer Hub Indicator Rod Adjustment

The only difference between indicator rod adjustment for these hubs and other Sturmey-Archer hubs lies in the location of the indicator rod adjustment indicator. On AM, ASC, and AC hubs, the indicator rod is in the correct position when the end of the rod is level with the end of the axle on the *left-hand* side of the hub. This is the side opposite the chain, or left side as you face the front of the bicycle.

Adjustment of the indicator rod should be made as shown above.

If gears still slip or change noisily after the indicator rod has been adjusted, wear on the internal parts in the hub is indicated. Take the bicycle to your dealer for repairs, or, if you wish to make them yourself, write to the bicycle manufacturer or see your dealer for assembly and disassembly instructions and the special tools that are needed.

Cable Change on Sturmey-Archer "Sportshift"

Sturmey-Archer also makes a gear-shift mechanism for their three-speed hubs, which is mounted on the top tube. Follow these steps to change cables:

STEP ONE: Loosen the locknut on the hub cable at the hub, and unscrew the knurled ferrule until the cable is free at the hub end.

STEP TWO: Remove the center screw from the control unit (gear-shift unit) and remove the cover from the plastic cover plate.

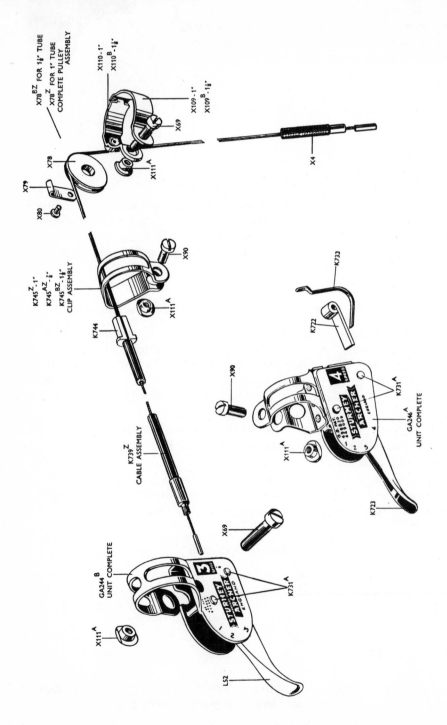

X78^{BZ} FOR 1¼" TUBE
X78^Z FOR 1" TUBE
COMPLETE PULLEY
ASSEMBLY

X110-1"
X110^B-1⅛"

X109-1"
X109^B-1⅛"

X69

X111^A

X78

X79

X80

X4

K745^Z-1"
K745^{AZ}-⅞"
K745^{BZ}-1⅛"
CLIP ASSEMBLY

X90

X111^A

K744

K733

K722

X90

K731^A

X111^A

GA246^A
UNIT COMPLETE

K739^Z
CABLE ASSEMBLY

K723

X69

GA244^B
UNIT COMPLETE

K731^A

X111^A

L52

Fig. 12-4: Trigger control gear-shift lever for three- and four-speed Sturmey-Archer hubs. If you cannot get enough adjustment with the cable locknuts at the hub, loosen nut X90 and slide clip assembly farther forward about a half inch, and retighten.

Code No.	Description	3-Speed Unit	4-Speed Unit	Description
K739Z	Trigger cable assembly—give length of both inner and outer cable	GC3B	GC4A	Trigger control complete less pulley
K744	Fulcrum sleeve	GA244B	GA246A	Trigger unit
K745Z	Fulcrum clip complete 1" diameter	L52	K723	Trigger lever
K745AZ	Fulcrum clip complete 7/8" diameter	K731A	K731A	Pivot pin
K745BZ	Fulcrum clip complete 1 1/8" diameter	L55	K722	Trigger pawl
X90	Clip screw	L56	K738	Trigger spring
X78Z	Pulley complete for 1" tube	X69	X69	Clip screw
X78BZ	Pulley complete for 1 1/8" tube	X111A	X111A	Clip screw, 1/4" diameter
X69	Clip screw			
X78	Pulley wheel only			
X79	Pulley arm			
X80	Pulley arm screw			
X110BZ	Clip with pulley stud (1 1/8" tube)			
X109B	Half clip (1 1/8" tube)			

STEP THREE: Push the control lever to the No. 3 position, and remove the old cable. Pull the old cable through the slot of the cable anchorage and over the pulley wheel to remove the entire cable.

STEP FOUR: Readjust the cable by moving the lever to the No. 2 position and adjusting the cable ferrule at the hub end until the indicator rod is in the correct location for the type of Sturmey-Archer hub involved. (TCW, AW, AG, AB, and SW hubs have a different adjustment from AM, ASC, the AC Sturmey-Archer hubs.)

Here are common symptoms of Sturmey-Archer hub problems, their causes and their solutions. If hub needs disassembly, I recommend you let your bicycle shop do it.

PROBLEM: Sluggish gear change.
CAUSE: Cable binding or worn toggle link chain.
SOLUTION: Lubricate or replace cables. Lubricate gear-shift unit.

PROBLEM: No gear at all; pedals turn, wheel doesn't.
CAUSE: Internal pawls stuck or held in place by too heavy oil.
SOLUTION: Add light oil. If this does not free up, dismantle hub. Clean parts. Reassemble and oil again.

CAUSE: Bent axle.
SOLUTION: Dismantle hub. Replace axle.

CAUSE: Distorted axle spring.
SOLUTION: Replace spring (requires hub disassembly).

PROBLEM: Hub runs stiffly, drags on pedals when free-wheeling, wheel seems to "bind."
CAUSE: Chainstay ends not parallel. When the axle nuts are tightened, this causes the axle to be "sprung" out of true, which, in turn, makes the internal hub parts "bind."
SOLUTION: Straighten the chainstay ends, or add packing washers on the left-hand side to align. You may also need a new axle.

CAUSE: Corrosion of hub working parts due to nonlubrication.
SOLUTION: Disassemble the hub. Check and replace worn parts. Re-lubricate. Follow lubrication instructions above.

PROBLEM: Slips in any gear.
CAUSE: On S5 hubs, this could be a kinked gear cable. On other hubs, internal parts are worn or incorrectly installed.
SOLUTION: Replace cable or reassemble hub with new parts as needed.

PROBLEM: On TCW (coaster-brake and three-speed) hub combinations *only*, brakes are noisy or "shudder" when applied.
CAUSE: Loose brake arm clip.
SOLUTION: Tighten clip nuts and bolts.

PROBLEM: On TCW hubs only, internal brakes in hub "grab" on application.
CAUSE: Lack of oil in rear hub.
SOLUTION: Add good-quality *thin* oil, SAE 20 or thinner.

General Instructions

Sometimes even when you take the steps to correct any of the problems listed above, you will still not have corrected them. If this happens to you, there is probably wear in the internal parts of the hub. I do not recommend that the average bicycle owner attempt to replace any of the interior parts of these hubs. But, if you want to anyway, troubleshooting charts and hub-assembly data can be obtained from the manufacturers.

In any case, do not attempt to adjust the rear wheel cones on multi-speed hubs. If the wheel binds, or shows side play, and you think that cone adjustment is the answer, let your dealer do it. Some hubs have factory-adjusted cones, and you can ruin the hubs if you try to adjust them yourself, without following a detailed instruction manual.

Sturmey-Archer Trigger (Gear-Shift) Control Maintenance

There isn't much that can go wrong with a gear shift (Fig. 12-5) unless you bend it accidentally. If you do, it should be replaced.

Cables do fray, wear, and break, however, and you should know how to replace the gear-shift cable (or cables, on an S5 five-speed hub).

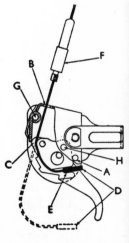

Fig. 12-5: Typical Sturmey-Archer gear shift. To remove control wire, it is not necessary to remove control from handlebar if the lever can be pulled back far enough to allow cable nipple to pass between pawl and ratchet plate. Procedure is (1) detach inner wire from indicator chain at hub, and (2) outer casing from fulcrum clip. Pull cable ferrule (F) upward until screw engages that of control casing at (B), then unscrew ferrule. Pull lever right back beyond bottom gear position to stop (A), push inner wire through to detach nipple from ratchet plate, then pull wire out between pawl and ratchet at (C) and finally through threaded hole (B).

To fit control wire, pull lever right back beyond bottom gear position to stop (A) and insert wire through threaded hole (B) and between pawl and ratchet plate at (C). Wire nipple (D) is then fitted into notch (E) and cable ferrule (F) screwed into (B) until it rotates freely. Keeping tension on wire, push lever forward into top gear position. Control is then ready for reconnection.

Trigger Control Cable Replacement, Three- and Four-Speed Hubs

STEP ONE: (Note: You do not have to remove the control mechanism from the handlebars if you can pull the lever back far enough to permit the cable nipple to pass between the pawl and ratchet plate.) Remove the inner wire from the indicator chain at the hub.

STEP TWO: Remove the outer wire casing (the spaghetti tube) from the fulcrum clip on the top tube (or, if it is a woman's model, from the top of the two downtubes).

STEP THREE: Pull the cable ferrule upward (so that the metal sleeve is entering the gear shift) until the ferrule screw (which you can't see because it's in the control casing) engages the control casing. Then, unscrew the ferrule.

STEP FOUR: Pull the control lever back beyond the bottom gear position as far as it can go. Push the cable (inner wire) through so you can remove the cable nipple (leaded end) from the ratchet plate, then pull the wire out between the pawl and ratchet and through the threaded hole.

STEP FIVE: To replace an old cable with a new one, reverse Steps One through Four, above.

Fitting Gear-Shift Cable to Frame (Sturmey-Archer)

When you install a new cable and its spaghetti cover on the bicycle frame, be sure to have the cable and cover long enough so you can turn the handlebars through their full movement in both directions. But do not overdo it. Make it just long enough for adequate handlebar movement.

Standard control wire length for most bicycles with Sturmey-Archer multi-speed hubs and handlebar controls is 54½ inches with a spaghetti cover length of 17½ inches. For controls mounted on the top tube, standard lengths are thirty-two, thirty-four, and thirty-six inches.

For Sturmey-Archer Five-Speed Hubs

When installing new cables on Sturmey-Archer five-speed rear hubs (Fig. 12-6), follow this procedure:

STEP ONE: For the right-hand gear-shift lever, follow the same procedure as for standard handlebar flick control. Screw down the locknut (Fig. 12-6).

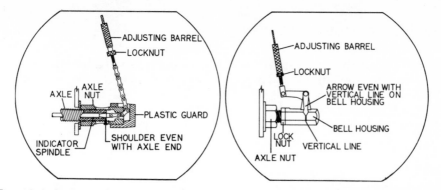

Fig. 12-6. Right- and left-hand gear-shift cables for Sturmey-Archer five-speed hubs.

STEP TWO: For the left-hand lever, push the left-hand lever to the forward position, screw the cable connector to the bellcrank (the metal connecting piece between the cable and axle, held onto the axle by a nut). Screw the cable connector (1) to the bellcrank just two or three turns, no more.

STEP THREE: Push the left-hand lever to the backward position, and screw the cable connector until all cable slackness is eliminated.

STEP FOUR: With light pressure, push the bellcrank arm forward and, at the same time, turn the wheel backward or forward. If the gears are not fully engaged, the bellcrank arm will move farther forward.

STEP FIVE: Screw the cable connector as far as possible, and secure with the locknut.

MAINTENANCE, ADJUSTMENT AND ALIGNMENT OF HUBS

Sturmey-Archer Hubs

For efficient cycling with minimum effort, as well as for proper operation of the rear hub, it is important that the rear sprocket of any rear hub, whether coaster brake or multi-speed, line up with the front chainwheel.

For more information on alignment, see the discussion in the section on derailleurs.

To align Sturmey-Archer rear hubs, all you need to do is change the rear sprocket a little, which is easy. You have an alignment adjustment of between 1½ inches and 1¾ inches in 1/16-inch increments. To change alignments simply follow these steps:

STEP ONE: Pry off the locknut (circlip) with a small screwdriver. (This is the round springlike clip that fits into a groove around the sprocket side of the hub—outboard of the sprocket.) Snap this ring out.

STEP TWO: Slide the sprocket off the hub, along with the washers on either side of the sprocket. To change alignment, you have a number of choices:

1. Face the concave side of the sprocket toward the outside of the hub. Put all the washers on one side or the other, or one washer on each side.
2. Put concave side toward the hub, washers as above. This gives you a total of six adjustments.

Incidentally, if you wish to change the gear ratio, up or down, on any Sturmey-Archer hub, simply ask your bicycle dealer to send to Raleigh of America in Boston for the sprocket with the number of teeth you desire. A larger sprocket with more teeth will give you a larger ratio (less speed in all gears but more hill-climbing ability), whereas a smaller sprocket will give you more speed, but hills will be more difficult to negotiate (all other factors, such as your physical condition, being equal, that is).

Shimano Multi-Speed Hubs

A number of American bicycle manufacturers use Japanese-made Shimano multi-speed rear hubs. The Shimano hub, in my opinion, is every bit as good as any American or European multi-speed hub and is a good deal easier to repair. If you plan to remove this hub, and disassemble and reassemble it, you will, however, need two special tools—a split snap ring remover and a ballcup remover—which you will have to order through your bicycle store.

The Shimano 3.3.3. three-speed hub is the most widely used of the Shimano units. Shimano publishes well-illustrated, easily understood, step-by-step disassembly, repair and reassembly instructions. Repair parts are available in this country. Lubrication is very important. Use a light oil, adding about a teaspoonful every thirty days and after each long ride.

There are two types of Shimano gear-shift levers for this hub, both positive "click-stop" types. The first is a handlebar "twistgrip" similar to a motorcycle speed control, and the second is a lever, usually mounted on the top tube.

To remove a frayed wire from the handlebar twistgrip:

STEP ONE: Loosen the locknut on the handlebar twistgrip and remove the ferrule and wire.

STEP TWO: Remove the cable cover from the fulcrum stopper on the top tube.

STEP THREE: Unscrew the locknut on the bellcrank on the rear wheel and unscrew the knurled cable nut from the bellcrank lever. At this point, the cable and cable cover should be removable from the bicycle. Install the new cable and cover, reversing Steps One, Two, and Three.

STEP FOUR: The adjustment for both the twistgrip and the lever-type control should start with the shift in the "N" position. At this position, the red "N" on the bellcrank should be centered in the "window" of the bellcrank or, on older models of this hub, the arrow indicator should be centered over the indicating line on the bellcrank.

STEP FIVE: If the centering in Step Four cannot be made, move the fulcrum stop on the top tube forward or backward, as necessary, to make more or less cable slack as needed; then readjust at the bellcrank end by loosening the cable locknut and screwing the cable ferrule in or out as required. This step applies for both twistgrip and lever-type controls.

   NOTE: Wire cables on any bicycle will stretch in time, so you will find it necessary to readjust the shift cable from time to time, as per Step Five.

PROBLEM: In the "H" shift position, the pedal skips or won't turn.
CAUSE: Pawl is worn or installed backward.
SOLUTION: Disassemble the hub and install new pawl and pawl spring (a job for the bicycle mechanic).

PROBLEM: Pedal skips at "N" position.
CAUSE: Planet cage pawl worn or broken, or pawl spring broken.
SOLUTION: Disassemble hub and replace defective parts (a job for the bicycle mechanic).

PROBLEM: Gears are stuck or do not change smoothly.
CAUSE: Broken parts are caught up in hub mechanism.
SOLUTION: Complete hub overhaul (a job for the bicycle mechanic).

PROBLEM: Hub is noisy.
CAUSE: Rusty mechanism due to lack of oil.
SOLUTION: If rust has proceeded far enough, a new hub may have to be installed. Try oiling the hub first. If this doesn't work, disassemble the hub and look for rusted part. Install new parts as needed (a job for the bicycle mechanic).

PROBLEM: Erratic shifting.
CAUSE: Control cable not set correctly.
SOLUTION: Adjust as described under Steps Four and Five above.

The Shimano click-stop shift lever is used on a number of 20- and 24-inch-wheel bicycles, as well as on 26-inch-wheel machines. To change the cables on the "stick" shift, follow these steps.

STEP ONE: Pry out the plastic dust cover on the round section at the bottom of the lever, which will reveal a screw in the center of the space.

STEP TWO: Remove the lever hub screw. The factory has this screw down rather tight, so use a good screwdriver and apply some elbow grease. Be careful not to lose the spacing washers under the nut, and to replace them in the same order.

STEP THREE: With the lever screw removed, the lever handle and wire will come off the lever slip in one piece. Remove the metal dust cover. Remove the cable nipple (leaded end) from its seat in the lever handle, and remove the cable and cable cover, replacing them with the new cable and cover by reversing the above steps.

The Shimano Combi-12 uses a combination four-speed derailleur and three-speed rear hub, for a total of twelve gear changes (twenty-four gear changes if a double chainwheel is used, thirty-six if a triple chainwheel is used).

Full instructions on the care, adjustment and alignment of derailleurs are given in Chapter 4. Because the three-speed section of the Combi-12 is identical to the standard Shimano 3.3.3. three-speed hub, maintenance and adjustment instructions already given in this section for this hub apply to the Combi-12 hub unit. Cable-changing procedures for both lever gear shifts have already been described.

There is, however, a difference between the derailleur lever on the Combi-12 and the conventional derailleur gear-shift levers. Standard levers have no click stops. The rider must adjust the lever position so that the derailleur is not pushing the chain part way off a cog and causing a grinding noise from the rear wheel while underway. The Shimano lever has click stops, so fine adjustment of the lever cannot be made to prevent the chain from running part way off a cog and causing a grinding noise.

The Shimano click-stop lever shift is a real boon for the adult who has to fix his child's bicycle. Once the cable adjustments are properly made so the click stops and you move the derailleur to the correct position for each hub external gear, you don't have to make any further adjustment of the lever. All you have to do is watch out for later stretching of the cable. When it stretches—and it will—you'll need to readjust the cable positions as follows:

STEP ONE: A stretched wire will cause an inaccurate setting of the click stop on the three-speed hub. Put the gear-shift lever in *top* position. If speed change cannot then be made to the *second* position, readjust by loosening the wire-adjusting nut at the bellcrank and loosen or tighten the knurled ferrule on the cable as necessary. Then retighten the lock-nut.

STEP TWO: Make sure the indicator on the bellcrank is pointing directly to the red indicator line, with the three-speed lever in the "N" position.

To adjust the derailleur wire:

STEP ONE: Put lever in *top* position. If the cable is not tight (taut), cable tension is correct.

STEP TWO: Now move the pedals (the bicycle should be upside down or hung from the ceiling) and change the gears through the four gear changes. Make sure the derailleur moves the chain from highest to lowest gear and back, smoothly.

STEP THREE: If the lever cannot be put into the *second* position easily, tighten the wire by loosening the locknut at the clamp on the seat stay and adjusting the knurled ferrule as necessary. Retighten the locknut.

STEP FOUR: Check adjustment by moving the lever to *top* position, as you turn the pedals. If the lever won't go into *top* position easily, loosen the wire slightly. Now, move the lever through all the gear ranges and adjust the cable as needed, if there is any noise in any of the gear-click stops.

Torpedo Duomatic Hubs

Some American and imported bicycles are fitted with a West German–made two-speed hub with a foot-operated gear change and backpedaling brake. This hub, which is called a Torpedo Duomatic, is similar in design to the Bendix automatic two-speed hub with coaster brake, and requires the same type of maintenance. Just follow the same instructions as for the Bendix unit.

I do not recommend your trying to dismantle this hub, unless you make sure you have complete step-by-step illustrated instructions, which can be obtained through your bicycle dealer.

Torpedo also makes a two-speed hub without the coaster brake, for use with bicycles equipped with caliper brakes. Maintenance instructions for this hub are the same as for the Bendix automatic hub; just feed it some light oil once a month after long trips, and if any strange sounds come from it, rush the bicycle to the nearest bicycle shop. If your mechanic can't (or won't) fix the hub, write to the Torpedo distributor or the bicycle manufacturer for the name of the closest *bicycle store* (not discount or department store) that can do this work.

As on most of the multi-speed rear hubs used on bicycles in this country, the sprocket on the Torpedo hub can be easily changed to one with more teeth for touring in hilly country, or to one with fewer teeth for faster riding where the going is flat and easy. If you do change sprockets, remember that you must order the same make of sprocket as your hub, because sprockets are not interchangeable from one make of hub to the other.

Apropos of changing parts, parts from different makes of bicycles and bicycle components are more likely *not* to be interchangeable, except for mundane things such as tires, seats, and spokes. Be careful about ordering everything else!

A Word of Warning

Before you take your multi-speed rear hub to a bicycle shop, phone the shop to make sure it has the parts on hand or can assure you it is willing to go to the trouble to order them for you from its wholesaler. The problem is that hardly any bicycle shop can afford to carry the tremendous number of parts it would take to be able to service all American, English, and Japanese hubs that are popularly used in this country.

A related problem is that not all wholesalers carry all parts, and if the bike shop proprietor can't find what he needs from his own wholesaler, the chances are very good that he'll tell you they aren't available. If this happens to you, keep calling dealers until you find one who says he can and does repair the type and make of hub you have.

Chapter Thirteen

Tandems

Tandems are fun to ride. They are much easier to pedal into the wind and uphill than single bikes because the weight of the tandem frame plus that of the two riders is, other things being equal, at least fifteen to twenty pounds less than the combined weight of two separate bicycles and their riders. But tandems do need special attention to ensure maximum safety.

Brakes

First, the brakes. I doubt that anything is more important for safety on a tandem than brakes, unless it is the proficiency of the riders and their own good judgment.

A tandem with two riders weighs about 350 pounds—and more if laden with camping gear. On a steep downhill run a tandem can quickly get up to really frightening speeds, easily to 50 miles an hour and greater. So it's vital that you control speed within the limits of your capability, and consider the nature of the road, its turns and curves and twists, its surface. If you have a straightaway drop, say of five miles on a 5- or 6-percent grade, you know there are no intersecting roads for ten miles and that you are descending into the desert or a sparsely populated rural area, and you are experienced tandemists, let 'er rip. But the usual descent involves winding mountain roads; and around the next bend may be a gravel-strewn road, an overturned truck-trailer, a child weaving around on a small bike, or even a herd of cows crossing the road! I've come upon all of these and so far have been able to stop in time to avoid a collision, because I had kept the tandem under enough control to be able to do so immediately upon making the curve.

The major problem in braking the tandem is heat. Friction generated by brake pads rubbing on wheel-rim flats can blow out tubes and tires with no difficulty at all.

323

You could use alternate front and rear caliper brakes to keep speed control, but the time will come when you must use both brakes, and then you could be in trouble. My solution is to use a good hub brake. The best brake I have found to date is made by Phil Wood (see Chapter 1), weighs one pound and costs $132, each. I use two. The heat of high-speed runs is dissipated in this brake's disc. So far I have had no problems with brake fade, a phenomenon that affects auto disc and drum brakes, and is due to heat squeezing some of the ingredients out of the lining which then turns into a lubricant. Letting brakes cool usually brings them back to normal. With the Phil Wood brakes I feel much more secure and confident during downhill runs, and when I see a straightaway run I usually let the tandem get up to 45 to 50 miles per hour. We have passed some pretty startled motorists. The $264 for two Phil Wood brakes is a lot of money, but the security is worth it to me.

To use the Phil Wood brake you must use a special Phil Wood hub designed for the brake. Schwinn uses these hubs on its Paramount tandem and sells the Phil Wood brake as an optional extra.

You could use just one Phil Wood on the rear, and use Mafac cantilever brakes fore and aft as well or, better yet, Phil Wood brakes on both wheels. The Phil Wood can be controlled by the stoker, while the captain uses both brake levers up front for the cantilevers. I have Mafac long-arm cantilevers on my Alex Singer single touring bike and I can report that I wish I hadn't ordered them. They work well enough, and are fine for tandems, but are big and ungainly for a single touring bike.

Shimano makes a drum brake (their Radiax), but it's on a low-quality steel hub, obviously intended for the youth market. Braking quality is excellent, though. It costs around $35, per brake, in your bike shop. Before considering it, measure the inside flats of your dropouts to make sure the Shimano hub will fit. The rear hub is 124 millimeters wide. The dropout-flat-to-dropout-flat widths on most of my one-up bikes is 124.5 or 125 mm, so the stays can be stretched that little bit or spacers can be used to receive this hub. However, there is no Shimano front-wheel hub for their drum Radiax Brake (see Chapter 1) so it can only be used on the rear wheel. I don't like the hub you have to use with this brake. It's steel, weighs 16.9 ounces, and is nowhere near as precision made and free spinning as Shimano's high-quality DuraAce aluminum hub, which weighs 10.8 ounces. I also don't like the fact that the Radiax brake weighs a good 20.8 ounces. So my overall objection to the Radiax is that it looks as though it belongs on a less expensive child's bike, uses an inexpensive hub and, in short, does not seem to me to be the kind of high-quality item that I would like on my tandem. This brake does not, as of this writing, come on any bicycle made in the United States.

I should point out that a hub brake, because it is enclosed, offers far better stopping power than a caliper brake. The same is true, but to a slightly less extent, of disc brakes. In the rain, discs take a few seconds to heat up enough to dissipate moisture, before full braking power is available. But discs are a vast improvement over caliper brakes in wet weather.

Bottom Bracket

The bottom-bracket assembly of cones, locknuts, bearings and spindle takes a beating on any bicycle. On a tandem the beating is doubled. It's not unusual for a bottom-bracket set to wear out in three or four thousand miles of hard use. The Phil Wood bottom-brackets sets, thus far, seem to hold up well; and they have the added advantage of being sealed, so there is one less component to worry about on a trip. The spindles come in 40- and 48-millimeter widths. See Chapter 6 for maintenance data.

Hubs and Spokes

Tandems are hard on spokes. On a trip the problem of spoke breakage can be a real headache, especially because you have to remove the freewheel when a spoke breaks on that side. Most spokes seem to break where they bend out of the hub, at the radius of the spoke under the head. One way to relieve stress at this critical point is to use a wider hub, one with wider flanges. Phil Wood hubs have such a flange (no, I am not a stockholder) and better yet, you buy them drilled for forty-eight spokes. Rims with forty-eight spokes are also available, so if you have had spoke problems, there's your solution! Five-cross lacing with forty-eight spokes is a good combination (see Chapter 10).

I don't like quick-release skewers on tandems: too apt to come loose, or not hold the rear wheel on tightly enough, so the wheel sometimes cocks to the left and rubs on the left chainstay. Yes, you can use dropout fittings to hold the axle where you want it. But it's safer to use a solid steel axle and bolt the wheels in place. And a solid axle is stronger than the hollow axle you need with quick-release skewers.

Handlebars

Use any high-quality bar for the front. There's some disagreement about what's best for the stoker. I would opt for dropped rather than flat or slightly curved flat bars because there are more places to put the hands, and so more ways to avoid fatigue and pressure. See Chapter 3.

Tires

The narrow-profile tire and the tubular tire can be used for tandem touring. But I prefer a slightly wider tire, such as the Schwinn Le Tour,

27 by 1¼ inches or 700 centimeters by 25 millimeters wide, or the Michelin T53, 27 by 1¼ inches with a tread designed for varied terrain. This is a fairly heavy tire, at 510 grams, versus the Elan's 300 grams, but the difference really is minimal when you consider the added comfort and reliability of the wider-tread, tougher tire. Another excellent tire is the Michelin T54 which comes in both 27-by-1¼-inch and 700-centi-meter-by-25-millimeter width. These tires range from $5 to $6 each. Another excellent tire is the Specialized Touring Tire in both 700 cen-timeters by 25 millimeters or 27 by 1¼ inches. It offers low rolling resistance plus a heavy tread for reliability and comfort. Its cost, around $7.50. You can also get a light folding tire (remember, when I say "tire" I refer to wired-ons; a "tubular" is a sew-up) to serve as a spare, that weighs only 235 grams, in the 700-centimeter or 27-inch size, for $12.50 from Specialized Touring Tire. If it's not available in your bike store, you can order it from Palo Alto Bicycles (see Appendix). Carrying a folding tire saves space, and if you blow a tube on a tandem it's not safe to patch it. It's much better to install a new tube. See Chapter 2.

The Super Champion rim, in either the 700-centimeter or 27-inch diameter, comes in a 40-hole drilling, which I would use for the front wheel, crossed-three lacing. This rim costs around $12. The Super Champion is also available with 48 spoke holes, which I would use on the rear, as I noted earlier. These drillings are not in wide demand as yet, so you may have to have your bike store order them from the whole-saler; or try shopping by phone first. See Chapter 10 for wheel-lacing instructions.

Derailleurs and Shift Levers

Since you should have wide-range gearing on your tandem, you will need a derailleur that can handle that range. I have tried all the super wide range derailleurs on the market and much prefer the Shimano alloy Crane GS, which has a long cage for handling up to 34 teeth on the rear cog. Shimano also has a new wide-cage front derailleur, their top-line DuraAce EX, Model EA-210, with a trapezium movement that makes shifting smoother and permits wider spacing design of the front derail-leur cage. The wider spacing frees you from having to make minute readjustments on the front derailleur when you shift a rear gear (usually needed because the chain angle is altered as it moves from one rear cog to another and the new angle causes the chain to rub on the derailleur cage unless such adjustments are made). The EA-210 weighs but 3.6 ounces. If you order a custom frame, you can have it fitted to a special Shimano braze-on. This fitting permits the front derailleur to be bolted down. A groove in the fitting gives the derailleur vertical adjustment, should you change the outer chainring. (The derailleur cage should be about ⅛ inch above the largest chainring.)

I prefer bar-end shifters because you can shift while still holding the handlebars, and you do not have to lean down to reach the levers on the downtube. Levers on the stem are strictly a hazard because you can snag a vital part if you come barreling down the top tube in a sudden stop and hit a shift lever. Up till now, the problem with bar-end shifters on a tandem is that no one made cables long enough to reach the rear derailleur. You need extra-long cables as it is for bar-end shifters on a single bike. I used to tie cables together and then solder the knot, a workable but ugly solution. You can now get extra-long cables from one California bike shop that specializes in tandems, tandem parts and supplies: Bud's Bike Shop, 217 W. First St., Claremont, California 91711. Bud also sells tandem framesets, and he reports that a new tandem frame builder, Santana, is doing a fine job, but so far only sells through that shop. If you have a tandem problem you might want to phone either Bill McCready or Darryl Le Vesque at their shop, 714/626-3285. They will even take calls on a Tuesday until 10:00 PM Pacific time.

CUSTOM TANDEM FRAMESETS

The better custom frame builders will make special sizes of tandem frame front and rear combinations, for about $500 a frame, minimum. Allow up to six months for delivery. Off-the-rack framesets by the English frame builder Bob Jackson may be ordered from the better of your local bike shops. The Bob Jackson touring tandem, with fork and headset, will run you about $500.

From surveying the better custom frame builders, I can recommend among them a few who build very fine tandems. They are:

• Tom Boyden, Fastab Cycles, 2706 Glenbrook Drive, Garland, Texas 75041
• Caylor Frames, P.O. Box 1793, Modesto, California 95354
• Colin Laing, 3454 N. First Ave., Tucson, Arizona 85719
• Bill Boston Cycles, P.O. Box 114, Swedesboro, New Jersey 08085

As for components to hang on framesets, I would leave this up to the builder, for two reasons. First, he knows what works best with his frames. Second, he knows how to put them on and which brazed-on fittings are needed. If you do much touring I would advise fenders, fifteen-speed wide-ratio gearing (see Chapter 3) and brazed-on fittings for panniers fore and aft. Two riders really will need front carriers and panniers as well as rear carriers and panniers, if you do cycle touring via the camping route. Fifteen speeds are necessary because you are lugging the weight of two riders plus a 40-pound frame plus whatever else

Fig. 13-1: This fine Bertin tandem has a very wide gear range necessary for touring. Note that the transmission is cross-over design (front drive chain on left, rear drive chain on right).

you carry. The fifteen speeds let you change into a wider selection of gears to cope with an infinite variety of wind speeds, road grades, and the physical condition of front person and stoker.

You have two choices of crankest configuration, though: the cross-over type (Fig. 13-1) or the same-side type (Fig. 13-2). The cross-over distributes pedaling forces more or less equally on each side, so bike balance is easier. That is, the torque or force of pedaling is on the left side of the rear bottom bracket and on the right side of the front bottom bracket, thus equalizing the power strokes and reducing forces that tend to flex the frame in one direction or the other.

The second of the two crank configurations is your choice between synchronized cranks, where right and left pedals are always in the same

Fig. 13-2: Schwinn mid-price-range tandem, Deluxe Twinn Sport 10-speed. This model has a transmission all on one side. Note chain tensioner just behind front chainwheel. More expensive models do not need a chain tensioner because chain slack on front drive is taken up by an offset bottom bracket which can be adjusted so that, in effect, bottom bracket is moved fore or aft as necessary.

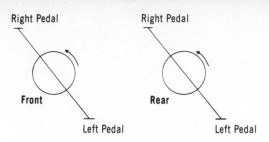

Fig. 13-3: When cranks are synchronized, pedals remain in the same relative position. When front right-side pedal, for example, is at two o'clock, rear right-side pedal will be at the same position. This makes it easier to take off from a standing start.

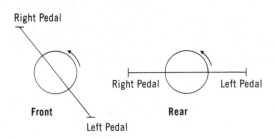

Fig. 13-4: Out-of-sync pedals make it harder to start off from a standing start but equalize pedaling forces better for a smoother, easier ride.

o'clock position (Fig. 13-3)—and where these pedals are out of sync, as in Figure 13-4.

An advantage with the sync crank arrangement is that it is much easier to mount the tandem and take off than when pedals are out of sync. For example, both right-side pedals can be at the two-o'clock position (Fig. 13-3) ready for takeoff. Captain and stoker each put their right foot in the pedal, push down with the foot and at the same time get into the saddle, pump three or four times, coast long enough to get the left foot into the pedals and continue cycling.

With pedals out of sync, it's a lot more difficult to get going if the right rear pedal is at 9 o'clock when the right front pedal is at the 11 o'clock (Fig. 13-4).

One disadvantage with the sync position is that there's a dead spot or null point in pedal power when zero or little torque is being applied to the rear wheel—when cranks are vertical to the ground, as in Figure 13-5. In this position, on an uphill climb, the tandem can lose momen-

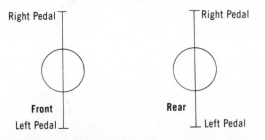

Fig. 13-5: In-sync cranks have a power "dead spot" during which little or no power is applied to the rear wheel, making for a loss in tandem forward momentum until pedals get past the 12-o'clock position.

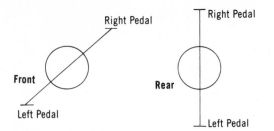

Fig. 13-6: Out-of-sync pedals do not have the "dead spot" of power transmission shown in Figure 13-5 because when the rear right-side pedal, e.g., is at the dead or zero torque transmission spot as shown, the front right-side pedal is at the power stroke at 2 o'clock. Pedaling is smoother.

tum, and in fact will alternately surge forward and slow up as the synchronized pedals are at 12 o'clock on the same side at the same time. On the other hand, when out-of-sync pedals are used, the pedals are never at a dead spot at the same time. When rear pedals are at the noon and six-o'clock null position, the left front pedal is completing its power stroke (Fig. 13-6). And as the right front pedal comes around to *its* zero torque position, the right rear pedal begins *its* power stroke. So with out-of-sync cranks, pedal power is applied much more evenly through-out the 360 degrees of pedal rotation, and you should find hill climbing easier. Also, with power being applied more smoothly, you don't have two riders putting maximum torque or pressure on the bottom-bracket bearing at the same time, at the same side of the bottom bracket, as in Figure 13-3. Tandem owners who use the out-of-sync pedal arrange-ment report longer bottom-bracket life. That's been my own experience as well.

How to "Out-of-Sync" Your Pedals

To move your pedals to the more efficient pedaling position where they are out of sync is simplicity itself. On a good tandem you do not have a front chain tensioner. Instead, chain tension is adjusted by an offset bottom-bracket fitting. All you do is loosen the bolts holding this fitting, rotate it until the chain is loose enough to slip off one of the front chainwheels, rotate one set of cranks until they are out of sync and readjust the front bottom bracket for proper chain tension. Now when the right front pedal is at 2 o'clock, the right rear pedal should be at 12 o'clock.

On the less expensive tandems without an adjustable front bottom-bracket assembly, front chain tension is taken up by a chain tensioner (Fig. 13-7). In this case just loosen the chain-tensioner jockey wheel where it slides in the fitting, slip the chain off the front chainring, and move the pedals to the out-of-sync position as shown above. Readjust the tensioner so there is about ¼- to ⅜-inch chain slack, at most.

Fig. 13-7: Schwinn Deluxe Twinn Tandem five-speed

Child Adapter

If you want to have your small child as your tandem "stoker" on the rear, but the child's legs are too short to reach the pedals, you can install a Phil Wood bottom-bracket adapter (see Chapter 6) at the appropriate place on the seat tube. This adapter is the bottom-bracket shell only and will require the spindle, bearings, and so forth.

TRICYCLES

The real difference between a bicycle and a tricycle of equal quality lies in the greater maneuverability of the two-wheeler and the consequent greater skill it takes to ride one.

Still, rather than give up the joy of outdoor pedaling, a tricycle can be an excellent compromise. One sees great numbers of tricycles in retirement areas.

Three Types of Tricycles

There are three basic types of tricycles available. One is a rather heavy (around 65 pounds) unit with 26-inch tires, complete with detachable rear wire utility basket; a trike conversion unit so you can convert a reasonably good ten-speed into a fairly lightweight (38 pounds or so) ten-speed trike; and a tailor-made tricycle with any gear ratio you wish, made of Reynolds '531' butted tubing and also with ten speeds.

If you want a tricycle because you have a balance problem and feel more secure on a trike, I recommend the Schwinn Tri-Wheeler as the best of the domestic models (Fig. 13-8). This model has a differential

Fig. 13-8: Schwinn Tri-Wheeler adult tricycle with differential transmission

transmission system, which means that the trike will corner more accurately because the rear wheels rotate at a differential speed, depending on the degree of turn. You can power this tricycle into a turn with less tendency to wheel lift, and if the wheel does lift it won't be the power wheel, unlike a conventional trike with direct chain drive.

If balance is not your problem, however, and you want a tricycle for winter use over snow or ice, or just for the fun of it, I can recommend a conversion unit that lets you change your lightweight ten-speed bicycle into a lightweight tricycle, with either direct drive (pedals turn as long as the trike is rolling; there's no freewheel) or ten-speed. I prefer direct drive because I can back up as well as go forward.

How to Make Your Own Lightweight Tricycle

I like to use a tricycle. It's fun, particularly in winter when the roads are ice covered and really too slippery for a two-wheeler. You can convert an old bike, or even a good bike, to a tricycle and reconvert it back to a two-wheeler in an hour or so.

There are two or three conversion kits on the market to transmute a two- to a three-wheeler. I like the one made in England by Ken G. Rogers, 71 Berkeley Avenue, Cranford, Hounslow, Middlesex. TW 4 6LF, for about $75, including U.S. duty. I converted an old Schwinn Super Sport lugless frame (a fine frame, by the way) into a trike for winter use (Fig. 13-9). To make the conversion:

STEP ONE: Lace up whatever wheels you want on the special hubs furnished (see Chapter 10). You must use these hubs, because they are made to fit a tapered axle. I would suggest Super Champion 700-centimeter-by-25-millimeter rims with narrow-profile tires (which are definitely not the type on my tricycle, but I was using up old parts at the time).

STEP TWO: Remove the rear wheel and derailleur from the old bike, as well as the seat binder bolt.

STEP THREE: Find extra links for your chain or install a new, longer chain. You will need about four extra links, the same make as your chain.

STEP FOUR: Remove the space bar between the cage of an old front derailleur, and install a jockey wheel from an old rear derailleur, for use as a chain tensioner. I did not use this setup in the trike, shown in Figure 13-9, until I figured out why the chain kept jumping off the rear cog: too loose. There's absolutely no way you can adjust chain tension otherwise.

STEP FIVE: Adjust the tensioner to your chainline, leaving a bit of slack on the chain.

STEP SIX: You do have your choice of using a five-speed freewheel or a single gear on the rear. If you use a five-speed freewheel you will, of course, not have to worry about chain tension, because the rear derail-

Fig. 13-9: A conversion of a two-wheeler to a lightweight, fixed-gear tricycle

leur automatically takes up the slack. Personally, though, I prefer a fixed gear on my trike, as noted earlier. This way I can back up as well as go forward, which shakes up motorists no end as I move back and forth while waiting for a stoplight, or back up out of a diagonal parking slot. The terrain is flat around Chicago, so I don't need multi-gears. You can, of course, also use the two- or three-plateau chainring setup on your existing bike so you can have the same number of gear changes that you are used to. My conversion added 12 pounds to the Super Sport, which, as a trike, weighs in at 38 pounds, or around the weight of one of the less expensive two-wheelers. Since there's only one brake on the Super Sport cum trike (there being nowhere to fasten a rear brake), I like the direct drive (pedals turn when the bike moves, no freewheeling). I can get more aerobic exercise by putting back pressure on the pedals when I want to stop. In fact, I almost never use the front brake, which is now a drum brake (not shown).

STEP SEVEN: Okay, now you are ready to fasten the adapter unit onto the bike. The unit slides into the rear dropouts (Fig. 13-10) and is bolted in place there.

STEP EIGHT: Now you fasten the two reinforcing stays supplied with the conversion kit. The upper part of the stays fastens onto the seat post binder bolt, and it may have to be a longer bolt than the one that came with the bike. The lower end of the reinforcing stays is clamped onto the axle housing of the adapter unit (Fig. 13-11).

STEP NINE: Make sure the chainline is accurate (Fig. 13-12). You have some leeway in chainline by using spacers on either side of the rear cog or freewheel.

The Rogers kit is very clean-cut and makes a very good-looking trike. You could, with some ingenuity, fasten a wire basket on the rear. For a ten-speed conversion, Rogers supplies an adapter which slips into a mounting fitting on the conversion unit, to which you can attach a rear derailleur (Fig. 13-13). Rogers also makes lightweight trike frames, in case you are interested in one for touring, or for racing, or for just plain high performance. Send for his latest price list.

Oh yes, the Rogers conversion unit weighs 7 pounds (3½ kilos), so whatever your bike weighs now, add 7 pounds, plus the weight of the spokes, rims, tires and tubes. As I said, I added about 12 pounds to my own Super Sport, including the weight of the rear wheels and the front drum brake, and it is a lot of fun. Somehow the conversion looks racy, which is fine by me.

Fig. 13-10: Conversion unit slides into rear dropouts.

Fig. 13-11: Two reinforcing stays or braces run from conversion unit drive shaft housing to the sear post binder bolt.

Fig. 13-12: When installing conversion unit, make sure chainline is accurate. This is especially important for single-speed, fixed gear. Not shown is a front derailleur with old rear-derailleur jockey wheel, installed on chainstay, used to take up chain slack. Keep chain under proper tension so it does not jump off cogs.

Fig. 13-13: There is a brazed-on boss on axle housing, just to right of the U-shaped cog bend, to fasten a derailleur if you want a five- or ten-speed tricycle.

A Tandem Trike

If you put a Ken Rogers special trike conversion unit on your tandem you can combine the features of tandem togetherness and comradely cycling, working in harmony close enough to hold a conversation, with the features of a tricycle—stability, no problems balancing, more relaxed cycling. I did and it makes tandeming, especially on wintry, snowy streets, much safer and, for me, more fun. One word of caution, though. Adding the Rogers trike adapter means, as noted, you have no brake on the rear wheel, and so braking must be done only on the front wheel, which cuts braking power in half. If you have enough fork clearance, and brakes with long enough caliper arms (they come in different lengths), you may be able to put a double set of caliper brakes on the front wheel, one set in front and one behind the fork. Or you can put a drum brake on the front wheel, plus the caliper brake that grips the rim. You'd better have a strong fork, though, because stresses in stopping with a hub brake plus a caliper brake can bend the fork. You can't put caliper brakes on the rear wheels because there's no place to attach them, and you can't substitute a drum brake on the rear wheel because you can use only the hub that comes with the trike adapter unit, and drum brakes are integral with their own hub. The same applies to disc brakes, used on some of the child "Chopper"-style bikes.

You might experiment with a Shimano disc brake next to a fixed rear cog on the adapter unit. I haven't done it myself, but it might just work.

Chapter Fourteen
Emergency on-the-Road Repairs

There's nothing like the feeling of supreme confidence of knowing that you can fix just about anything short of a bent frame that is likely to malfunction on your bike while you are commuting to work or out touring. After all, it puts a real damper on a bike tour to have it come to a halt because no one can fix a busted bike. Remember, too, to bring along the necessary tools and spare parts. Here are some tips on the emergency repairs and maintenance that you should be prepared for *prior* to going on a trip.

TOOLS

You should be prepared for every type of minor mechanical disaster that can befall your steed, both in terms of having the right tools to make the repairs and in knowing *how* to make the repairs. Here's a recommended list:

- Spare spokes to fit front and rear wheels. Two spokes per wheel, with nipples (total, 4; 1 oz.)
- Spoke wrench (3 oz.)
- Two spare tubes and one patch kit (12 oz.)
- Two tire irons (1.5 oz.)
- Freewheel remover (3 oz.)
- Small adjustable wrench (3 oz.)
- Two brake blocks (1 oz.)
- One brake cable, long enough to reach the rear brake. You can cut to fit the front brake (½ oz.)

- One rear derailleur cable (½ oz.)
- One foldable lightweight tire such as the Michelin Elan, particularly important if you use 700-centimeter tires not readily available in small-town bike stores, the usual hardware stores or auto-parts stores that sell bikes (11 oz.)
- Small screwdriver (2 oz.)
- Chain lubricant (4 oz.)
- Hub lube (if you do not have sealed bearings) (2 oz.)
- Allen wrenches to fit rear derailleur, seat post binder bolt stem (if Allen bolt fitted) (3 oz.)
- Chain rivet remover (chain "breaker") (4 oz.)
- Four spare chain links (same make as your chain) (2 oz.)
- Set of hub wrenches (unless sealed bearings) (4 oz.)
- Spare rim tape (1 oz.)
- Roll of black electrician's tape (a patch-all you will not appreciate until you need it) (2 oz.)
- Set of lightweight box wrenches 8-, 9-, 10-, 11- and 12-millimeter sizes (3 oz.)
Total 63.5 ounces = 3.97 lbs.

Bikecology, and probably your local bike shop, has a lightweight set of tools handy consisting of three tire irons, 5-, 6- and 7-millimeter Allen wrenches, spoke wrench, three open-end wrenches from 6 to 13 millimeters, and a 6-inch crescent wrench, two headset adjusting tools (won't fit new Shimano DuraAce headsets), tire patch kit, chain rivet tool, all in a zippered case for $12.88. Bikecology, P.O. Box 1880, Santa Monica, California 90406. This is item TL8. The entire kit weighs only 1 pound.

EMERGENCY REPAIRS

Because the sections on various bike parts and their maintenance, adjustment and/or replacement are quite complete I won't duplicate this information here, except to list the kinds of things you might expect to go wrong on the road. Please refer to the specific chapter involved for repair data:

- *Flat tires.* Of course. Chapter 2
- *Broken spokes.* Preventive maintenance can pretty well eliminate them. Chapter 10
- *Broken chain links.* Replace the old chain before you go on tour. Chapter 6
- *Broken, frayed cables.* Ditto. Chapters 1 and 4
- *Wheels out of true.* Align first, before the trip. Chapter 10
- *Brake blocks worn.* Replace beforehand. Chapter 1
- *Sand or dirt in the wheel hubs.* Listen for grinding. Spin wheels of upside-down bike each day, especially if you have traveled over dirt or sand-covered roads. If you hear gritty sounds, disassemble, clean, repack and readjust hubs. Better yet, install Phil Wood, Avocet or Durham sealed-bearing hubs before you leave. Chapter 5

- *Gritty sounds from bottom bracket.* Follow the same procedure if you hear gritty noises from the bottom bracket. Slip chain off first. Spin cranks. Listen. If you hear gritty sounds, you have trouble unless you brought along a set of bottom-bracket spanners and crank puller. But be of good cheer. This is a fairly rare occurrence. You could install an Avocet, Phil Wood or Durham sealed-bearing bottom-bracket assembly before leaving home. Chapter 6
- *Gritty sound from freewheel jockey and idler wheels.* Clean and relube if necessary. Better yet, install a set of Durham sealed-bearing derailleur wheels beforehand. Chapter 4
- *Loose carriers.* Check every day. Tighten nuts and bolts as necessary. This chapter
- *Loose headset. This is serious.* Check by gripping handlebars, keeping bike steady (use a helper if necessary to hold the bike) and feel for looseness or "play" in headset. Lift front wheel off ground, turn the handlebars with one finger. They should turn easily. Remember, a loose headset can flatten headset bearings and score bearing races, because tremendous pressures are exerted in this small area due to road shock, weight of rider and his belongings and the bike itself. A loose headset can also cause or contribute to high-speed "shimmy," especially on downhill runs, and cause loss of control—definitely not a healthy situation. Chapter 7
- *Loose cranks.* Grip crank at pedal, try to move laterally, from side to side. If loose, retighten. The crank is aluminum, the spindle is steel. A loose crank will soon wear the beveled flats inside it, and you will need a new crank. On the road this is guaranteed disaster unless you are lucky enough to find a bike shop with a spare crank that fits your bottom-bracket spindle and is threaded to receive your pedal. Well, sure, a French-threaded crank can be rethreaded English. On a new bike, or if you have removed the crank for bottom-bracket maintenance, the cranks should be tightened every fifty miles for three or four sets of fifty miles. After that the crank should be well seated and need no further retightening. Before a trip, check it anyway. If you are lucky enough to have one of the new Shimano cranksets that goes on and off with one Allen wrench, you can save a pound of tools, such as a spanner and a crank puller. Well, a half pound anyway. Chapter 6
- *Check hub-cone adjustment* by gripping the wheel with both hands on opposite sides and move gently from side to side. If you feel looseness, remove the wheel and readjust the hub cones. Better yet, remove the wheel and spin the axle between thumb and forefinger. Axle should spin freely, without binding. Holding the axle the same way, try to move it from side to side. There should be no side play. Readjust as necessary. Chapter 5
- *Make sure the seat post and stem are inside their respective tubes.* Chapter 3
- *If you get dirt in the freewheel,* or have used too heavy a lubricant (use chainlube, or a *very* light oil) the pawls can hang up (they are spring loaded) and the freewheel will rotate but you won't. The bike will stay put. If you're lucky and can get to some kerosene or other nonexplosive solvent, try pouring some on the freewheel. Do not get any on the tire! Solvents eat tires. If this doesn't free up the freewheel, remove it and soak it in solvent, spinning at the same time, holding it from inside, where it threads onto the hub. *Of course*

you brought along a freewheel remover, didn't you, and a wrench to fit it? See Chapter 9

HOW TO MAKE YOUR OWN CARRIER

Anyone can easily make his own rooftop bicycle carrier with a little ingenuity and effort. Start with any ordinary pair of metal bar roof carriers, the kind that clamp to rain gutters or bolt to the roof, *not* the suction-cup type, which can come loose.

L. L. Bean carries an aluminum alloy load bracket with drip eave clamps and carriage bolts for your own wood crossbar, costing about $15 for a set of four (Fig. 14-1). These are made by Quik-'n-Easy Products, Monrovia, California.

Chick Mead, a bicycle dealer in Marion, Massachusetts, has designed a fine homemade carrier. His instructions, which follow, are simple (Fig. 14-2). They call for:

1. One set of brackets, L. L. Bean "Quick-'n-Easy," or Sears Roebuck rain-gutter type
2. Two 9-foot two-by-fours
3. One quart wood preservative
4. 12 carriage bolts ¼ by 1⅝ inches
5. 12 feet of ⅜- or ⁷⁄₁₆-inch aluminum round (stock) for pegs
6. 64 1-inch-wide rubber bands, made from old inner tubes
7. Two pieces of ⅛-by-1-by-32-inch aluminum flat or ¾-inch angle stock for adjustable struts (total 62 inches)
8. One pint weatherstrip adhesive to glue on padding
9. Scrap ends of thick felt or carpeting for padding
10. One quart exterior-grade preservative finish paint, such as Rustoleum
11. One quart liquid Neoprene for waterproofing top of pad

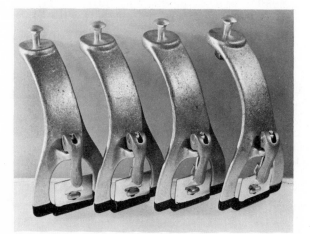

Fig. 14-1: Brackets for homemade bike carrier. *(L.L. Bean)*

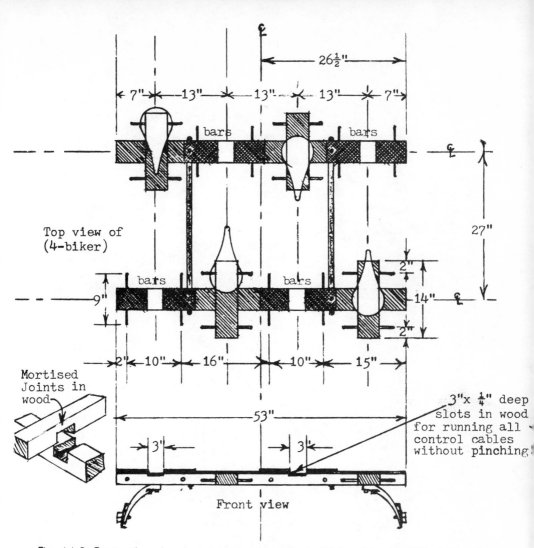

Fig. 14-2: Design for a homemade bicycle carrier holds four bicycles. *(Chick Mead)*

If you can't scrounge old inner tubes from a gas station, try a foreign-car dealer, such as a Peugeot garage, where inner tubes are used with radial tires.

Plans should be self-explanatory. An unexpected side benefit was the fact that after about a thousand miles of driving, the slight bouncing up and down movement thoroughly broke in all our saddles! Note that the adjustable struts of aluminum flats or angles permit saddle position to be changed to conform to wheelbase of bicycle.

The nine-inch dowels of the aluminum rod should stick out about two inches from the two-by-fours.

Allowing thirteen inches apart for each bicycle, you will be able to carry up to four bicycles on this carrier. Be sure to pad the two-by-fours

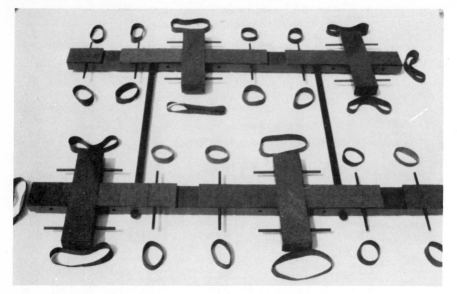

Fig. 14-3: Finished homemade carrier. Note that hold-downs are from old tire tubes. *(Chick Mead)*

Fig. 14-4: Finished carrier mounted on car. This is the homemade model. Total cost about $20, not counting your time. *(Chick Mead)*

liberally with old hose or other soft but durable material, to avoid marring the handlebar finish.

When ready to tie down the bicycle, use the rubber holders (or leather straps) to tie both sides of the handlebars and the seat to the carrier. Stagger bicycles on the carrier, as shown in Figure 14-3. And make sure the carrier is securely fastened to the car roof!

I made one of these Chick Mead carriers myself, and I am able to carry four bikes on my car (Fig. 14-4). My expenses totaled about $15 for everything, and the result is a very useful and practical carrier indeed.

Incidentally, the Chick Mead bike carrier is also very handy for transporting luggage and other miscellany. The aluminum rod tiedowns are very convenient for securing almost anything. My carrier is always fitted to my car, though it could be removed quickly and easily.

INDEX